Quarterly Review of

EDITED BY T. & R. WEISS

Literature

Poetry Book Series
VOLUME XXXVII–XXXVIII

JAMES RICHARDSON
A Suite for Lucretians

SUSAN YANKOWITZ
Phaedra in Delirium

J. D. SMITH
The Hypothetical Landscape

PHILIP DACEY
The Paramour of the Moving Air

ANN GOLDSMITH
No One Is the Same Again

RICHARD SEWELL
The Mischief at Rimul

26 HASLET AVENUE, PRINCETON, NEW JERSEY 08540

ACKNOWLEDGEMENTS

PHILIP DACEY: Poems in this book have appeared, sometimes in earlier versions, in the following periodicals: *Eureka Literary Magazine, Farmer's Market, Flyway, Georgia Review, Great River Review, Hard Love, Hurakan, The Journal, Kestrel, Laurel Review, Mid-American Review, Midwest Quarterly, Minnesota Monthly, Mississippi Valley Review, National Poetry Competition Winners 1995, Nightsun, North Dakota Review, Poetry Northwest, Poetry Now, Seneca Texas Review, Shenandoah, Sing Heavenly Muse, Talking River Review, Tampa Review, Texas Review, Two Cities, What's Empty Weighs the Most, Widener Review, Wolf Head Quarterly, Xanadu.*

ANN GOLDSMITH: I thank the editors of the following journals, in which some of these poems have appeared: *The Niagara Magazine* and *On Turtle's Back: a Biogeographic Anthology of New York State Poetry*, "American Gothic"; *Pembroke Magazine*, "Famine: Ethiopia Hits the TV News Again"; *Poets at Work: Contemporary Poets—Lives, Poems, Process*, "Light Arms Around You"; *Poets at Work* and *The Quarterly*, "Tales from the Archipelago: the Keeper of the Light"; *Helicon Nine* and *The Helicon Nine Reader*, "Red Riding Hood: Her Story" and "Red Riding Hood: the Mother Speaks"; *Buffalo Press Anthology I*, "Two Blocks from Home the Lions Moan," and *Scarecrow Poetry*, "Vanishing Point." "The Roller Coaster Child" was a runner-up in the 1996 Orillia International Poetry Festival.

JAMES RICHARDSON: *A Suite for Lucretians* was begun with the assistance of a 1993-1994 Artists Fellowship from the New Jersey State Council on the Arts.

J. D. SMITH: Certain of these poems have appeared, in some instances in slightly different form, in the following magazines: Ascent, Black Buzzard Review, Buffalo Press, CutBank, Denver Quarterly, Dickinson Review, Folio, Great Midwestern Quarterly, Gulf Coast, International Quarterly, Kaleidoscope, Kansas Quarterly, The Ledge, The Maverick Press, Mudfish, New Delta Review, No Exit, Painted Bride Quarterly, Phase and Cycle, Poem, Rain City Review, Rio: A Journal of the Arts, River City, Seneca Review, Small Pond, Sou'wester, Spoon River Poetry Review, Stone Country, Talking River Review, Tomorrow, and Visions International.

SUSAN YANKOWITZ: Ms. Yankowitz has been honored for her writing by the Berilla Kerr Foundation, NEA, TCG, the Rockefeller Foundation, Guggenheim Foundation, Opera America, the McKnight Foundation, NYFA, and others. She is a member of New Dramatists, The Dramatists Guild, PEN, WGA, and The Women's Project.

Assistants: Mary Capouya, Karen Emmerich, Tiffany Fung,
   Helen Labun, Jonathan Queally, Nicholas Silinis
Designer: Mahlon Lovett
Cover Monotype: Roselyn Karol Ablow, *Forms In Blue,*
  Water soluble paint stick, 30x54 inches

JAMES RICHARDSON

A Suite for Lucretians

JAMES RICHARDSON's collections of poetry include *Reservations, Second Guesses, As If,* which was chosen for the 1992 National Poetry Series. He is also the author of two critical studies, *Thomas Hardy: The Poetry of Necessity* and *Vanishing Lives: Tennyson, Rossetti, Swinburne, and Yeats,* and his essays and aphorisms have appeared in *Poetry, Yale Review, Michigan Quarterly Review, Ontario Review, Boulevard, The Formalist, The New Criterion, Paris Review, Poetry,* and *US 1.*

A SUITE FOR LUCRETIANS

A Suite for Lucretians

The new molecular philosophy shows astronomical interspaces betwixt atom and atom, shows that the world is all outside; it has no inside.

Emerson

1

Because the oysters I sucked down
were swished with Red Tide,
the fleeing of the stars
shifts red tonight.

Running a red
with the radio loud
or singing under a green,
even my brain's less mine—

Ah, Long Island wine,
and my new taste in ties!
Like you, I've seen what no one else has seen.
The universe will die before I die.

2

So it is spring, the season, as Lucretius says,
of Desire, skill of the world. Alas, so hurtfully young,
rumple of sheets still faintly on her cheeks,
she wanders, flushed, one button half out,
like a tongue just touching the back of the teeth,
or tangles on the floodplain's picnic blankets
in tableaus the iconographer would call
Venus enveloping hardbody Mars,
sleepily appeased, Love sapping War.

I like the other allegories better:
ice binding fire; or form and matter;
or sympathy and. . . whatever keeps us at our ourselves
when we are licked at, lapped at by desire.
The sand is swept downstream in toughening waters,
the breeze grows keen with smoke, the evening dense
with lovers its half-closed eyes have blurred together.
Listen up. And I will disclose to you the laws of heaven.

3

If there were no such thing as empty space, Lucretius says,
no atom could move, no new thought enter this universe:
there is no fecundity without emptiness.
Yet nothing can come of nothing without seed or cause.
Otherwise bluebirds, shaking off dust,
would hatch from the harrowed fields, and cattle,
lowing, amble from the storm-green sky.
All things randomly would greet and deny us, feed and fail us,
and creatures would flood rockwaste and woods indifferently,
gnashing at leaf and stone and nothing at all,
mistaking hunger for their food, and for their joy, austerity
        and pain,
but none of this can be imagined.

Men would stride out of the river, memoryless.
They would imagine themselves immortal,
and ride the trains bird-eyed, imploring, homicidal.
They might mistake love for a deadly thing
and batter children to save themselves from pity,
or shoot from a rooftop a crone swaying behind a laundry cart
as you might practice your deadly topspin serve.
But none of this can be imagined.

4

Between the Millstone River, just downstream
from the Sewer Authority,
and the Delaware and Raritan Canal
(disused) which two warm days
turn much too green

is a towpath, where you might surprise
a tangle of bikes
or a carp some laid-off fisherman, aghast
at its sheer albino size

has left to a mannerly crow
that lifts, as from gift wrap,
quivering scarves,
rose-dust, and smoky blue, and mauve,

or the pink-eyed
guy with skinzines,

or me with my roar of a walk
and Walkman, head wide
with ten-in-a-chain moon-glossy
(oops I've been singing)
junk mail songs

O reader, dear!
(You have already won)
Never, O never before
(Our sympathy. . .)

Water, water, everywhere. . .
Though it probably wouldn't kill me.

5

For if each thing did not have its essence and seed
nothing would prevent a single tree from bearing
all fruits ridiculously, or each in its season,
and the mind would be lost in every image crossing it.
Parents would shudder and revert to infancy,
old men, mouths softening, turn into women.
Just by closing your eyes, you could distinguish the planets
by taste (those rocky herbs, red and green and blue),
or six pistons superheated, or each friend's failure,
but none of this can be imagined.

You would thrill with the narrow wind of the beast's desire,
glass wind of the stone's.
You would know how the deer's mind, leaping,
tones like the air in a flute, silver
and sudden as the long lake glimpsed through trees.
You would know through desire how to become anything,
as the lake holds any cloud, each sad migration,
each wooden bottom, each suddenly outcast line
it seems to itself to conceive of.

6

Because my immunity was compromised
I was invaded by living particles,
because I stepped ankle-deep through the ice
I was cirrus, keen across the moon,

because of stress,
because I scorned two aspirin and bed rest,
resigned myself to the poverty of pure relation,
neglected my office, hardly propitiated
Fever, the rock-bound Titan,
or because,

I have every disease.
I have heart shutting down.
I have noon, my brow hot lily.
I have evening's
repeating crickets, metastatic.
I have the bulls-eye rashness.
I have the undone.
I have August, terminally.
I have sleeping on an open magazine.
I have white, chronic dawns.

7

Nothing we know, Lucretius says, is nothing:
the unseen wind, he reminds us, must be bodies
small and soft enough to stir single hairs on your wrist
or find places on your skin so secret and grateful
you cannot tell the feeling of them from your feelings.
Yet surely they have hardness and strength in concert,
since they can herd a bank of clouds sky-long without
derangement,
erect from the sea eighty-foot walls, or slide a ship
with the flat patience of continental drift,
just as rivers whisk houses from their foundations,
or wear canyons so slowly it hurts to think of the slowness,
even though water seems the softest thing to us
because we are water, and touch ourselves, touching it.

Similarly, downwind of a burning house,
you smell the fire-tang and your eyes water
though you saw no odors approaching, their ambush
so sudden, so much like remembering,
you have to remind yourself they are not everywhere.
No, they're a lake you can wade into, or walk out of:
as in the car I hold myself in the wind,
with your swift, O too swift, silence next to me,

and smell lilac for a mile, then henhouse,
diesel, mildew, laundry and what else,
as if a book went by too fast to understand,
or a runner's ripe heat, running just behind her.

8

Nothing is easier than that you assume me,
though if I squeezed next to you on the bus, smelling
of wool and rain,
we might smile tightly and never look to the side.

You would not want to overhear my bitter prayer,
my thought of your perfume, least of all your name.
Like you I walked with my family and was helpless love.
Like you I wished for their destruction, not knowing
I was wishing.
Like you I was granted perfections and did not feel
them undeserved.
Like you I dreamed of making love to myself,
wondered if anyone saw exactly the blue I see,
knew no one was moved as I was by that love
that song that season
and no one was bored as I was by that love, song, season,
knew you as myself, and did not know myself.

This entire warm front was breathed last week in Omaha,
rebreathed in Cleveland, and already
see how these long sentences lie down in you, knowing,
is it, or already known? You cannot stop hearing them,
though I am modest, I am polite. How is it possible
to be alone, since someone is always speaking
in the head, someone is always reading,
with a chancy candle, the middle of a sentence
that begins and ends in darkness.

Here, I am long gone
from behind these words, yet you hear them talking,
as the gull's cry seems to be coming from far behind the gull.

9

Nothing is just *out there*, Lucretius says;
its particles must enter us to be known.
Smell, for example, is the lounging of inhalations
along receptors complementary in form,
like fingers spreading for a difficult chord,
or the whole sky sliding soundlessly to dock
in the fine-toothed harbors of a fern.

That softly-repeated *plinking* on a jar,
distant at first? Listen more closely:
the rain's tower rises, and you walk,
steps echoing, in a huge cathedral
of hearing that has somehow entered you.
Hills left carelessly under the horizon
like someone sleeping, the sky, cloud-sifted sun
settle like fine gauze on our open faces
as if we were daisies, blind in the fall of pollen.

As for your slow extrusion from the ocean
failing colorlessly down your sides,
lift of your thighs against reluctance:
I *feel* it, I say, as if the eyes were hands,
for it is true, as desire tells us, that the world is touch,
or being touched—no telling the difference.
Always the shifting of tumblers, the whisper *Open*,
just as, moving against you at dawn, and lightly,
I am gray windows slowly lightening.

10

I can't get it through my head that the day is just in my head:
that I don't see *things*, only reflected light.
That I don't see light, actually, flitting between perches,
just the splash on my retina, the ripple
inward, of chemical potentials,
which isn't seeing at all—I mean, as I think of it.
It's as if I were watching behind video goggles
a movie of exactly the path I'm taking,
hearing on tape exactly what I hear,
though to God, looking down in trans-sensual knowledge,
it's darkness and silence we walk in,
the brightness and noise only in our heads,
which are the few lit windows in a darkened office tower.

11

But Lucretius, who does not believe in light,
not really, says that we see because things broadcast
images of themselves, continuous, that are material.
That jogger is shedding skins of herself like frames of a film
entering my eyes. The revolutions of the moon send down
husks of a moon, tree calls endless *treeeee* into the wind.
So the moon is itself a wind, the tree is a wind of seeing,
and the rose throws *rose* and *rose* down your welling eyes.

Naturally, the air is crowded with these films.
Your image, for example, and a wayward horse
superimposing, *centaur* might come to mind, though faintly
since such a thing never was. Imagination, we call it,
or dream, because these simulacra are so fine
they can enter through the skin, asleep, or any opening.
So, too, when *rose* and *moon* and *jogger* blend like winds:
I feel running in the skies, and a thorn of breath,

a gust of sweat and roses passing,
a body of moon my hands of moon pass through.

Images of all that has ever happened, further,
and all who have ever been, alive or dead,
persist in every place, at any time.
I concentrate, and your paleness rises through the throng
of clamoring shades. I.e., I remember you.
For the air itself is memory, everything's stored there:
faces we seek and recognize, all those strangers
who populate our dreams, or rise to become the faces
in books we read. It is all the air on our faces.

This is why no one asks you for your secrets.
Your whispers of love and shame in apparent privacy
are already heard, but so faintly who can be sure
whether it's you, imagination or the air,
in this life or the last, that whispers in them?
Now, as my past grows longer, things I did
in my faint youth are fainter than someone else's,
and things I have dreamed of, over and over,
stories I've read, lives scented on the wind
or distantly adored, history, imagination,
are strong as what was mine. I call them true. I call them
truer.

12

The sun is bright because its images dive steeply
into our eyes, ninety million miles.
The breeze they drive before them
is how distance, Lucretius says,

is sensed in the eyes. Can you feel this
when you open to my gaze:
how the eyes themselves are wind,
wind with a question's rising intonation?

13

This is how it goes: all you are saying
expands in a sphere, an organized explosion,
though blurring, with distance, into wordless intonation,
until its vagueness, at last encompassing everything,
becomes unhearable motions, displacement of a pane,
rocking of airborne particles, faint heat in the walls
that not even a god's hearing can turn back into words.
Nor can you take them back, no more than remove
the blush from a cheek, these your root
in the world, your touch of everything again.

There is no standing that is not sending everywhere,
no waiting that does not rush out at lightspeed.
Even the un-happened, the never-told,
for these gave form to all you did, are raying out
to shape the future, though impossible, though unheard,
as my call ringing and ringing in your room,
and ceasing, leaves the silence ringing.

14

The film of brass from the sax's raw throat,
or the singer's smoky, torchsong bronze,
or your voice, lapping me
with the soft, wet inside of your throat:

no wonder I talk such trash, as distraction
from the nakedness of talking.

How we must struggle not to understand
all that is said to us, not to be covered with it,

just as here, head in on your hands,
hair falling over them,

you focus on these words, thinking *I get it*,
though any words say everything: I mean *everything*.

15

Dust of singer on singer, bird on bird,
dust of their images, broadcast,
dust of their songs that settles
on monitors and end tables
and in me, residuals of wind,
so I must be seen again, to grow light
after much fatness of seeing,
must speak, not to drown in hearing.

16

If everything is touch, then what's this soft
devouring of your drifts and drives, this blowing
through your tops and outlooks, under your shuddering doors,
this smoothing you like a map, or folding you small
to fit you into all these stories
I have to tell, this feeling you fit me into yours.
this saying O you *this*?

If I am the trillion fingertips of air
you form beneath, if we are waters blended,
perfumes unstoppered, gone and everywhere,
have I reached you, do I hold you?
If I stand in you, my eyes behind your eyes,
if I underlie your breathing, rising where you rise
and cleaving where you cleave? Is it knowing

at all, this saying
that tries to be like seeing, this seeing trying to be heard,

these sentences, which are one further sense,
straining to vanish into something they call you,
or to be vanished *into*, as a lake makes
so much of its forgetting of the rain?

17

And if, as I dream, I touched you microscopically
as smoke touches air, if I entered you
at the level of the molecule, your carbon chains
stretching like power lines into a starless sky,
it would be dark, for there are no eyes on this scale,
and there's nothing to see, anyway, no face of yours
in no beneficent sky, no windy soul,
no signatory flourish of your limbs,
just atoms, like invisible constellations,
and light waves, propagating past me darkly,
as if I stood blind and deaf, even my thoughts turned off,
on the shaken platform of the Express.

This inside I've imagined would be an outside,
this merger I've desired, a further distance,
lucid, stellar, cold.   O you *you*
who are a galaxy that has never heard of you,
as words have never heard of a beautiful line
or the beautiful line of its explanation.

18

Neutrinos through the thickness of the planet, undeflected,
shine invisibly, touching no atom, and sans diversion
of a rock's thought, or any thought of yours,
though what's more sensitive, what's more easily
distracted—forking, scattering? It's the void in us,

Lucretius says, that revels in discovering
planets translucent, waters, shadowy woods,
since these are most like looking back into the mind.
Thus car and sycamore and kiosk dimming at evening,
half-memory already, and the child, half-seen,
who fumbles at a lock, half-seeing,
are a loss we feel as ours, or a coming-again,
since to repeat is also to lose.
My thousand hurries along this block,
like your thousand turnings of the page,
reduce to one. Each sunset,
settling in, abolishes the last,
as wind will blow the wind away,
as all memory of obliteration your one kiss,
like a sky coming down on me, obliterates.

19

Probably they had it right, those ancients
who thought the soul was in the chest. They knew
where the real life was,
terror and love and awe,
their chasms, and quakes, flash floods.
But we who are smarter know it's all in the brain,
a little dark room there, behind the eye,
where someone littler watches and remembers,
talking to himself as the picture changes.

Aren't you sick of it,
this video, don't you want
exaltation like a cliff, passion or eagerness
in your hands, like loaves of stone
that stay where you put them?

20

If this is what we are like, then the gods,
who have to be what we fear,
must be stillness and clarity,
some star-like coffee-high that does not need to hold anything
as the world-sea holds none of its shores,

and nothing in their lives is heavy,
no pain or obstacle that does not vanish
when they cease to think of it
as if it were snow falling touchlessly through the air,
as if that air were the high blue vault of their eyes.

21

Thus for our lightly, fluently repeated
wish to be light or wind or water—to be pure *move*
and blend as movements—wind and light and wind—
and no more rage at our massiveness and boredom,
that not-wanting-to-be-loved
undoing all our dreams of who we were,
wind in light and cloud in light in wind.

But then: the pillar taller than my body, the slammed door,
the light on the sill, the cliff between two notes,
a shelf booked up in size-order, even the oft-sung pear
that reminds us, as everything else does, of the body,
and yes, even its truly boring
and sad oft-sungness,
and a tire's hot squeal, letting go,
are desire, and difficult, and difficult desire.
Why should I not have a garage,
a swabbed counter, a geode,
why should I not have a dog for a heart?

22

Why touch me, anyway, if *nearness* is just a metaphor
that leaves us in the cold?   But to feel what planets feel,
holding each other to their swift ellipses,
their swinging out a form of their falling in: speak

around me, then, let me misunderstand
deeply, fail to compare yourself to me,
smiling stubbornly. Rise so steeply
I can clamber up, scatter my equipment,
sleep, and wake to mountains of the dawn.

23

For we have never, strangely, been within ourselves.
Never have I sailed the red arterial grotto
to my thick hand, have never and never
seen the mauve noon there, like the sun through squeezed lids.
I imagine the air mid-palm as dense and tropical,
but there is no air; breathing there is sub-marine,
continuous but hidden, molecular like time,
and, like time, runs without our willing

as even our will does. I say *I will walk*, but given the power
over walking, I would fall debating which nerves to fire,
which of a score of muscles to contract in order.
If I were responsible for everything in my body,
I would pass out from mismanagement of glands,
I don't even know the names of. As for the legions
of mitochondria and ion channels, how would I supervise them,
and still remember to draw breath in, to beat my heart,
as if I were charged with counting *a million, a million and one*
in a million voices simultaneously?
The body is what is done for us. From it
our dream of the world's beneficence derives,

from it, too, our helplessness, since, floating above it,
we do not know what we do or how we do it.
Thus our intensest pleasures, alone or together,
are pleasures, too, because they lose us in our bodies
with a slow perfection. I taste and fail,

or let music sway me with the wide slowness
of a plucked string in strobe. *It is rich to die*, I say,
torrents of darkness filling my closed eyes.
Old metaphor, but true, since it is true in dying,
whether from gunshot, heart attack, or cancer,
the last thing is: cells starve for oxygen and go down.
All deaths, in the end, are drownings in the body,
as what desire desires is drowning in desire.

24

Pretty convincing, what the brain's
original darkness, guessing what light was like,
came up with: eye.
As for the ear?
Ah, what it thought of air.

This plane in turbulence, dropping abruptly,
this one-more-stair-than-I-thought,
my foot sunk in the mole-soft lawn,
the wounded falling towards their wounds,
these swallows, hitting the sunset, gone,

must be what I've made of you: November,
white-blue and high
chamber in the catacomb
desire has hollowed, prisoner for life.

Come the thunderbolts, such is their suddenness
who knows whether they made us afraid, or our fear
or guilt summoned them, wrath of Zeus?
Thus when we hear what we least wanted to hear,
which means, of course, that we expected it somehow,
we say *It hit me like a thunderbolt.*

For the mind is not a point, as we sometimes think,
or the little theater where we sit alone, but many nations,
eye, ear, memory, knowing, knowing of knowing,
each in touch with the others by long distance,
and there's no one Place that is us, no single Present,
only the order in which we hear their calls.

So much that happens to us is ourselves, is timing.
A man who seemed to *think* of lightning, birds, a face
a millisecond before he knew he had seen them
might feel he was a god and had called them down,
or, take the milder case, might grow up feeling his power
because so much took place as he foresaw, or milder still,
might feel the world as a friendliness of happening.

Whereas the one who heard himself speaking words
a millisecond before he knew he'd chosen to say them
would find them like lightning. Would think
Even my own words happen to me.
I lie here, dead, listening for the voice of the god,
though even my listening is His Will in me,
as on the tip of a downbent branch, a dampish sparrow
opens its throat to admit a cry.

26

When I bend to dial, and your number comes to mind,
who has gone down what stairs, along what aisles,
and stood tiptoe to get it off what shelf,
third from the right? I say my words, it is true,
but where they came from, how they rose
to the very tip of saying, that I have never seen.

For the mind, I admit, is even outside itself.
I see a knife, and sense how I would grip it:
my eyes have spoken to my hands in some third language
they both understand, but it is not my language,
just as I can say only very crudely
all that I know from your face, or all the reassembly
of your torso, as you shift, says other ways.

Poor reasonable creature, I say *I understand*
but cannot tell you what is meant by that,
except that I seem to. Even those memories
I most call mine, they, too, must belong to others
I timeshare with, constantly missing,
as like me and unlike me as my moods,
since they do not fool me into thinking I am them,
or then, or there. We think what's in our heads

is ours, is us, and that what we don't know,
or can't have, must be outside: real.
But it is not imagination that wants what you want
and not some constant world that constantly prevents,
since both are you, since neither is.
It's yourself you can neither find nor talk to,
force to listen, change. And what's the story of time
but that Edenic moment, lost forever,
which was a window you looked out contentedly,
which was you looking out of it, content?

Hawks, rockets, lightning are fast, but the mind
concludes these journeys almost before they are thought of.
To Sirius? A matter of milliseconds. Ah, but how
do the continents remember to keep drifting
at a rate that imperceptibly becomes an inch a year,
how does the frost with a week's pressure,
such delicate and terrific pressure from every side at once,
harden and brown a weed without breaking a single stamen,
or in fifty years turn a hair gray? Slow's the wonder.

So many phenomena it pleases us to think of
as beyond process or performance, help or hindrance—
the reassertion over scarred ground, for example,
of the weeds, or the congregation of the clouds—
because to think of them this way (which means not
to think of them) leaves something in us free
and the world wild and full of gifts, what we call *real*.
Slow's the wonder; slow's the relief. But even wonders
have their essences and seeds, and patiently grow from them,

for time also is particulate, as Lucretius tells us, atom by atom.
Thus your wedding ring, over decades, slims with wear,
and a plowblade down the sillion shines and dwindles,
as a knife with sharpening disappears into the air.
Lanes blacken gradually with the passing of tires,
and the stone stair is worn in the middle as if sagging
with heavy feet, and when it rains the water courses there.

Even the legendary lightning, slowly seen,
is a man descending a ladder, stopping to look down,
starting again to descend. Even light,
scrupulously imagined, is gradual,
though when will you calm, when will you ever gaze
with the steady openness that would slow its radiation,
showing the smooth striving from streetlamp down to street
of the individual waves, over and over?

Ah, everything happens for cause, and gradually,
and nothing disappears at once, or totally:
this is the thing Lucretius seems to tells us
that we most wanted to be told. That time
is also touch, and touches us again,
and always the *having been* leaves traces of its being,
as if it remembered us, and would never leave us alone.

Or that's what we believe, regardless, we who trek
to the stairs the poet's foot wore, or look out the windows,
strangely askew now, of our childhood homes,
or weep for pleasure in apartments of old pain,
or greet the traveler who once stopped to listen
to crickets in the field, where, rumor has it,
the lover of the goddess rained down, blasted,
though reason insists coincidence of place is nothing.

For the mind itself is suasions of erosion
if we could pay attention—but that is the point,
isn't it?   No one notices, in all the backing and forthing,
how the beach re-contours. "Suddenly," it is changed,
something is gone you thought was a love forever,
something lifted you thought would be heavy forever.
In the novel the children grow up in a sentence
and a young man wakes up gray and over, and Lucretius
. . . but now—gods, make me slower!— I cannot remember

how it took forty-odd years to get here,
page whatever, a matter of inches from the beginning,
and if I can't re-live it, second by second,
feeling the constant assurance of faint time
like the slight burn of kite string paying out through two
        fingers—
as, alas, who can?— then it is not mine,
and there is no such thing as a life, and my next step
may thrust into blankness white as the end of a line

28

Just as Zeno with his arrow that must travel
half the distance to your heart, then half of what remains
and half of that, and never arrives,
proves motion impossible, since how could the arrow remember
over the huge chasm between instants
that it should be moving: so I am always half-way
to half-way to understanding: that the present does not exist,
though once it must have, since. . . see
all I cannot move back to!

Or maybe it's that we do not live in the present,
which is the rock in the stream
that splits us as we flow around it.

29

All things have an essence, and a time, and take their time.
Otherwise, why could not Nature produce men of such power
they could traverse the ocean as if it were nothing more
than blue carpet, dampish on a humid morning,
and break off Andes like the heel of a loaf?
They might eat the planet clean, or replant it
with aluminum forest and weep at its ruin.
They might, in whimsy, channelize our Southern rivers,
leaving them straight and navigable—
what could be simpler or clearer?—
and if they were also scoured of life, silt-choked, flood-prone. . .
well, here is the law of the universe, first,
that everything we can imagine would be too simple for us,
and second that our desires, given their way,
are powerless to undo their own undoings.
For desire simplifies and forgets, and Lucretius reminds us
things are more easily taken apart than put back together.
How could we live in a world that abided our consent?

I think of you turned to mine, to me, to yours,
to someone else's, to what you wanted.
I think, don't you, of our grade school art class—
how we waited in line to pour in the sink our rinsings,
how all of our visions, finally mixed,
made, every week, the same brown disappointed waters?

30

For all things are made also of what resists them.
Otherwise each Atlantic wave, incoming,
might spread over the prairies like a sky, and never stopping,
meet the Pacific, or each single, barely perceptible
spore of a fern might suddenly unfold
over us a green map the size of the world.
The peach, in its seed-instant, already turns and turns
as if the opposing air were coded in its dream
of how roundly it will ripen against the sky:
the essence of things is foreknowledge of their limits,
as the mime's body shapes itself backwards from finger
to shoulder with the touch of a wall it will never touch.

Thus for imagination, thus for desire:
time is the enemy they deepen against,
though it alone denies the return of the dead
they ached for, and all those loves unhappening.
It alone saves us from subjugation to freedom, it alone
prevents the fruitless practice of perfection.
Otherwise all stories are equally true
and there is no success or failure, heroism or shame,
no love some other story won't undo.
Otherwise nothing is left to the imagination,
otherwise there is no otherwise.

AFTERWORD

Lucretius is one of those authors I can't imagine not having read, though he came along late in my virtually Latinless education, in the last course of a Ph.D. program I happily survived by completely failing to understand what was expected of me. In the Mantinband translation of *De Rerum Natura* we used back in the 70's, he sounded like this:

> For nothing can touch or be touched, unless it possesses body
> And garments hung up by the sea-washed shore grow damp,
> but, spread out in the sunshine, they become quite dry.
> Yet no one has ever seen how the water came into them,
> or how it went away again in the heat of the sun.
> Therefore water consists of tiny particles
> which it is impossible for our eyes to see.

A scientist at a time when science, philosophy and poetry were not necessarily different, Lucretius explains the atomic theory of matter in language as plain and literal as possible. But how plain is that? "Plain" and "literal" are themselves metaphors, and even rationalism's most scraped-clean explanations are stories: in passages like this I found a strangely disembodied body, the secret ministries of invisible particles, an austere but heartening animation in the mere drying of beach towels. And how much stronger the sense of transparency, of Presence, when Lucretius pulled out all the stops and turned the sturdy present into a panorama of secret and lovely erosions:

> Moreover, in the course of many revolving years,
> a ring on someone's finger is made thin by wear,
> and dripping water hollows a stone, and an iron plowshare
> imperceptibly diminishes in the fields.
> The paving-stone of the highway is all rubbed away by human
> feet,
> and brazen statues near the gates often have the right hand
> partly worn away
> as people pass along and touch it for a greeting.
> We know these things diminish, since they are rubbed away,
> and yet which particles fall off, and at what times,
> our jealous faculty of sight prevents us from seeing.

This landscape was the one I lived in, or needed to, and I had found something like it in the Victorians I most loved. Hardy's novels and poems are full of worn stairs, shoulder-brushed jambs, haunted places. When he traveled to Europe, he gravitated to the graves of Keats and Gibbons, the field where Shelley's skylark might have crashed. He refused invitations to America: it had no ghosts of interest to him. What he felt was what Tennyson called "the passion of [not *for*] the past." I trust in this context I won't have to explain, as I often did to incredulous friends, why I thought "Transformations" was his best poem

> These grasses must be made
> Of her who often prayed,
> Last century, for repose;
> And the fair girl long ago
> Whom I often tried to know
> May be entering this rose....

or why these lines of Whitman

> This grass is very dark to be from white heads of old mothers,
> Darker than the colorless beards of old men,
> Dark to come from under the faint red roofs of mouths.

seemed to me his most moving. No, say his most touching. For Hardy and Whitman, though two thousand years later, live in a Lucretian community of touch. To minds both literal and superstitious enough (and what mind isn't enough of both?), time's recoverable. Those eroded particles are the trail of bread crumbs back to where we were. Everything that's gone touched something that touched something else that we can still see and touch. Isn't it all still there, then, trying to remember itself in us? That's a desperate world-size metonymy we can't quite believe, of course, skeptics and rationalists that we are. But then, of course, we can't stop believing it either.

Lucretius is a brilliant scientist and a teacher just as brilliant. I don't pretend that "A Suite for Lucretians" qualifies as scientific, though its reader will not be surprised to hear that I subscribe to more science magazines than literary ones, or even that it's more than tangentially Lucretian, an homage, a fantasia. As for teacherliness: I call my tone "faux-didactic." There's a deadpan faintly amused at itself, a kind of lecturer who fairly often runs off the rails being over-logical or over-lyrical.   I'm aware the poem makes points about metaphor, about the isolation of the mind, about imagination and the adequacy of the world thereto, but they weren't The Point.   If there's an overall argument, it came late and was elicited largely by changing the order of sections written for their own sakes until their sequence made as much sense as it could.   It was like doing one of those games on the old HoJo place mats: connect the dots in the right order and you've drawn a face, or spelled out d-e-s-i-r-e.

What's it like to be, physically?   To be alone?   Together? What's in, how's with, where's to?   I suppose the need to think those basic terms over and over is what makes one what's called a "nature poet," a term I detest.   When I was a young man, my story was that I'd started out wanting to be a physicist or chemist and that adolescence had diverted me into poetry. In actuality, I was always terrible in the lab.   There was always some measurement I knew would be interesting that I didn't have the tools or the discipline or (over and over) the patience with reality to come up with.   Now it seems to me that what I really wanted was to be something more like an alchemist, and that I kept right on.

To my only husband, Herbert Leibowitz,
and my only son, Gabriel Sky-Leibowitz,
with unbounding love

SUSAN YANKOWITZ

Phaedra in Delirium

SUSAN YANKOWITZ is the author of *1969 Terminal 1996*, a collaboration with Joseph Chaikin and ensemble; *A Knife in the Heart, Under The Skin,* and *Night Sky,* seen throughout the country and currently being translated for productions in France, Spain, and Germany. She is the librettist and lyricist of *Slain In The Spirit: The Promise of Jim Jones,* a gospel-and-blues opera with music by Taj Mahal, to be produced in 1999.

PHAEDRA IN DELIRIUM

*A New Version Inspired
By Variants Of The Myth*

CAST OF CHARACTERS

Phaedra, *a woman in her forties*

The Friend, *an androgynous person of either
gender, aged thirty to thirty-five, who plays
both Phaedra's Female confidante and
Hippolytus' Male friend*

Theseus/Hippolytus, *a single actor who plays a
man of forty-five and his own son at twenty or
two actors who convey their physical
similarities as father and son by using the same
inflections, postures and gestures at key
moments in the play.*

SETTING

*A large canopy bed and the wild outdoors
outside, visible through a window; or, more
abstractly, a world of beds and mirrors,
surrounded or invaded by lush, brutal nature.*

PHAEDRA IN DELIRIUM

*The Friend, an androgynous figure who appears more
feminine in scenes with Phaedra, and masculine in those
with Hippolytus, addresses the audience. Nearby is a four
poster bed with a canopy, surrounded by curtains. These now
are closed.*

FRIEND:
> Phaedra's sick. For weeks she's been in here, rooted to her
> bed. Sleeping. Not sleeping. Lady of leisure, or lady of
> lamentations: lady layabed. She needs me now—I know
> she does—and so I packed my bag and settled in to keep an
> eye on her. Not that it helps, not that she cares. She barely
> answers when I talk to her, doesn't drink, doesn't eat,
> doesn't really see me, and doesn't budge from that bed, as
> if she didn't know the difference between night and day,
> day and night. Sometimes I hear her tossing and turning,
> full of moans and sighs; and the rest of the time—

*(The Friend pulls open the curtains that conceal the bed.
Phaedra sits there, supported by pillows, looking at herself in
a mirror.)*

FRIEND:
> —she stares in that mirror, stares and stares, as if she's
> married to it. But she's not. She's married to Theseus, a
> wealthy man, a powerful man, Theseus who is away,
> frequently away, I hear, on business, he says, always on
> business—but what business can that be? He's almost
> newlywed, and he lets business seduce him from his home?
> *(Moving closer.)*   That's what's eating her up, it must be.
> I'm a woman and her friend; I know these troubles. She
> feels abandoned, she longs for him, she worries that he
> regrets the marriage already, that in six months' time he's
> bored with her, lost himself in a strange woman's lap. . .

PHAEDRA:
> *(Delirious.)*   It's so hot in here, I'm suffocating   Asleep,
> awake, my dreams are heavy with him, my tongue is
> parched, my lips can't open without his lips near   The

mountains! I want to go with him to the mountains, to be
with him in the air, with the wind on my skin and the
rustle of leaves and the silence that has wildness in it, the
sense that something could happen   anything could
happen   in the night, in the dark.

FRIEND:
(*Touches her forehead.*) Shh. Shhh. The fever's making you
talk like this. You're burning up.

PHAEDRA:
Good. I'll be consumed, I'll turn to flame, to ash, I'll become
pure   yes, pure spirit.

FRIEND:
You're sick, that's all. People live through sickness and go
on to love their lives. Let me call the doctor, get you some
medicine.

PHAEDRA:
There's no medicine for this.

FRIEND:
It's been three days. You have to eat something.

PHAEDRA:
I can't! I'll live on nothing—or better still, not live at all.

FRIEND:
Now why are you so morbid!? The man adores you,
worships you. Everyone knows that. So he's away for a
while. So it's hard to be without your husband. But it's no
tragedy.

PHAEDRA:
You! What do you know of tragedy?!

FRIEND:
(*Offended.*) And what do you know of me? I understand
suffering, believe me. I'm not ignorant of life. So I never
married. Haven't you ever suspected that sex might be
better without a ring on your finger?

PHAEDRA:
It has occurred to me.

FRIEND:
I'm not exactly a virgin, you know. I'm just... discreet.

PHAEDRA:
So that's your secret. That's why in all these years I've
never once seen you possessed, taken over by a passion.

FRIEND:
Would I compete with you? Thank God one of us is balanced. I know how to enjoy myself without going crazy. Without driving everyone else crazy! You may love your extremes but I prefer the middle ground.

PHAEDRA:
How comforting for you.

FRIEND:
You could be comfortable, too. But you won't let yourself. You give in to every feeling, you wallow in your misery as if it were pleasure. What's wrong? Tell me.

PHAEDRA:
Please. Go away.

FRIEND:
I won't. I'll wait right here until you tell me what's happened. Why else did I come to stay with you? I've been up all night, worrying, worrying; my nerves are shot. What awful news have you heard? *(Silence.)* Oh great suffering angel, great mum's-the-word, great martyr of the bleeding silence, talk to me! Is Theseus hurt? In danger of some kind? Speak up! Is he dead?

PHAEDRA:
I've heard nothing about Theseus. Nothing at all.

FRIEND:
Well, then, why all the fuss? Some women would be thrilled to have their husbands out of town for a while, then suddenly, excitingly, turn up one lonely night and slip between the sheets.

PHAEDRA:
Some other woman, maybe. Some other sheets.

FRIEND:
So he *is* with another woman. Don't deny it, I see it in your eyes, that green flame. What did you expect? We all know Theseus. That man never could resist a woman! So what? Who cares if he's having a fling? Look at the fabulous life you have! I've never seen such luxury: this beautiful house, the gardens, horses, a lake... *(Strokes the bed linens.)* In my entire life, I've never even touched sheets like these.

PHAEDRA:
Trust me, you wouldn't want to lie in this bed.

FRIEND:
Oh yes, I would. I'd delight in everything you have! Why can't you? You don't have cancer, your heart is strong; I can hear it pounding from here. You're too young for this "sickness unto death".

PHAEDRA:
Too old, you mean, to suffer the petty griefs of love. Come here. Closer. Look. Gravity has her hands on me, she's pulling at my skin, pulling down down down, turning muscle soft and falling off the bone.

FRIEND:
(Touching her cheek.) I like your skin.

PHAEDRA:
My cheekbones are vanishing. And my hair is losing its color. Do you see? There's a stripe of grey right here.

FRIEND:
That's not a disease. It's nature.

PHAEDRA:
I hate nature! I hate what she does to us. You'll understand soon enough. Every woman who's reached my age knows what I mean. Suddenly, overnight, we become invisible. We could walk down the street naked and no one would notice. Oh, yes, we can celebrate our "glorious, our liberating maturity"—but who burns for us now? Who pours out his heart in poetry and midnights? No one. Never. It's obvious: we're the fate that every woman is trying to escape.

FRIEND:
You have great character in your face.

PHAEDRA:
Thank you so much. That's what every woman wants to hear.

FRIEND:
No-one's ever said *I* have great character.

PHAEDRA:
Maybe you don't.

FRIEND:
I beg your pardon!

PHAEDRA:
Why would anyone care about your character? You're still young enough to catch the eye. And pretty, too.

FRIEND:
 You think so?
PHAEDRA:
 Does it matter what *I* think? The world has its standards.
 You meet them.
FRIEND:
 You're very beautiful.
PHAEDRA:
 Beautiful, oh yes—for a woman my age. That's what people
 say and think they're being kind. "How beautiful she is for
 a woman her age!" But I can't fool myself; I have eyes.
 Everywhere I go I see them, the girls with glowing skin,
 their faces and throats like unmarked paper, their stomachs
 little bowls turned inside out. That's where men go to fill
 themselves.
FRIEND:
 They'll get older, too, you know.
PHAEDRA:
 But they have time! They have time now, when they need
 it! Oh God, how fast it goes. Only yesterday I walked down
 the road, sending up clouds of musk. My breath was an
 invitation. No man would have refused me.
FRIEND:
 Who would refuse you now? No one, no one.
PHAEDRA:
 Really?
FRIEND:
 Is *that* what happened? You met a man and you wanted—?
PHAEDRA:
 Wanted?! Me? What could I possibly want?! I'm a wife, the
 wife of Theseus, a great figure in the world, an important
 man!
FRIEND:
 And he should be with you. I'm going to track him down. It
 shouldn't be too hard. He leaves a strong scent. Men who
 love women always do. *(She exits.)*
*(Phaedra turns around on her bed to face the audience, her head
bowed forward under the weight of an enormous mass of hair piled on
top.)*
PHAEDRA:
 (Tries to lift her head; she can't.) This hair   I can barely lift

up my head   so neat, so proper, no wisps flying   it
weighs me down *(Occasionally she succeeds in raising her head
but slaps herself down.)* Girl   run through the fields
hair flying   unbraid the braids   raise the sails   let
the horses loose   slap!   grow up!   running   toes
like worms, feet like birds   where are your shoes?
slap! slap! grow up!   can't see the stars the sun the skies
the floor is grey and dirty, the ground hits my eyes   lift!
slap me down!   pins in my scalp a torture, pins like
needles, needle in the haystack, jumping falling hay in my
hair slap!   can't go wild, can't go child   stop! slap! sit
still   grown up   heavy heavy heavy the head that
can't move can't dance can't throw back my head for song or
love or   heavy   heavy   heavy
*(Theseus has entered and watched her. He moves closer and grips her
hair, pulls back her head, kisses her on the lips.)*

THESEUS:
I love your hair, your eyes, your mouth, your lower lip, the
way it quivers now, your throat, and how you offer it to me
now. *(Kisses her strained throat.)* It was always you I
wanted, not Ariadne. But Ariadne showed me the way, she
kept me from death, I owed her my love; I did what was
right. But you were the one I desired, it was you, Phaedra,
behind my eyes while I gazed into hers, you I held in my
arms at night, you, the sister. Time waited until I was
free—and finally you belong to me, you share my bed, my
breath. *(Kisses her lips though her head is still arched
back.)* You wanted me, too, when I wasn't yours. And now,
now that I'm here and in the flesh, tell me: is reality better
than your dream? Tell me, darling. How do you feel now?
*(But although he releases her, she is left with her head
flung so far back that she can't lift it forward or speak. She
makes a strangulated sound.)* You don't have to say a word.
I know how you feel. Don't change. Stay the way you are.
I'll hold this image of you in my heart. *(Kisses her again
before leaving.)* I'll be home in a week.
*(Phaedra again can't lift up her head. After several attempts,
she raises her hands and begins to pull the pins from her hair.
One by one she plucks them out and drops them to the floor. Her
long hair begins to hang loose. As the floor, perhaps the whole
stage, becomes littered with pins, lights come up elsewhere on*

Theseus in a rhapsody.)
THESEUS:

Women women women. What do I love best about them? The odors that waft from them, the odors of deserts and of seas, of wildflowers and of fish, odors that aren't odors only but personalities, each one an invitation, a pure yes, a yes and no, a maybe, a husky no. What does it matter if their skin is like silk or like sandpaper, if their thighs are loose or tight as violin strings, there's music in all of them, in their voices and in their hips, inside where the darkness hums. Women, with their eyes opened like windows or narrowed to squeeze a man's breath away, eyes that shut in self defense when the fire burns too hot, eyes that take you by the hand and lead you in, far inside, where it's always a mystery, and if you take your time, the mystery doesn't disappear, it deepens. And where are you when you're in there, in women, surrounding yourself with them, sliding into darkness that is your own darkness, too, a darkness that you can't find alone.

(The last hairpin falls as Theseus vanishes from view.
Finally Phaedra can lift her head. She is facing the audience.
She takes a deep breath, then swirls her hair around and
around her with increasing freedom. She pulls down her
nightgown so that her bare shoulders are exposed, and lets her
hair move over them. Her eyes are closed, and she is smiling,
standing in a field of hairpins.)
PHAEDRA:

This is how he saw me when he saw me first. This is how I felt, this is how it felt when he saw me first. *(Swirls her hair.)* This is how I want it to feel   like hands on me like fingers playing on my skin. This is who I was when he saw me first. This is how I felt when-

(Spotlit elsewhere, Hippolytus appears, dressed in a white
linen suit. Phaedra turns in his direction. Slowly, as if against
her will, she walks toward him. She stands directly in front of
him.)
PHAEDRA:

So. You're Hippolytus. *(He nods and stares at her awkwardly. Transfixed, she takes his hands in hers and holds them for a long time.)* Hippolytus. You have your father's hands.

(Hippolytus grabs back his hands and stares at her as she backs away from him, her eyes fixed on his, until she is once again ensconced in her canopied bed and pulls the curtains shut. During this, the Female Friend has entered with a broom to sweep up the hairpins.)

HIPPOLYTUS:
(Staring at his hands.) Why did she touch me?

(The Friend turns around, in his Male aspect now, Hippolytus' Friend.)

HIPPOLYTUS:
Why did she touch me?

FRIEND:
You know how it is with women.

HIPPOLYTUS:
No, I don't. She sends me away on ridiculous errands; she makes sure we're never in the same room; she avoids talking to me, eating with me, even looking at me—but when we happen to meet, she puts her hands on me. She puts her hands on me.

FRIEND
So? She doesn't have leprosy.

HIPPOLYTUS:
I don't like people touching me.

FRIEND:
She's not `people', she's your mother.

HIPPOLYTUS:
No, my step-mother, my father's wife. I'm no part of her. She doesn't want a son; she's been cold to me from the start. So why does she touch me?

FRIEND:
Why? Put yourself in her place. She's probably lonely, scared. She's not used to being alone. And here she is, in a big house in the country, too much land, too few people, no neighbors, no visitors, no shops even. Your father doesn't let her know where he is, how he is. I don't think she's heard one word from him. She's worried to death, I bet.

HIPPOLYTUS:
My father's been around. He knows the world. What could happen to him?

FRIEND:
Women. Women could happen to him. You **know that**.

Women have always been his problem.

HIPPOLYTUS:
When he was young. That's all over now.

FRIEND:
You think so? A man like him? Come on, use your imagination. He's in a desert, right? It's hot. He's thirsty, looking for water. He's all alone. He sees a woman, any woman. Aha, an oasis! What does he do? He drinks!

HIPPOLYTUS:
He's not in the desert. He's in Europe.

FRIEND:
Oh. There are no women in Spain, on the beaches in Nice.

HIPPOLYTUS:
He loves Phaedra.

FRIEND:
Sure he does, sure. But love isn't the problem, it's sex, my friend, desire, that body itch, that lowdown cry, nothing to do with conjugal sheets. And when that rises up, when passion grabs hold of a man, it makes him forget everything else, it murders what you call love, it kills loyalty, it—

HIPPOLYTUS:
Put it in jail, then.

FRIEND:
You don't know what I'm talking about, do you?

HIPPOLYTUS:
I have better things to do than study diseases of the heart.

FRIEND:
Diseases, you call them. Well, Hippolytus, one thing's for sure: you are not your father's son.

HIPPOLYTUS:
When it comes to women—I guess not. I think I'll take a ride.

FRIEND:
Alone?

HIPPOLYTUS:
No. I'll have my horse.

FRIEND:
Oh. Great company, a horse. Much better than a human being.

HIPPOLYTUS:
That's not it. I don't have anything against people. It's just that I like nature better.

FRIEND:
Rocks don't try to touch you, huh? Trees don't expect you to share their troubles. The moon stays far above you, cool, distant and cool.

HIPPOLYTUS:
You understand me perfectly.

FRIEND:
What am I going to tell Phaedra when she finds out you're gone?

HIPPOLYTUS:
The truth, what else? Her husband's son is staying in the mountains for a few days. She'll probably sleep better, knowing I'm away.

FRIEND:
She doesn't sleep at all. Once or twice last night, and the one before, I heard her footsteps down the hall. They stopped outside your door.

HIPPOLYTUS:
Why?

FRIEND:
How should I know? Maybe she's afraid *you're* lonely now that Theseus is gone. Maybe she's listening for your tears or nightmares, ready to comforrt her young charge.

HIPPOLYTUS:
She'll have to find someone else to mother. I won't be here tonight.

FRIEND:
You promised your father to look after her. Do it, then. Give her a few minutes of your attention. Bend a little. People admire a man who goes his own way—but they don't like him. Not really.

HIPPOLYTUS:
I don't care.

FRIEND:
Maybe you should learn to care. You're part of the race.

HIPPOLYTUS:
A man can't change his nature.

FRIEND:
But you aren't natural.

HIPPOLYTUS:
Not natural? Me?

FRIEND:
No. Look at that body of yours, all those muscles and economy. Beautiful, sure—but like a statue, chiselled, cold. And inside, I sometimes think, you're made of marble, too. You don't let anyone close. Tell me: who do you laugh with? Who holds you when it's dark at night? Who consoles you?

HIPPOLYTUS:
I don't need consolation.

FRIEND:
Come off it. Everyone needs consolation; everyone wants love.

HIPPOLYTUS:
Everyone, everyone! I don't give a damn about everyone! Why should I pretend to be someone I'm not? If I were a dwarf, you wouldn't keep pushing me to grow another three feet. If I were blind, you wouldn't insist I see. I'm not going to twist myself out of shape. Not for you, or anyone. I am who I am and I'm happy that way.

FRIEND:
People hate arrogance like yours. Take my word for it: set yourself above the rest of humanity and humanity will do everything it can to bring you down.

HIPPOLYTUS:
But I don't feel better than other people; I just feel... separate. I want to be a man as powerful as my father but closer to sky than to earth, like air or light, cut loose from everything, from fevers and tomorrows, deserts and fish, sea and caves. Why should people hate me for that? It's what we all become at the end.

FRIEND:
But why hurry there? This is the world, this is life, and we're not air. As for me, I like bodies... (*Traces the line from Hippolytus' neck to shoulder.*) ...how the neck flows so smoothly into the shoulder, and the shoulder curves into the arm. I think it's beautiful the way we're made. Don't you?

HIPPOLYTUS:
(*Confused.*) You mean... aesthetically, right?
FRIEND:
(*Embarrassed.*) Right. (*Moves away.*) I'll see you in a few
days. But while you're gone, think about what I said. Go
easy. Relent. (*Exits.*)
(*Hippolytus remains on stage and addresses the audience.*)
HIPPOLYTUS:
Relent, he says. Bend. What he really means is, curry
favor. That's what men do when they're dependent on
others. I can't wait till my father gets back. If he were here,
this would still be our house, the fields our fields, and the
days would be filled with our steps and our horses racing
side by side in the mountains, and our talk at night. He'd
smile at me, he'd grip my shoulders in his hands and study
his face in mine, he'd tell me of the years before we met,
when he was just a name to me, an image, a big man with
a beard, like God. Where is he now? Where has he gone?
Without him, I don't belong here. Since he married
Phaedra, everything's changed. When he's home, the door
to his bedroom is locked, I hear him laughing at night with
her, he forgets me, he forgets I exist. And when he's away,
the house feels... contaminated; it reeks of Phaedra's
perfume. She's everywhere! In the sink, on the tiles,
sometimes on the china, I see strands of her hair; her
stockings are draped over the chairs; I find her slippers on
the stairs I have to walk to reach my bed. She's like an
enormous slug, swallowing all the oxygen, spilling over
into every inch of space. It's disgusting.
(*Slowly, without his awareness, the curtains begin opening around
Phaedra's bed. Little by little, she can be seen listening to him,
completely gripped by his presence, his words.*)
HIPPOLYTUS:
I have to get away, into the hills and the mountains behind
the hills, the covering leaves and the surprise of flowers
where there seemed only dirt, and the paths that seem
made for my foot, or the hooves of my horses. We graze
and gallop and never stumble. I'm strong in the hills, I
know who I am and where I am, I never lose my way, I just
keep mounting higher and higher till there's no sight of

this house at all, not even of the smoke rising from the chimney. That's where I belong: above the swamps and marshes and the perfectly ploughed fields of farmers, the perfectly groomed lawns of perfect families, high up, alone, where the air has no perfume, no perfume at all...

PHAEDRA:
(Steps out from her bed, startling him.) Hippolytus!

HIPPOLYTUS:
What?! What is it?

PHAEDRA:
I heard you're going away.

HIPPOLYTUS:
Yes.

PHAEDRA:
Overnight?

HIPPOLYTUS:
Maybe a few nights.

PHAEDRA:
A few. Two? Three?

HIPPOLYTUS:
I'm not sure yet.

PHAEDRA:
Would you like something to eat before you go?

HIPPOLYTUS:
No, no thank you. I'm fasting today.

PHAEDRA:
Fasting. So am I. I haven't eaten in days.

HIPPOLYTUS:
I heard. I'm sorry. You've been sick.

PHAEDRA:
Running a fever. Burning up. Here. Just feel my forehead.

HIPPOLYTUS:
(Steps back; nervous.) I don't need to do that. I can see for myself. And you're doing right. It's better not to eat when you have a fever.

PHAEDRA:
Oh, it is, it is. There are advantages to fasting, I've discovered, at least for me. I gained so much weight in the last few months. And now, well, as you can see, I'm quite a bit thinner. *(A silence.)* Don't you think so?

HIPPOLYTUS:
I can't say. I don't think I noticed.

PHAEDRA:
Does that mean you never thought I was overweight?
(Hippolytus doesn't know what to say.) Or that you didn't
look. In all this time, you never really looked at me. Is that
what you mean?

HIPPOLYTUS:
I'm sorry, I just don't know anything about women's...
weight.

PHAEDRA:
But there must be a *type* of woman you find attractive.
Curvaceous ones, for instance. *(No response.)* Or slim boyish
ones. Or motherly types with big bosoms and round arms.
(Still no response.) Most men have a definite preference.

HIPPOLYTUS:
I guess I'm not most men. *(A silence.)* I think I should go
and pack.

PHAEDRA:
Already? Why? What time is it?

HIPPOLYTUS:
I'm not the kind of person who lives by the clock. I never
notice the time.

PHAEDRA:
But you can't escape it. Time passes. It passes like a dream.
(Almost to herself.) It passes and leaves you behind. With
everything broken.

HIPPOLYTUS:
I won't break.

PHAEDRA:
You're very strong, I know.

HIPPOLYTUS:
(Proudly.) You can see that?

PHAEDRA:
Anyone with eyes can see it. And to tell the truth, your
body, your physique, I suppose I should say, makes me
wonder if I... if maybe *I* could become stronger, too.

HIPPOLYTUS:
I don't know about that.

PHAEDRA:
But you could help me. The problem is I've gone all soft:

my arms, my legs, even my neck. Sometimes I can't even lift up my head with all this hair on it! When I was growing up, girls didn't exercise; it wasn't feminine. But things are so much different now. Oh, I'd love to be a young girl today. I'd run, I'd swim, I'd ride horses, bareback—I could ride with you! in the mountains! with the manes of the horses wild in the wind! *(Lets her hair fall against her shoulders.)* I'd learn to keep my seat and hold on tight with my thighs, I'm sure I could do it! I could build up the right muscles. You could teach me. *(No response.)* Well, what do you think? Tell me. Is it too late?

HIPPOLYTUS:
I don't know. Probably.

PHAEDRA:
You mean I'm too old.

HIPPOLYTUS:
If you've let your muscles get too weak...

PHAEDRA:
I'm not sure they're *too* weak. *(Holds out her arms.)* Here. Feel.

HIPPOLYTUS:
(Backing away.) I think you should talk to my father about this. *He* knows how a woman's arms should feel; I don't, I don't have any idea. Now please, excuse me. I have to go.
(He wheels away and leaves, as Phaedra yearns after him, recapitulating her prior remarks.)

PHAEDRA:
Would you like something to eat?
I was very casual; my voice was relaxed, a mother talking to a son.
Would you like something to eat?
Then on to the inevitable:
Am I too fat? Too thin? What kind of woman do you like best?
I embarrassed him. But he was polite; he tried to answer. And then he tried to go. I wouldn't let him.
What time is it? I asked. Time passes, it passes like a dream.
He didn't know what I was talking about; he's young. So young.

I'm too soft, I said. But you could teach me, I could learn.
When I was growing up, girls didn't exercise; it wasn't
feminine.
    I think I smiled when I said that.
It wasn't feminine.
    Then:
I could ride with you. Bareback.
    Oh God, I didn't say that!
Ride bareback. With you. Do you think it's too late?
    Probably, he said. Probably it's too late.
(The Male Friend enters.)

FRIEND:
Excuse me. I'm looking for Hippolytus.

PHAEDRA:
Looking here? Why? How should I know where he is?

FRIEND:
I thought I heard his voice. If he needed my help, I was
going to saddle his horse for him. I wasn't sure when he
was leaving.

PHAEDRA:
Immediately, I assure you, and without looking back! He
was in a terrible hurry to get away.

FRIEND:
That's Hippolytus. Can't wait to be alone, out of reach, out
of touch, no embraces or goodbyes. He's probably off
already—

PHAEDRA:
Probably.

FRIEND:
—saddle or no saddle. *(Goes to window; looks out.)*

PHAEDRA:
(Overlapping.) Saddle or no saddle. Bareback. Probably.

FRIEND:
He's headstrong, stubborn, won't be reined in, just like his
horse. I wish I had more influence on him—
(Turns around, transforming into the Female Friend.)

FRIEND:
—and on you, sweetheart. Are you feeling better now?
Have you eaten? Slept?

PHAEDRA:
No. No. And no.

FRIEND:
>   You can't keep this up, can't keep testing the edge; you'll
>   fall over one of these dark nights.

PHAEDRA:
>   Good. Then it will be finished.

FRIEND:
>   For you. But what about me? What will happen to me?

PHAEDRA:
>   Who knows? Maybe you'll marry. There are always new
>   widowers popping up. Maybe you'll marry Theseus.

FRIEND:
>   *(Touches Phaedra's forehead.)* You do have a fever! Lie down.
>   You need to rest.

PHAEDRA:
>   If I rest, I'll give in. I have to keep fighting.

FRIEND:
>   Fighting what? Why? Tell me. Please. Maybe I can help.

PHAEDRA:
>   No one can help. It's in my blood, I can't escape. You know
>   my history. All the women in my family have been ruined
>   by love: my grandmother, my mother, and my sister, my
>   poor sister....

FRIEND:
>   Why dredge that up? It happened years ago.

PHAEDRA:
>   A lifetime ago. Theseus was young then. And so was I.
>   Ariadne fell in love with him at first sight—and so did I.
>   *(Moves into a separate light, lost in a repetition of obsessive*
>   *memory; the Friend listens from the distance.)* But she was
>   the one he chose. I was only fifteen years old. He seemed
>   like a god to me, so tall and slim, his skin bronzed by the
>   sun. Golden, that's how he looked, golden, walking toward
>   us through the sand. I'll never forget. I kept praying he
>   would change his mind and turn to me, I kept waiting,
>   waiting for someday, for somehow, all my girlhood,
>   waiting, in the daylight thinking of him, in the night-time
>   dreaming of him, wanting him, in my bed, in my white
>   sheets, in my white nightgown, dreaming of white and
>   waiting for it, and how it would feel, and love, and love-
>   making, and love-words, to me, for me. But he made a

pact with my sister. She helped him through the maze and in return he married her. He gave her a night or a week, made her pregnant with his child, and left her on an island all alone. And then what happened? What happened then? No one knows, no one was there, no one is certain how she died, in the agony of childbirth or by her own hand. No one was with her at the end.

FRIEND:
(*Leads her out of her isolation.*) She was far away and you were just a girl yourself; it wasn't your fault.

PHAEDRA:
It was a monstrous fate! And what did I do? Avenge her, murder him? Oh no. On the contrary. I took her place, I filled her absence, I married the man she married.

FRIEND:
You wanted to be happy.

PHAEDRA:
I believed I would be happy! And now the wheel turns to torture me.

FRIEND:
I'll stop the wheel, I'll send the torturers away! (*Tenderly.*) Tell me now. Tell me everything.

PHAEDRA:
(*Sorrowfully.*) What do you think love is?

FRIEND:
Something sweet, something bitter.

PHAEDRA:
It's only the bitterness I've known.

FRIEND:
How can that be? Theseus would give you the world. He's a great man in this country and he's made you his wife.

PHAEDRA:
Why do you keep jabbering about Theseus?!

FRIEND:
What? (*Silence; light dawns.*) You mean it's love—but not Theseus?

PHAEDRA:
How did you ever guess?

FRIEND:
Who is he?

PHAEDRA:
I can't say.

FRIEND:
Why not? Worse things have happened. Don't hold back now. Tell me who it is.

PHAEDRA:
A boy.

FRIEND:
A boy? . . .You mean someone young? *(Phaedra nods.) Much* younger than you? *(Phaedra nods.)* Well, that's lucky. Right in fashion, too.

PHAEDRA:
I could *set* a fashion with this one.

FRIEND:
Who is it?

PHAEDRA:
A relation. But not a relation.

FRIEND:
Don't tease me.

PHAEDRA:
My husband has loved him longer than I. But there's no sin in that for him. No, not for him.

FRIEND:
You don't mean—

PHAEDRA:
He has a room in this house. At night I hear him breathing. What divides us? Walls.

FRIEND:
Him!?

PHAEDRA:
Walls of wood and plaster. Even with my own weak hand I could strike them down. Then he would be next to me. In the darkness. Then he would be in—

FRIEND:
No.

PHAEDRA:
—my arms and his lips would be on mine and I would whisper into his mouth his name.

FRIEND:
Hippolytus!

PHAEDRA:
You're the one who said it, not I. Not I.

FRIEND:
And he, does he say he loves you too?

PHAEDRA:
How could he? He doesn't know how I feel. I'm so ashamed.
Oh, what should I do? What?

FRIEND:
You ask *me?* I have no husband, I have no son. How
should I know?

PHAEDRA:
Just imagine yourself in my place: you have years of
experience doing that!

FRIEND:
I don't think I have the imagination for this! Hippolytus?
Oh, how could you do this to yourself! Don't even try to
answer. Let me think. You can't put him out of your mind
now, I assume. No, it's gone too far; he's a fever in your
body, in your heart. You can't give him up, and you can't
give up your hopes either. Well, then, is there a chance he
wants you?

PHAEDRA:
How could I even guess? He's so shy, so proper, so virtuous.

FRIEND:
There must be some way to find out.

PHAEDRA:
It can't happen. It shouldn't happen! For God's sake, he's
almost my son.

FRIEND:
Almost. One little word that makes all the difference.
There's a solution for everything. Let me see what I can see.

PHAEDRA:
No. Please. Don't give me away.

FRIEND:
(Already hurrying out of the room.) I won't say anything. I
promise.

(The Friend exits; Phaedra is left alone.)

PHAEDRA:
I never meant for it to happen. But it did. On the very day I
stood beside the man who was to be my husband, on that
same day, another man. . . possessed me. Not in body, no,

I don't mean that, but my heart, that had been so cool, so still, went mad. In a minute I was changed, in a foreign land, heaven, hell, I don't know, but filled with knowledge, a new and terrifying knowledge. Theseus turned to slip the ring on my finger—

(Theseus reappears; puts the ring on her finger.)

PHAEDRA:

—but as I gave him my hand, I saw a young man, dressed in white linen, standing at the edge of the garden in the high grasses so he seemed to grow out of it, his hair curling like vines, his face like marble. *(To Theseus.)* Who is that boy?

THESEUS:

Him? I told you about him. That's my son, Hippolytus.

PHAEDRA:

(Echoing.) Your son, Hippolytus. I should have guessed. I see your face in his.

THESEUS:

Good-looking, isn't he?

PHAEDRA:

Beautiful.

THESEUS:

But stiff. Tight. Life hasn't shaken him up. . . He has my eyes, doesn't he?

PHAEDRA:

Your eyes. Yes. But clearer.

THESEUS:

Colder. There's ice in his blood.

PHAEDRA:

Is there?

THESEUS:

Nothing melts him. Not yet anyway. By the time I was his age, I'd had a dozen women in as many cities, I'd risked my life for a chance at immortality. You remember. You were there. But this boy! This boy still drinks milk.

PHAEDRA:

He looks the way you did the first time I saw you. When Ariadne and I saw you. You had no beard then, you were thin, and your shoulders looked like knives, knives or wings, yes, you looked like an angel; I thought I was hallucinating. Am I? Am I?

THESEUS:

What's the matter? You're trembling.

PHAEDRA:

I've never felt like this before.

THESEUS:

You've never been married before. What woman wouldn't feel nervous? Come closer, darling. Lean on me. Use my strength. *(Takes her in his arms.)*

PHAEDRA:

He's watching us.

THESEUS:

(Irritated.) You wouldn't know if you weren't watching *him.*

PHAEDRA:

You're right, I'm sorry.

THESEUS:

Almost everyone's gone. He'll leave, too. *(Starts to kiss her; she pulls away.)*

PHAEDRA:

He hasn't moved. Ask him to leave.

THESEUS:

I don't know why it's so important to you.

PHAEDRA:

It's my wedding day. I want to be with you now, only with you, alone with you. Please. Send him away.

THESEUS:

(Gestures at Hippolytus to go.) There. He's off and running. Happy now?

PHAEDRA:

He has such long legs....Who was his mother?

THESEUS:

It doesn't matter. The past is past.

PHAEDRA:

I want to know.

THESEUS:

Well, I am consecrated to satisfy you. But you will not be satisfied, I'm sure; there's so little to tell. I barely knew his mother. She was a woman I slept with one night because we were both in the mood. Oh, maybe it was two nights. Or five. She was hot-blooded and so was I. Sometimes, you know, no force on earth is as strong as human passion.

PHAEDRA:
Nothing on earth. Oh yes. I know.

THESEUS:
The affair meant nothing.

PHAEDRA:
How can love mean nothing?

THESEUS:
But it wasn't love. Not for me or for her. She didn't care a damn for men, only the pleasures they gave her. She had no feeling for me—and less for Hippolytus. She couldn't wait to give him up.

PHAEDRA:
He must have been hurt by that.

THESEUS:
Hippolytus? I don't think so. He's a stoic, that boy, always was, from the day she sent him to me when he was twelve. I took him in, that scrawny thing. What else could I do? But as time went on, he grew on me. We spent days together, sometimes weeks.

PHAEDRA:
(Echoing.) Days together, weeks together.

THESEUS:
Now don't tell me you're jealous!

PHAEDRA:
I won't tell you anything. *(Kisses him. Then:)* I think he has your mouth, too.

(Theseus pulls Phaedra down on the bed and draws the curtains. There is the sound of the bedsprings moving rhythmically, and thick breathing. These sounds continue—even after Phaedra slips out from the curtains and talks to the audience.)

PHAEDRA:
And whenever I kissed my husband after that, I felt the son's mouth on mine, and whenever I wrapped my arms around him, or my legs, it was the younger body I enclosed. From the first moment I saw him, I was incurable. I did what I could, sent him away, and when he was near, avoided the sight of him, the sound of his voice, the casual touch in the hallway, but then in secret I hid so I could watch him lifting weights in his room, naked, his muscles

tensing and relaxing, opening and closing, and all the while I held my breath, terrified of being caught. But he never saw me, so intent was he upon his discipline, that severe young man, that beautiful boy. And every night I tried to drown myself in Theseus' love. Then he left, on business, he said, urgent, essential. He shouldn't have gone. He shouldn't have left me here with this dreadful feast on my table, tempting me, forbidding me—fatal! fatal! To put on the plate of a starving woman the only food she craves, and the only one that will poison her—fatal!

(Theseus emerges from the bed, rumpled, and embraces her.)

THESEUS:

I'll be home as soon as I can.

PHAEDRA:

Don't go. Stay here. Please.

THESEUS:

Before you start missing me, I'll be back.

PHAEDRA:

I'm frightened. I won't feel safe.

THESEUS:

Don't be absurd. There's nothing to be afraid of here. Anyway, Hippolytus will be around. He'll look after you.

PHAEDRA:

Hippolytus? No. No. That's not the answer. No.

THESEUS:

I imagine he seems young to you but he's very strong. Really. He can take charge. Don't worry. *(Kisses her.)* I'll talk to him now. He'll be proud to be the man of the house in my absence. There's nothing he wants more than to prove himself to me. It's really very touching, don't you think?

PHAEDRA:

I don't want to be touched! I won't be able to sleep. Don't go. I beg you! *(But Theseus has gone.)* Take me with you. Or take him. Oh, God, don't let me drown in this terrible sea! Why won't you understand what I'm saying?!

(It's already too late. Hippolytus appears, beardless, awkward, a youthful version of his father.)

HIPPOLYTUS:

Excuse me, but my father just asked me to make sure that—

PHAEDRA:

(Draws herself up haughtily.) Your father was mistaken. I

don't need anything from you. *(Starts to turn away, then stops. She brushes her hand against his cheek, almost a caress.)*

HIPPOLYTUS:

(Jumping back.) What are you doing?

PHAEDRA:

I thought   I think   there was a mosquito on your cheek

HIPPOLYTUS:

(Incredulously.) A mosquito? In November? *(He backs away from her and exits.)*

PHAEDRA:

(Staring after him.) On the edge   swaying on the edge in the country, on the mountains and the cliffs   don't push me!   tempted by the edge   cold sweat, thunder heart, brain on fire   where are you?   day dawns wake up   empty pillow   where are you?!   no one home   door creaks, wind howls, racing pulse, fever high stay with me! *(Lights up dimly on Theseus taking off his clothes in candlelight.)* You cast your shadow over my life   I was lost in it   lost

(Phaedra watches as he speaks to someone unseen.)

THESEUS:

I swore to be a faithful husband. I thought I would lose myself in happiness with her, and I did, I did. For a week, a month, maybe more. But life is cruel: it makes us bored with the passion we know best. It doesn't kill the appetite, though. No, it just leaves you craving a different taste, a new delicacy. The older I get, the hungrier I am. I like a full meal at breakfast, a bite at lunch and a nibble at dinner, with a wide variety of specialities on the side, and then a nightcap, always a nightcap.

(Phaedra watches with anger and disgust as he takes off his trousers.)

PHAEDRA:

Theseus' hair is turning grey. He doesn't see it, or maybe he thinks it looks distinguished. His waist has thickened, like mine, veins braid his legs, gravity has a grip on him, too, his skin is loosening, as flabby as mine, he has age spots on his cheeks and hands, and soon he'll have a turkey neck, like mine—but that doesn't stop him from gobbling!

THESEUS:
So I'll break a promise. Why should I fight it? Lie down.
Yes, lie down here. *(Naked; bends over someone not seen.)* I
want your taste on my tongue, making my dinner sweet. I
want to be in your arms, between your thighs, in the deeps
of your belly. *(Straddles the other.)* Stay open for me. Yes.
Like that. We'll pull the night over us, we'll make the
darkness sing. A man can't be a saint. *(Seductively.)*
Anyway, women don't want saints, do they? *(Begins a
sexual rhythm.)* No, no, they don't want saints; they want
men. Race with me, darling. Rage with me. We'll get there
together.
*(Phaedra steps into the near darkness and picks up the candle, carries
it toward her bed.)*

PHAEDRA:
Why should I be different? I love the heights and the deep
places, too. I know the song and I want to sing it, now, now,
before my candle goes out, before I forget that I was
beautiful once, before I forget my name, before time goes
out with the candle and I forget my dreams, forget that
night follows day and shades into day again, forget what a
button is for—*(Begins unbuttoning the neck of her robe.)*—and
what's underneath the clothing, and underneath the skin
where the blood runs fierce and my spirit shows its pulse,
before the darkness steals in and I forget my face that loves
his face, my face that might grow young in the light of his
eyes before it becomes a stranger, even to myself.
*(She picks up the mirror again and studies herself intensely. Her
Friend enters, watches, then breaks the silence.)*

FRIEND:
Can't keep away from yourself, can you?

PHAEDRA:
It's written on my face: my life as a woman is over. But
Theseus, Theseus is in his prime!

FRIEND:
(Gently takes mirror away from her.) I love those little laugh
lines at your eyes.

PHAEDRA
Crows' feet.

FRIEND:
You call them that because you don't laugh anymore.
Because you don't even remember you laughed. I remember.
PHAEDRA:
Write it on my gravestone. "She laughed, once."
FRIEND:
Oh stop! You can't push time back, you can only disguise
its mischief. Women have always used artifice. Cleopatra
did, Nefertiti did; there's an entire history of art devoted to
these female tricks. Henna for the hair and cheeks. Kohl for
the eyes. Sand. Mud. The sting of bees on the lips.
PHAEDRA:
Forget the bees.
FRIEND:
You can make age an illusion, too. It's a grand tradition.
Why shouldn't you take your place in it?
PHAEDRA:
I need a miracle, not some fiction in a bottle.
FRIEND:
I'll cover up those little flaws you hate so much. Tilt your
head back, sweetheart, yes, good. *(Takes out Phaedra's
cosmetics; starts working.)* We can conceal these shadows
under your eyes; they look like graves, for pity's sake. Of
course if you slept at night...! And I can hide a few of those
crinkles you detest, too.
PHAEDRA:
I don't think he's ever been with a woman.
FRIEND:
(Applying mascara.) There's a first time for everything.
Keep your eyes open. The mascara will give you a more
open, vulnerable look. *(Looks at her handiwork.)* Yes, yes, it
does. Now *you* look like a virgin. *(Takes a hairbrush and
brushes.)* Let's fluff out your hair, make it full and soft
around your face. There. Like a halo. He'll like that.
(Employing rouge and lipstick.) Now for some color, a sense of
excitement in the flesh. A warm radiance on the cheeks.
And on your mouth, a deep rose or burgundy—yes,
burgundy is better; it suggests wine, intoxication. I'll put a
little gloss, right here in the middle of your lower lip, a hint
of petulance—excellent! because petulance reminds us of
sulking and sulking reminds us of adolescence. And

adolescence, as we know, adolescence reminds us of sex. *(Can't help herself; kisses Phaedra on the mouth.)*

PHAEDRA:
What?!

FRIEND:
Just testing. Making sure you get the response you want.

PHAEDRA:
You mean now I'm... irresistible?

FRIEND:
That was the idea, wasn't it?

PHAEDRA:
You have my burgundy on your mouth.

FRIEND:
Does it make me irresistible, too?

PHAEDRA:
It makes you a stranger. *(Hands a tissue to Friend.)* I liked you better the way you were.

FRIEND:
(Wipes lipstick off her mouth in a tense silence.) All right, sweetheart. Listen to me. Here's what I've been thinking. Everyone lives for love, right? And what good is love if it kills? Or if it dies, strangled in its own cord? If you put your ear to the wind, you hear, in all corners of the world, in all its mountains and valleys, in mansions and in slums, women sighing, men wailing—and for what? The glorious pains of love.

PHAEDRA:
Not glorious to me.

FRIEND:
Only because unsatisfied.

PHAEDRA:
Satisfaction! As if that were everything! We're human, not animals. I feel what I feel, I can't help it, but I can hold myself back, I can rise above my passions, and I will, I swear I will—or die!

FRIEND:
Better to lie beneath Hippolytus and live!

PHAEDRA:
You? You tell me that? You who almost collapsed when you heard my confession?

FRIEND:
   I was upset, it's true, but I've had second thoughts. I want
   your happiness above everything.

PHAEDRA:
   Above morality. Above law. Above natural law.

FRIEND:
   Love and desire, that's what's natural.

PHAEDRA:
   My only desire is *not* to desire.

FRIEND:
   And what would *I* do, then?

PHAEDRA:
   You could get your own life.

FRIEND:
   But I prefer yours. It gets so boring walking back and forth
   on the middle ground. Besides, I'm terribly fond of that
   little softening under your chin. *(Touches her there.)*

PHAEDRA:
   Don't! It's repulsive.

FRIEND:
   No: human. Everything changes, everything life touches.
   Even this mattress. *(Moves near to it.)* It isn't straight or firm
   anymore, as it was the first night you slept here. It's taken
   the shape of your body—where you lie, where you roll,
   how your weight distributes. It's a little lumpy now,
   uneven; not a perfect model, but one that bears your
   imprint, right for *you*.

PHAEDRA:
   And for Theseus? If I lay here with his son, would that be
   right for him?

FRIEND:
   Who knows? Maybe Theseus will do what thousands of
   husbands do: see and not see at the same time.

PHAEDRA:
   Love may be blind. Theseus isn't.

FRIEND:
   Of all people, Theseus knows that it's natural to sin. Tell
   Hippolytus. Tell him and be rid of your obsession.

PHAEDRA:
   You must be insane.

FRIEND:

No: selfish. I don't want to go through another week like the last one. I couldn't find him when I searched. I ran here and there for hours. Why would he come to me, anyway? He can't guess what's in your heart.

PHAEDRA:

And in his? He trains horses; he breaks them, makes stallions obedient to the bit in their mouths—but with me, he's afraid. His voice cracks like a boy's at puberty; he looks everywhere but into my eyes.

FRIEND:

If wild animals can be tamed, so can he. Criminals and saints, both extremes have surrendered to love. Why not Hippolytus? Take the chance. Tell him, I say.

PHAEDRA:

My tongue would go dead in my mouth.

FRIEND:

Use my tongue, then.

PHAEDRA:

You'd speak for me?

FRIEND:

I would.

PHAEDRA:

No! Go and find your own love! Then you won't have to worry so much about mine.

FRIEND:

(Stung.) All right. If that's how you feel. I'll pack my bags. Believe me, the last thing I want is to interfere. Sleep well.

PHAEDRA:

I'll never sleep again.

FRIEND:

There you go again, so melodramatic! Don't you know by now that only death is forever, nothing else--not even this anguish you suffer today? Or my anguish. *(Turns to leave.)* Goodbye.

PHAEDRA:

No. Don't leave me.

FRIEND:

Make up your mind.

PHAEDRA:

My mind is torn.

FRIEND:
Well, get it together then. Fast. Hippolytus is coming.

PHAEDRA:
You hear him? *(The Friend nods.)* What will I do?! I can't see him; I'm too weak. Send him away. Tell him to get his saddle, mount his horse and ride, ride far away. Tell him I'm deathly sick, and all because of him. No, no, don't say that.

FRIEND:
Let me feel him out. Trust me.

PHAEDRA:
But once you put my feelings into words...

FRIEND:
I won't. I swear. I'll talk around it. I'll lead him on and see how he follows. But he can't know you're here. Hide. Hurry. Hurry!

(Phaedra runs to her bed. The Friend quickly draws the curtains, just as Hippolytus appears.)

HIPPOLYTUS:
What are you doing?

FRIEND:
Oh, nothing. Straightening up. Phaedra left her bed such a mess. She's really been sick, poor thing.

HIPPOLYTUS:
She's not here?

FRIEND:
You don't see her, do you?

HIPPOLYTUS:
It's just as well. Tell her that I came to say goodbye.

PHAEDRA:
(In a whisper.) Goodbye?

FRIEND:
(Overlapping.) Goodbye? But where are you going?

HIPPOLYTUS:
I have to find my father. Something's happened to him, I'm sure of it.

FRIEND:
Really? What makes you think so?

HIPPOLYTUS:
My dreams. They wake me at night, show me blood on the waves, foaming on the mouth of my horse, show me black

wings swooping. If I don't go for him now, I'm afraid the worst will happen. *(Tries to leave, but the Friend detains him.)*

FRIEND:
But Phaedra's on the case. She's sent messages everywhere, across every sea, to track him down. Her devotion will turn the tide. Wait a little.

HIPPOLYTUS:
I can't. He's never been gone this long before. I have to help him!

FRIEND:
But you promised your father you'd stay with Phaedra. He'll be furious if you leave home.

HIPPOLYTUS:
It isn't my home now; it's hers. I can't stand it any more. Anyway, she has you to care for her. *(Starts to leave.)*

FRIEND:
(Restrains him.) She'll fall apart if you go. Don't you understand? The man who possesses her heart seems indifferent to her. Other women might lose themselves in drink or drug themselves to sleep: not Phaedra. At night her eyes don't close, and on the screen that darkness brings, she sees her lover's face. She cries out for him, she reaches out her arms, she's wild with love and longing.

HIPPOLYTUS:
I never doubted the depths of her love.

FRIEND:
But have you understood its true nature?

HIPPOLYTUS:
Why ask me that? I'm no authority on women, or on love.

FRIEND:
Exactly. And there is the crux of the problem. You don't know the power you exert on her.

HIPPOLYTUS:
I?

FRIEND:
Yes, you. You, the son.

HIPPOLYTUS:
Oh.

FRIEND:
Your father's son. Here, in this house, while he's away.

HIPPOLYTUS:
Oh. Oh. I see.

FRIEND:
Do you?

HIPPOLYTUS:
Yes, yes, I do. How stupid of me! No wonder she can't bear to have me around, gets flustered when our paths cross.

FRIEND:
Yes? Yes?

HIPPOLYTUS:
My presence, my very existence, reminds her of him. But I'm here—and he isn't.

FRIEND:
Yes, that's right.

HIPPOLYTUS:
And I never suspected! It never occurred to me that I brought her pain! Well, she'll soon be free of all the grief I've caused. When you see her, tell her I've gone to search for him, and I won't rest, won't sleep, until I have him safe at home and back where he belongs, in her arms. *(He turns to go. The Friend grabs his arm.)*

FRIEND:
You still don't understand. Nothing will please her if you leave now.

HIPPOLYTUS:
You make no sense! Please! Take your hand off my arm.

FRIEND:
Oh, why won't you listen?!

PHAEDRA:
(Draws curtains and steps out.) Yes, please, listen.

FRIEND:
Phaedra, wait. Don't—

PHAEDRA:
It's too late. I have to. Leave me with him. *(As the Friend hesitates.)* Do as I ask. Go. *(The Friend exits; to Hippolytus.)* What she said is true. I do miss your father, terribly, not as he is now, with his great swagger and pride, but as he once was, a young man, brave and gentle, even a little shy, and handsome—as handsome as you are now.

HIPPOLYTUS:
As I am? What do I have to do with it?

PHAEDRA:
He had your eyes, the curve of your lips, the smooth
marble of your skin, shadowed then with its first beard.
Everywhere he went, women threw themselves into his
arms. Who could blame them? My own sister deceived her
family and taught him how to cheat death with a thread so
he would take her for his wife. I wanted him for myself but
held my hopes in check, was patient, made another life. But
I would have abandoned all my scruples, if it had been
you; I would have stolen her place and stood by your side
all the way to the end—

HIPPOLYTUS:
What?

PHAEDRA:
—facing death with your hand in mine; and if we'd died
then, together, I would have been happier than living a
thousand years with someone else.

HIPPOLYTUS:
You don't mean what you say. You're feverish; you're sick.

PHAEDRA:
Sick with love, yes, yes, I am. I've put myself into your
hands; do what you want with me.

HIPPOLYTUS:
What I want? *(Pushes her away.)* What I want is never to
have heard the words you've spoken today, never to have
laid my eyes on you—no, no!—had your eyes fall on me.

PHAEDRA:
But if the food is tempting, why shouldn't I taste it? Why
shouldn't you?

HIPPOLYTUS:
Tempting? It's disgusting—for you to come to me like this,
your body uncovered, shameless, shameful! Your "love," as
you call it, is horrible to me! Get back! The sight of you, the
smell of your perfume, even your breath on my face, make
me feel dirty.

PHAEDRA:
Shhh. Shhh! You're shouting.

HIPPOLYTUS:
After these confessions, do you expect me to be calm? Get
away from me. Don't infect me with your corruption! God, I
hate you.

PHAEDRA:

I fought it, I did, I swear I did!

HIPPOLYTUS:

What am I going to say to my father when I see him?

PHAEDRA:

...You'll tell him?

HIPPOLYTUS:

I won't have to. Don't you think he can see the difference between a clear glass of water and a polluted one? *(He exits. Phaedra stands in shocked silence, then walks to her bed and opens the curtains. The disarray of her bed confronts her. She begins pulling off the bedclothes and folding them in neat little piles. The Friend enters and watches in silence, increasingly worried.)*

FRIEND:

What did he say? *(No reponse.)* What are you doing? *(No response.)* Stop that folding, stop it, please! *(Phaedra rebuffs her.)* Please, sweetheart, tell me what happened. You're making me afraid.

PHAEDRA:

(Coldly.) You? Why should you be afraid?

FRIEND:

Don't keep secrets from me now. Please. What did he say? What happened?

PHAEDRA:

(Mimicking.) "What happened? Tell me what happened." You have to know everything, don't you? Be involved with everything! You, with your insatiable curiosity! You'd ask a corpse to describe the guillotine that cut off her head.

FRIEND:

No. It can't be that bad. Maybe he was shocked—

PHAEDRA:

(Handing her a pile of bed linens.) Burn these sheets.

FRIEND:

What are you going to do?

PHAEDRA:

You've done everything else I asked—even what I didn't ask. Burn them, I said! *(The Friend doesn't move, distraught.)* Why do you stand there paralyzed? My faithful and loving friend! You couldn't wait to "help" me before. Why won't you help me now?

FRIEND:
You make my heart stop, you look so cold.

PHAEDRA:
It's good to be cold. *(Continues folding.)*

FRIEND:
All right, I misjudged him, I failed, but it was all for you! For love of you! If he had run to you and taken you in his arms, then you would call me your best, your only, your one true friend. You're not angry because I did something wrong; it's because I didn't succeed.

PHAEDRA:
Finally, a moment of truth.

FRIEND:
I'm sorry, so so sorry.

PHAEDRA:
I'm sure you are.

FRIEND:
I never meant to hurt you, I swear it.

PHAEDRA:
I believe you. So?

FRIEND:
So? So? . . . I have something else to tell you.

PHAEDRA:
What else can there be? I have nothing now, not my self-respect or *his* respect, not my pride or the little flame of hope that lit my darkness. And *you* were the one who tempted me; *you* sang of the glories of love and I listened. If not for you, would I have spoken at all? You've destroyed me. Cry, yes, cry.

FRIEND:
It's not for myself I'm crying. Theseus is back.

PHAEDRA:
What?!

FRIEND:
He arrived last night; he means to surprise you, I heard. He could be here at any minute.

PHAEDRA:
What will I do, what will I do? Where are your solutions now, my friend!

FRIEND:
Stay calm, you must be calm.

PHAEDRA:

Do you think Hippolytus will be calm? No, no. My words will pour from his lips and then, and then—Theseus will break me between his hands; my life will be over. Because of you. Because you pushed me to this.

FRIEND:

I wanted what you wanted; I moved your desire forward. For you, for your happiness. I was sure you'd overcome his impossible pride, his fear.

PHAEDRA:

Fear? Loathing, you mean! It was insane to think I could seduce him from his chastity, me, with these furrows on my forehead and my body stinking of desperation!

FRIEND:

Use your head. Be clever. Go to Theseus the minute he arrives and—

PHAEDRA:

And what? what brilliant plan have you hatched now?

FRIEND:

Accuse Hippolytus.

PHAEDRA:

Place my crime in his mouth?

FRIEND:

What choice do you have?

PHAEDRA:

Accuse Hippolytus?

FRIEND:

You woke last night to find him leaning over you. Terrified, you cried for help and I, hearing your voice, went to you just in time to see the monster running from your room.

PHAEDRA:

I'd cut out my tongue before I add lying to my sins.

FRIEND:

If you're afraid to speak, write it down. Send Theseus a letter before he meets his son or God knows what will happen! You know his temper!

PHAEDRA:

I know my crime.

FRIEND:

But Theseus doesn't. He'd never suspect. He, with his stupendous ego. *(Brings pen and paper.)* Here. Write.

There's not much time.

PHAEDRA:
I can't.

FRIEND:
Hurry, or Hippolytus will betray you first. He'd denounce you in a minute to keep his father's love.

PHAEDRA:
Haven't you done enough harm?

FRIEND:
I want to make it up. Why should you let Hippolytus get the best of you twice? Didn't he laugh at your confession? Humiliate you? To hell with him. Save yourself.

PHAEDRA:
Don't you understand yet? I can't be saved.

FRIEND:
You want to sacrifice your life for Hippolytus? What good will come of that? Think it over. *(Exiting.)* I'll keep Theseus at the door to give you time. But don't delay. Write the letter!

PHAEDRA:
(Alone; sits, stands, paces.) He stared at me with such contempt. There's no time, no time! How can I? But if I don't ...?! Time, time is running out! *(Begins to write.)* "My dearest Theseus, If only I could greet you with open arms and open heart but I barely have the strength to tell you what has happened or to name the guilty one." *(Pauses; stops writing.)* And whose name do I write? Whose? *(Begins writing again. Theseus enters, unseen, a stack of gift-wrapped boxes in his arms, and listens.)* "All the ties of blood could not hold him back from me. When he first accosted me in the garden I ran from him in horror. For days I resisted his pleas. I took to my bed, feverish. The household worried for me, believing I was sick. To insure my safety, I sent for my friend and had her sleep in the next room." *(Pauses; writes.)* "Ask *her* what happened on that fateful night, in the hour just before dawn, when she heard my screams and, running to my bed, saw the intruder bending over me, his naked body glowing in the moonlight, that body you, his father, created, that beautiful boy you trusted and—

THESEUS:

(Has dropped his packages, startling Phaedra, and now runs in to grab the letter.) Hippolytus? It's my son who has done this? *(She stands mute, paralyzed.)* Answer me!

PHAEDRA:

I can't, I can't!

THESEUS:

So that's it. That's why he didn't run to meet me. Oh God, it's unbelievable. My own son. *(Phaedra collapses. Theseus kneels beside her.)* Dearest. Darling.

PHAEDRA:

Don't touch me.

THESEUS:

Let me carry you to your bed.

PHAEDRA:

No! You mustn't touch me. No. Not now.

THESEUS:

Are you taking his sin upon yourself?

PHAEDRA:

No. Yes. Please. Please forgive me.

THESEUS:

Forgive you? You? This is intolerable! No, my darling, no, my sweet, you mustn't blame yourself.

PHAEDRA:

I didn't want you to go away, I begged you!

THESEUS:

Now I see! How blind I was! He never looked at women because he was obsessed with *you!* And you knew it. You were afraid, all along, you were afraid of him. And I was too slow to understand. *(Draws himself up.)* I won't be slow now.

PHAEDRA:

What do you mean?

THESEUS:

I will be swift to justice. How dare he put his hands on you!

PHAEDRA:

He's young. He didn't know what he was doing.

THESEUS:

You would plead for him? I won't hear of it! *(Thunders.)* Where is my son?!

PHAEDRA:
He's not here, he left the house to search for you.

THESEUS:
So you'd imagine you were safe and he could steal back at night. Oh, I could do murder!

PHAEDRA:
No. Please. Don't hurt him.

THESEUS:
How could I have stayed away so long? If I'd been here, nothing would have happened. *(Embraces her.)* I'll never leave you again. *(Lifts her up and carries her to the bed.)* You can sleep now. And when you wake, my son will not be here to cast his shadow over you.

PHAEDRA:
You'll send him away?

THESEUS:
You will never have to see him again. And he will never lay his eyes on you.

(Leaves Phaedra on the bed and moves behind it. The rear canopy conceals him. Only Phaedra reacting to every moment of the following scene, can be seen.)

THESEUS:
Hippolytus!

(From this point on, only the voices of Theseus and Hippolytus are heard.)

HIPPOLYTUS:
I'm here, father. I'm so happy and relieved you're safe. I told Phaedra—

THESEUS:
Phaedra! How dare you mention her name?

HIPPOLYTUS:
What?

THESEUS:
Hypocrite! Even snakes shed their skins in the open air but you, you hide in the grass and blend with it, and call it nature! Well, I see your nature now!

HIPPOLYTUS:
You're talking in circles.

THESEUS:
Then you should understand me. You're used to double-talk, to the twisted tongue, the crooked road. If a traveller

HIPPOLYTUS:
used you for a star, he'd wind up in a bottomless pit—
HIPPOLYTUS:
Father!
THESEUS:
—or in his mother's bed!
HIPPOLYTUS:
What? Who told you this lie?
THESEUS:
Do you accuse your mother of lies?
HIPPOLYTUS:
My mother?   ... No. I accuse no-one. But remember who I
am. I never wanted any woman; you thought it was a fault.
Other boys took their girls into the bushes. I rode into the
mountains alone to find my raptures and meet my Gods
face to face. My Gods, not yours, Father.
THESEUS:
Get out of my sight. Leave my home this instant!
HIPPOLYTUS:
How can you believe—?
THESEUS:
(Thundering.) Go! And never let my eyes light on you
again!
HIPPOLYTUS:
I'm your son, Father. I'll do as you say. And I forgive you.
(Crosses in front of Phaedra; pauses.)
HIPPOLYTUS:
Even a pig, wallowing in its own shit, is cleaner than you.
(Exits.)
PHAEDRA:
He would never have spoken, never betrayed me. As I
betrayed him. *(Steps down from her bed; shouts.)* Theseus!
THESEUS:
(Enters.) How amazing that guilt can sound so much like
innocence! Oh Lord, what could be worse than a father
cursing his own child? *(Moving toward Phaedra.)* Here, come
into my arms. *(Folds her against him.)* I have been your
revenge and now I will be your refuge.
PHAEDRA:
There will be no refuge for either of us. Call him back.
Quickly. Quickly!

THESEUS:
You're burning up.

PHAEDRA:
Yes. Burning as I burned when you were gone. Not in fear as I told you but—Quick! Call him back before it's too late.

THESEUS:
But you're safe now. Your enemy is gone, and gone forever.

PHAEDRA:
No, no, the enemy is here, here—(*Strikes her breast.*)—in me.

THESEUS:
You were the victim, you were helpless against him.

PHAEDRA:
He is the victim, he, your son! Go after him, I beg you. He's taken his horse; I hear the hooves in a gallop. They'll head for the cliffs. I know the path he favors. Hurry. He'll kill himself to prove his innocence.

THESEUS:
Innocence?

PHAEDRA:
Call him back, call him back before it's too late.

THESEUS:
(*Shakes her roughly.*) What possesses you?

PHAEDRA:
He! He possesses me! Not through any act or wish of his but . . . but I. . . I wanted him. He never touched me. That's the truth, I swear it.

THESEUS:
He never touched you?

PHAEDRA:
Never.

THESEUS:
But your letter... ?

PHAEDRA:
Lies.

THESEUS:
He never came to your bed?

PHAEDRA:
Only in my dreams.

THESEUS:
You say that to me?! Better die than dream such dreams!

(Strikes her.) You filthy thing! You animal!

PHAEDRA:
Don't.

THESEUS:
To lust for your own son!

PHAEDRA:
Your son, yours! It was you I loved, your youth, mine. I don't blame Hippolytus for despising me. But you—you with your married women and little girls!—you have no right to hit me.

THESEUS:
I have every right! Since time began and women were false, men have taken law into their own hands—taken their wives' throats into their own hands! *(Starts to choke Phaedra.)*

PHAEDRA:
Nothing happened, don't you understand? Only words, only desire.

THESEUS:
I'll tell the world what you desired. Wherever you go, people will point their fingers at the woman who forgot to look in the mirror, who tried to seduce a boy, her husband's son. Yes, the world will laugh at your ridiculous "love." *(Slaps her.)* Slut!

PHAEDRA:
Oh yes. Only the great man is entitled to a great passion, fury or love, it doesn't matter which. It's natural to give way to primitive emotions with that . . . battering ram between your legs.

THESEUS:
You're proud of what you've done?

PHAEDRA:
The stars in my heaven have all gone out.

(Hippolytus' Friend enters.)

THESEUS:
Have you found him?

FRIEND:
Yes.

THESEUS:
Thank heaven. Where is he? Well? Well? Won't he come to me? *(The Friend shakes his head.)* Never mind then. I'll

go to him.

FRIEND:
It's too late for that.

PHAEDRA:
Too late? Already?

THESEUS:
That's impossible. He knows my rages, how I lash out. I was wrong, I'll admit it. I'll go down on my knees, I'll beg him to come home.

FRIEND:
You may beg for the rest of your life but he won't hear.

THESEUS:
What terrible thing are you trying to say? Tell me!

FRIEND:
Your voice was still thundering as he jumped on his horse. He was crying, he couldn't see for the tears. I was afraid for him; I got my horse and followed, shouting warnings against the wind. But Hippolytus was hellbent. His hand cracked the whip and together they climbed the cliffs higher and higher, galloping so fast that the trees disappeared. In no time there was nothing but icy air and bare rock. The clouds lowered themselves onto his head and made a kind of wreath for him. At least that's how it looked to me.

THESEUS:
So that's where he is? On the peak?

FRIEND:
Not anymore. Suddenly a snake darted out from under a rock, its forked tongue hissing, and the horse reared back. Hippolytus fell, and got tangled in the reins.

PHAEDRA:
My doing. My undoing.

FRIEND:
The horse bolted and charged forward, dragging the helpless rider over the stony ground, and on they raced as if they were a single creature, the poor boy hanging upside down, his head crashing against rocks and turning them bloody, the skin tearing from his body in strips.

THESEUS:
Enough! My son, my son... I gave in to my anger, I condemned him on Phaedra's word.

PHAEDRA:
I could rip my tongue out by the root.

THESEUS:
If only I'd held back!

FRIEND:
Hippolytus, too: the way he leaped on that horse.

THESEUS:
Quiet! How dare you speak ill of him now?!

FRIEND:
I loved him as much as you. But his purity brought him down.

THESEUS:
Show me where he is. I want to hold him one last time.

PHAEDRA:
Let me go with you.

(She freezes at Theseus' expression. He turns away and exits with the Friend. Phaedra begins to pin up her hair.)

PHAEDRA:
You fear it—and it comes to pass. You try to escape—and it comes to pass. You weep and you struggle and you bargain with your Gods—and still it comes to pass. Lost. Everything. Lost.

(In a moment, the Friend returns in her female aspect.)

FRIEND:
If only I could go back in time, undo what I've done.

PHAEDRA:
No more words now. Please.

FRIEND:
I was too eager to make you happy. I let my reason find excuses.

PHAEDRA:
Can't you be quiet even now? Hippolytus is dead; and it was I who killed him. My love that killed him.

FRIEND:
I should have known. One deceit always leads to another, and then we're trapped for good.

PHAEDRA:
You're not trapped.

FRIEND:
Won't you forgive me?

PHAEDRA:
Yes. But who will forgive me?

(Her hair is tightly pinned up now. She begins to knot a sheet.)

FRIEND:
What are you doing with that sheet? *(No response.)* Phaedra, what are you doing?

PHAEDRA:
Theseus will have his freedom; it's what he loves most, you know. I can give him that, at least. Now that I've thrown everything away. *(Ties the last knot in the sheet.)* I'm almost finished. You should be relieved: I'll be able to sleep again.

FRIEND:
But you can't! No. You can't do that.

PHAEDRA:
Quiet. I've had enough of your advice. *(Throws the sheet over the canopy frame, tightens it.)* It's better for you to leave now.

FRIEND:
No.

PHAEDRA:
All right, stay. Be with me to the end. *(Makes a noose.)*

FRIEND:
I *do* have a heart, you know.

PHAEDRA:
Come here. A kiss will keep me warmer than words. *(Kisses the Friend.)* Thank you.

FRIEND:
Isn't there another way?

PHAEDRA:
No. *(Takes off shoes and steps on the bed; smiles.)* So. This is how I'll escape old age.

Blackout.

NOTE: PHAEDRA IN DELIRIUM *premiered on January 20, 1998, co-produced by Women's Project & Production and Classic Stage Company. It was directed by Alison Summers with Kathleen Chalfant as Phaedra, Peter Jay Fernandez as Theseus/Hippolytus, and Sandra Shipley as the Friend.*

AFTERWORD

It is always intriguing to consider what draws a writer to certain material. In my own case, the immediate and apparent attraction, the story, usually turns out to be a pretext, and the real fascination some subtle strands beneath the surface, at the outset not even apparent to me. Only in the writing of the play are these revealed.

The myth of PHAEDRA in its various versions by Euripides, Seneca and Racine engages many compelling subjects — the obsession of an older woman for a young man; the relentless power of the irrational; the danger inherent in extremes, whether of eroticism or chastity — but as it turns out, my deepest attention was engrossed by several less conspicuous themes.

During this era of Winfrey/Rivera spectacles and best selling memoirs of lucrative disgrace, in which every intimate feeling is exposed and publicized, nothing could be less fashionable than the notion that restraint and privacy are virtues, not symptoms of psychological or emotional parsimony. I was very much drawn to this idea not only for its moral sentiment, but because as a writer I am in love with language and do believe that words possess power. In PHAEDRA IN DELIRIUM, it is the *expression* of illicit passions, not the passions themselves, that lead to tragedy — a conviction implicit in Euripides' HIPPOLYTUS, where Phaedra says:

> This is the deadly thing which devastates well-
> ordered cities and homes of men — that's it, this art of
> oversubtle words.

Phaedra's greatest conflict is the struggle between keeping silent and speaking out. Had she succeeded in keeping her feelings to herself, the play would have no tragic dimension. No one dies of self-control — but unlike the sing-song reassurance of childhood's adage, 'sticks and stones won't break my bones,' words *can* kill.

The tension between words and silence informs much of my work in the theatre, as does the Dostoevskian motif of freedom and subjection in both its political and metaphysical forms. Sometimes, if luck or fate is holding hands with me, language and image meet to illuminate one another.

Like most women, I am always fretting about my hair, so I was struck by the fact that each of the classical playwrights mentions Phaedra's hair as a weight, a burden that oppresses her. Racine has her say: "What busy hand, in tying all these knots,/ Has taken care to gather on my brow/ This heavy load of hair? Now all afflicts me,/ hurts me. . . " Seneca gives her these lines: " . . . my hair—/Let it be loose and free of Syrian perfume. . . / falling anyhow about my neck. . . Down to my shoulders. . ."

On the stage, we have the luxury of actually seeing the image contained in the phrases above, seeing the hair bound and then released. In my version, Phaedra physically liberates herself from the oppression of her hair in an almost hallucinatory scene:

(PHAEDRA turns around on her bed to face the audience, her head bowed forward under the weight of an enormous mass of hair piled on top.)
PHAEDRA: *(Tries to lift her head; she can't.)* This hair I can barely lift up my head so neat, so proper, no wisps flying it weighs me down *(Occasionally she succeeds in raising her head but slaps herself down.)* Girl run through the fields hair flying unbraid the braids raise the sails let the horses loose slap! grow up! Running toes like worms, feet like birds where are your shoes? slap! slap! grow up! can't see the stars the sun the skies the floor is grey and dirty, the ground hits my eyes lift! slap me down! pins in my scalp a torture, pins like needles, needle in the haystack, jumping falling hay in my hair slap! can't go wild, can't go child stop! slap! sit still grown up heavy heavy heavy the head that can't move can't dance can't throw back my head for song or love or heavy heavy heavy
(She raises her hands and begins to pull the pins from her hair. One by one she plucks them out and drops them to the floor. Her long hair begins to hang loose. The floor, perhaps the whole stage, becomes littered with pins.)

In its rhythms and choice of words, as well as in its suggested stage imagery, this theatrical monologue is clearly an expression of a twentieth-century sensibility. What is most satisfying for me is to have found my own connection to a masterpiece and its metaphors, and to focus the spotlight on a few of its facets that sparkle more than plenty in our own time.

For my parents and teachers

J. D. SMITH

The Hypothetical Landscape

J. D. SMITH was born and raised in Aurora, Illinois and currently lives in Chicago. After taking an undergraduate degree in Latin American Studies at American University, he completed graduate programs at the University of Chicago, the University of Houston, and Carleton University in Ottawa, Ontario. His poems and writing in other genres have been published in a variety of journals throughout the United States. *The Hypothetical Landscape* is his first book of poems.

CONTENTS

THE HYPOTHETICAL LANDSCAPE

I

OFFERING

I am the offspring of mixed marriage.
My father came from the tribe of Grown Men.
My mother, from the tribe of Grown Women.
I began as neither,
sitting between them in the car
as if I were a corpus callosum
that joined their hemispheres of thought.
I began as neither, walking between them,
a hand given to each
like ends of a vine bridge that spanned
the canyon between two great countries.

But, unchosen, my true colors unfurled
in hair's thousands of banners—
even my toes could not lie.
My voice broke, then lowered
with a confession of manhood.
The Y of my chromosome wrote itself large
and led me in the dowsing
passed down through my father's lore.
With sweat outside and thirst within
I sought the moist well of woman, any woman.

I still thirst, having found
volume doesn't quench me—only a true source.
So look on me as an emissary from my tribe,
a repentant member, and take me in.
Take me hostage if you must,
take these limbs as pale olive branches,
and we'll negotiate day and night, mainly night,
a portion of peace in our time.

UNSENT LETTER

By now, I may not seem
like a monster, or even
a man who strayed but,
perhaps, a nickel-wide vaccination
against misplaced love

or, if not that,
a stain on your blouse,
hidden under a shawl

or the red speck
scraped from an egg-yolk,
if that.

CREDO

I believe, besides the volumes
I'll never know of you,
that your brow is a tablet
of new laws

and from your hands'
mirrored continents extends
the slender and fabled Florida of each thumb,

while your clavicle describes the one yoke
I would labor to take on.

In honor of your left calf alone
an ancient people would have raised altars.
I mourn the passing of their time.

SHORTNESS

You are king nowhere,
not even in your skin's space
that one large hand can
drag away or crack.

Your coins are thin, picked up off the ground,
and no one will take them
when you reach the bar, debate your age,
strut length into toy legs.

You look close, seeing things
parallel to flight below radar range—
the way maple seeds fall,
the flutist's tapping foot,

how a lie hides in the extra half inch
you tell your blind dates.
You keep a second soul on hand
in case the first grows large and breaks.

SUNDAY DAWN

Coming home half-drunk I wonder
if I leave the hours' fields too fallow,
wasting the years' sun, growing idle,
when I have time to see how
my fingers end in my grandfather's flat nails,
the spades he dug his grave with, drink by drink,
or trace desire's itinerary: the unvisited states—
Virginia, Kentucky—in my keys' shapes.

With every minute strained through a schedule
the blocked and plotted hours would yield
more of the world's like and measured goods,

dollars in bushels, if I liked them that way,
a cleaner cut of suit. At best,

the gilt-bound agenda might show how
the stress that raises sierras of warts from my
    hands
could manure the passing unique seconds when
I read the fortunes in my nails,
the state of every key on a loose chain.

FIRST GRADE

My friend was cycling
as I walked down the road,
she waved and yelled.
I shouted back long enough
to delay her looking straight.
A truck came head-on;
the body flew twenty feet.
I don't remember her name.
The funeral was brief.
Thirty years have intervened
without a metaphor.

UNEMPLOYMENT

For months I haven't put on a suit;
Discipline comes from need. Wearing a bathrobe
is easy these days, when I stay in the house.
I let my limbs search for their length, free
from hems, pacing circles that never end
in the front room. My feet are broad from walking

barefoot. Three days ago I went walking
with no place to go. It hardly suited
me: idleness is a private part. The end
of ten minutes found me in my bathrobe,
waiting for the mail. Perhaps a free
offer or love letter would find this house.

Neither came. A curse is on this house,
I swear. I went to college one day, walking
away from this town where only sweat is free,
only weddings and funerals bring out suits—
except for some—I cringe in my bathrobe
at the thought—like Grandfather, who met his end

drinking and gambling down to the end
of his children's money, when he lost the house.
Some days I think I would have left this bathrobe
behind by now and found work, walking
to my office in a gray tailored suit,
if he had left a legacy, a free

beginning in gentility. The free
time holds me. Dishes, placid to the end,
sit in the sink for days, and all my suits
stay at the cleaner. I have my house
and don't really need to take off walking
when I can relax here in my bathrobe,

although today I would wear no bathrobe,
dance naked in the kitchen, my body free,
instead of watching TV and walking
out for the mail—that may be a dream and end.
At times my mind swells as big as this house
with daydreams of playing cards in five suits,

walking to a canyon to drop my bathrobe.
Then the house would let go. I will be free
when I can spend my days working in suits.

ULCER

This ragged asterisk
shares only its name and surface
with the textbook lesions,
kicking in me like a fetus
conceived by bills and deadlines,
thriving, a night-blooming flower
whose petals are
the tetragrammaton's
sharp letters, pointing
toward a fulfillment
unknown as its vowels,
as the number of my days.

ENGLISH AS A SECOND LANGUAGE

Prepositions
He is in front of the desk.
She is behind the desk.
The desk is between them.

Again. *Repitan.*

He is in front of the desk.
She is behind the desk.
The desk is between them.

Repitan otra vez, con ánimo.

I turn to questions:
Where are we right now?
We are in the school.
Where are your friends?
They are in Mexico.
Where is your brother?
He is in Los Angeles.

Where is your mother?
She is dreaming with the saints.
Do you mean sleeping?
No, dreaming, I think.

On Break

Segismundo tells me that a play
in his culture claims
all of life is a dream.
His parents named him
for the protagonist so that
if he suffers, if he is tired,
it isn't real.

Sergio takes notes all class
in a draftsman's block print—
he says, when he studied
engineering in Monterrey,
every letter, every number meant something.
One error, and a whole equation
would collapse.

With his degree
he welds on the first shift,
by night sketches circuits
and solar panels around my words.

Composition

While my students write,
I try to empathize, starting a letter,
but have no news.
I alternate between the sports pages
and a novel where nothing happens—
people only sort out their lives.

After an hour, we read
what the class would have done
if they hadn't come north.

Jesús would have started a trucking company,
and Alejo would have grown marijuana
because corn and beans never made his parents
   rich.
Griselda would have studied accounting.

Ana—who would have become a nun
to help people already born
instead of having her husband's children—
turns the question around.
What would you have done
if you couldn't have stayed here?
The answer might fill an essay, or a novel
where anything could happen.

   Course Summary

I imagine one of my numerous Marias
making love to her husband,
whom I've never met.
They know what they need to know,
they are where they need to be,
and out of their night
a baby will come, or not,
a gift plain as faith.

I use her husband's unknown face
like the mirror in *Las Meninas:*
to look in is to join the picture,
to stand in the king's place.

I set myself in the festival of bodies,
begin the exercise with a few words
before casting off words:
I am with Maria.
Maria is with me.
There is nothing between us.
I am in the king's place.

BEFORE RISING

A part of sleep escapes remembering,
the thin coin of a few seconds
when the mind, done with dream,
drifts on a current of dozing thought,
knowing itself at rest and whole.

Then it waits,
potential as a seed, as if
swaddled in an ark
that could be taken up at any moment.

HANDS

Meat-woofed looms,
they flex and glide
fluently as the false
dogs and wings
hands silhouette
on a blank screen.

Sometimes their knuckles
cross purposes
and send up digits
to search the air
in skewed planes.
A finger's touch would
shatter them
in their webbing.

My writing hand clutches
dogs and wings,
and the silhouettes
of what falls through it.

II

The boy in love—
the incipient man who looks
into a desert canyon
and plans to pass through
with heels cool and unbruised—
takes strength from devotion.

He finds in himself the heroism
to face how slight a lever
his love is against the world.
(For him,
to buy a candy bar and a comb is heroic;
for now,
his beloved will see in that act
an honor and a glow.)
He admits his loving won't repeal his death,
won't turn back the tides.
It lacks the force
of the billion Chinese
who, jumping, might budge
the earth and its axis.
His is an adjective love.
He would state, if he had the words,
"This is my loved-in world, O
possible and inconceivable planet
where she and I might combine."

Wanting words, he pockets the comb,
eats the candy bar
and whistles through nougat
on the way to her house.
It is a whistled-in world,
the world where he is whistling.

Sometimes, on the hollowest boulevards
the world confirms him
with echoes or a dog's bark in reply.
Sometimes.

BACHELOR

Lying down he thinks, having tried not to think,
Orpheus had better luck with women.
Not a complaint—a fact,
like the freezing point,
though it took time to learn:
magazines and massages reminded him
that, once, there had been someone,
but things happened—
it was hard to describe.
Anyway, the memory of her
may have improved by fading.
He finds comfort in this thought
as, on other nights,
comfort in thick socks, and in sleep.
Drifting off, he notes
that the pillow is cool,
that Orpheus had better luck with women.

MASTURBATOR

On the sands by Onan's bed
I maroon millions of homunculi,
busted, luckless,
each spoonful a half generation—
potential poets and pederasts,
shadow candlemakers, fragments of vandals,
kings and their chroniclers

left hypothetical, like whether
they would have shaped an era
or, following their father,
filled in its blanks.

LITTLE BUCHAREST

America is a state of mind, like any country.
Our people came from another.
Its memory stands before us, filtering what we see
Like a sun-scar on the retina, a vision of the absent.
Dead great-grandparents still seem to lodge with us,
their broken English and rank sausages left behind
as they lightened their steerage to the next world,
journey and end vague enough to resemble
the old country, for all we know, the redemption
of Rumania's failed rages, or
a revision of what must have been its emblem,
a grounded falcon's downcast head.

How do we fare here? A whisper wraps around fact and
        guess.
George's car was repossessed, George gambled away
the wages intended for his children's coats.
He trumpets by night to cover the loss or forget it.
This is true enough. Most of our men are Georges.
It could be any of them, or all,
clock-punching at the roundhouse, forging ties,
painting the boxcars, upholstering the passenger cars,
sharing in our tradition, subsistence.
Our mating and our fighting rise
like half-forgotten dances
from the depths of payday drunks;
tomorrow night could find a man unmanned or thumbless.
No one denies demons. We know of lathes and presses.
And we believe in a hell sure as the layoffs

where savings are sheared like dandelion heads in wind.
Under T-shirts, half-proud, our beer-guts swell into
    hemispheres,
a visible sign of our fathers' faith
that lean days will return.

Sometimes the rails are vacant.
We don't hear the still, but a memory of hooves
carrying Hussars one night, Cossacks another—
two kinds of hat, uniform in malice.
One of our own rides along to guide the torches, point the
    lash
as confessions are signed with inked thumb and X.

THE JAILED PAINTER

When he let his eyelids slip down
the iconography of Justice, with her scales'
equal and empty pans, fell away.
Instead, his urine etched on porcelain
the baroque pastries that were his one vice,
his one substantial crime against the State.
After thirty pounds melted away like meringue
the guards still chanted the cherished names—
eclairs, petits fours—in time with the broomstick's
thwacking against his soles.

On the concrete floor his fingers
trailed in their own delible oil
a fantasy of florid wrought iron—
trellises, and gates that would open from inside.
He could landscape an estate or two
between Tuesdays, when he was required to mop
his townships into nothingness.

He could presuppose, in any land
where such delicacies prevailed,
a whole judiciary of Solomons
or a multiple of the Seventy Just Men,
so many as to defy a lifetime's portraiture—
in fact, a whole people presiding at their benches,
producing lush acquittals from beneath robes
all abundant folds, green as hope.

THE BLINDED FILM CRITIC

The dark used to mean anticipation,
even a shudder, before the first frame,
and the satiation of end credits.

Now the hours are canisters
sealed over new releases,
and he is left with screening revivals.

Time and again, Rick Blaine chooses
his salvation on a runway.
Charles Foster Kane builds Xanadu
into a capitol of need.
Toshiro Mifune draws the long sword
to cut down challengers like willow twigs,
and Patty Duke draws her finger across a page,
looking to make sense of it.

It's a hell of a thing to carry
a thing that's mainly space, amazing for its bulk.
You can think about it and go crazy,
or you can have some fun with it.
Holler through the hollow tunnel—
the guy at the other end will holler back
with a low echo, like he's lost.
Imagine the monstrous joint you could roll inside.

The fun stops, though, when the storm
kicks in its long spurs from the west.
The land lies too flat for perspective,
and you hedge your bets: everything is close.
You balance the length like a huge spirit level.
If the huge bubble slips one end tips
to salute the bolts and forks above;
they could return the gesture drastically.
Trading dangers, the end could tap a power line
in one turn, like Mo or Curly's, with a plank.
The risks stem from being grounded.

The in-town struts and shuffles disappear,
saved for Rock Island tonight.
Knees bent, you hold the length low from straight arms
as if to stay some rogue current
that missed Franklin's key,
that would reach waist-level to strike.
You set the tube, fit to its neighbor, in the trench,
spade on the quick dirt, then get your ass inside.
Both will be buried sometime. And deep.

"Sometimes they play a little hard to get,
and you have to call them up.
Just like women. Every carp
thinks it's a goldfish, and you know
it's the other way around."
Dave, who never bought the lures for wifing, winks.
He thumbs the scales weighing unknown loss and gain.

I say nothing, I've come to join him
in the exclusions of men excluded by women.
My ballast, clean jokes and hygiene,
falls away. It couldn't steady a home
or fill the space in one house that widened
between my river town and a wife's North Shore.
Her embrace wore the shine off her city,
and the marriage split in two.

Wearing yesterday's clothes,
I've come for the affection of things
that stand apart, their dependable indifference.
The riverbanks and water moccasins take in
cussing and broken wind, Dave leaves me alone
to search the tackle for some solace.
When we talk, it's about the common times
as if no one had broken them
with a promise of pooling lives
and the holding back that followed.
Her damning father set his sights on
fitting heirs for his futures,
and a downstater's living couldn't yield enough—
my work is flesh, the sure swift killings
he gambles on, feeders and steers.
With nothing in my hands but skill I made my trade
and put my stock back in home soil.
Our words drown out the break with tales
of how we skipped stones and school

until my travels widened like ripples from a stone.
I learned when the ripples die the stone stays,
fixed as a birthplace. You have to dive
and hold your breath to find it.

On the dredged bends where we played hooky
Dave churns a charge from an old gangster phone
as I feed down the illicit wires, made
accomplice by convenient reason.

An oarlock could take my place with no qualms;
and the game warden, an out-of-towner
who hasn't learned his place,
saves his binoculars for deer behind the bluff.
We trespass outside his vision's twin tunnels.

Our alien current, quick as guile,
flows into the Mississippi
without operator or human voice
but a small song to fit
sealed ears and lateral line.
We have the sawfish and channel cat's number;
our rusted anchor drags from the hauled
weight, muddy bunches studded
with lidless eyes, foreign coins that buy
nothing in our country of air.
A catch outside the law has no limit,
no fin slashes back overboard
without children to save the small fry for.
My line ends here, untied
to the next generation.
I count only the gains in sight.

Again we cast in the dark
without the old, unbaited nets of obligation.
Our nets are down, with no rules for sport,
calling any partner that will join our drift.

THE NIGHT WATCHMAN'S DAWN

The world starts at four or so
without me.

Milk bottles clink
in shrinking number, down
to little more than
a *ching* in memory;

and the city's remaining paper
thumps onto doorsteps
with doubled weight
and the authority of a single voice.

For two years
the green hummingbird has left untouched
the feeder near my window.
Without his low-hanging flight,
a spirit in the early hours,
the cup of nectar hardens,
and morning is for sleep:

for a man of my age
daylight comes not bright
but pale, like fat claiming
the top of a stew gone cold.

I shudder.

WRITER'S BLOCK

All I can say
about the world
is that it's round.

Sunrise doesn't speak to me,
and bird-song suggests
only itself.

What remains to fill the hours
are the literal tasks—
groceries, walking the dog.

No wonder emanates from them.
I work, and I consider
what lies out of my hands:

time, the randomness of love,
the existence of men
whom no poem will move,

who take up every day
the sheer task of handling
things in themselves

so that, bare of memory or hope,
bolts mean bolts,
beams mean beams, and

bridges of pure denotation
connect points of land
across water or a valley.

How does one speak to these men,
with their language written in number four pencil,
their appointments kept to the minute?
They are a strange people.

But for now I have joined them.
Their roads are what I walk on,
not the air.

III

THE GREETING CARD

Held at the fold,
a V is outlined along the edge,
a gull that crosses the distance
between correspondents
then alights.

Hands are joined:
one traces where another
left cells of skin,
a loop or whorl in oil.
A tryst is made in the page's
blank plazas, ink alleys.

LOBSTER

In its last days its significance,
    A kind of metaphor, emerges
In the tank—claws like bound castanets

Or Popeye's forearms scrabble on the glass;
    For hours antennae sound
The finite water, finding no release

But a lifting of the body, a brief
    Exile in the air and immersion again
Before changing, from green to red, like a leaf.

IOWA

They prefer their Old Style
in abundance, spiked with tomato juice,
string cheese on the side.
It is a land of odd strengths.
Farmers lose their young faces
as they feed the soil, filling
barges that pull the Mississippi behind.
There's one Bible from God,
one *Register* from Des Moines,
and the truth hides in them both.
Corn grows beyond the sunset, parallel to nothing.
The fields give their ears,
and the stalks turn brown.

MARGINS

The park's old men play their checkers
under a sun imported from the Mediterranean
and never sweat in their flannel shirts—
their flesh, shrunk close to the bone,
quickly loses heat.
They pinch off gobs of Red Man,
ruminate before each move.
One wins now and then;
both would like more pieces,
a bigger board, a longer game.
One may stop to spit and tell a story,
now bigger than what it recalls—
the last bear in these parts,
flush days before the Crash,
limbs lost in the tractor plant.
At six they go home to wives or memories,
dead or dying in various degrees,
a shot of bourbon out of Social Security,

papers and TV.
After the anthem they sleep a few light hours,
again wearing new spats and gold cufflinks,
living high on margins.

IN A TRAIN CAR

At times, almost everyone talks
as if words were a meal

laid out among the narrow aisles
and stiff-backed seats.

The passengers savor thick d's, rich n's,
crunch crisp x's.

They take sparingly the bitter t's
and relish the vowels' condiments.

A few abstain to sleep, or read,
to hear their headphones' private music;

others look out the window for wisdom
in the bushes and the right-of-way.

They may have spoken their fill before leaving,
or save an appetite for their destination.

Some, enclosed in the habit of silence,
may recall accounts of besieged towns

where people dreamt
of nothing but bread

until the gates opened and their rescuers
bore regiments of loaves.

The citizens bolted them, to the last crumb,
and perished from the shock of nourishment.

THE HYPOTHETICAL LANDSCAPE

Imagine a study in the genre,
warehoused in the reach of mind
where the remnant autumn leaf
rustles on the oak,
where the scattered cattle graze
in a tidal rhythm, stasis
at the heart of their repetition.

Look through the impossibility
of foreshortening a countryside,
compressing vision into a rectangle
where the day's late light is given
by the sun of a muted palette.
The impasto *campagne* billows
with broadly-drafted grain,
and the road is knife-graded from near to far

where, almost walking into cloud
and a furl of mahogany frame,
a figure, a smudge of life,
bends away and heavenward
under his bundle of sticks.

We can follow with the eye,
with the question of what fire
he might kindle, might fuel by sale
at his always-waiting destination.

Passing him, we vanish into the distance
at a point where a man loses
his perspective, his measures of depth,
and every safety of enclosure.

STILL LIFE WITH NO APPLE

The perfect light was waited for.
Waited-for, it passed, like
the last harvest day before frost,
and the meticulous shadows
let no single light
be cast on the composition.

Each element must hold its own.
Walnuts born hard and wrinkled
disperse on the walnut table.
Three oranges phosphoresce,
and lobsters are laid on
either side of an absence.
The half-drained glass of burgundy
meets with no like tones in the palette
but is paired in want
with half a loaf
hard by a wedge of cheese.
The table is set
as well as it will be.

Behind it, a parchment globe
alludes past the frame
to a completeness wherein
the fullness of knowledge grows on trees
and a second equator, followed as incision,
shows five seeds arranged in a star.

SCRUB PINES

We are jointed, gerontocrats, a geometer's dream,
bolder than lichens, we square and skew

our limbs into a slow addition of angles,
increasing the world's degrees.

Like the mushrooms, that grow round-edged
and flaccid on manure,

we conform to our soil,
the compost of monks who fed on water, salt, and bran,

the matter for the meager annual rings
we squeeze into our thin corsets of air.

Needless of needles, or the light they convert,
we are the limbs we go out on,

neither leading nor following,
staying out of the way,

pivots of the spinning which men at our side
see when they look over the cliff.

We are above all, inedible,
Melchizedeks on our ground.

Blight and rot starve;
in winter, as they emaciate like us,

browsing deer pass by on their acute bones,
repelled by our fixity.

THE ACORNS HAVE FALLEN

The acorns have fallen.
Frost spiders its way
up the windowpane, then
drains the blood of gourds
until they rattle, many-voiced
as the inside of a dream.
Peering through a martyrdom
of wilted leaves,
the low pumpkins are on fire,
swollen with persistence,
secretly terrible
through their centers' dark growth,
the creatures of uncounted limbs
they will feed.

SHE

There is a woman in the world
who lives between places,
the woman of the cleft
in the sprouting bean.
The moon tugs at
her ebb and flow.
She walks boundary lines
to gather fern-tips for food,
slips through kitchens
to steal the flavor from bread,
leave the loaves.
Her skin does not touch
its dress, that shifts with lighting,
outside one color's hold.
Unmanned, unchilded, she
bears private seasons,
saves her flesh for the cattails,
the seashell breeze.

SOMEONE

Even the faithless will tell you
to believe in someone.
Someone to fall in love with
who will return the favor.
Someone to give you a job,
or a jump-start in winter.
Someone to thrust beneath your ribs
with both hands, interceding
between your life and a fish-bone.

The list grows with time.
Someone to secede from your life
out of boredom or lack of money
and leave you with half a marriage,
dry and silent as a castanet.
Someone to call in the small hours
and hang up without speaking,
to let the intravenous pouch run dry.
Someone to seal the coffin,
having slipped off your rings,
having lifted the cool coins from your eyes.

IV

These beads aren't told with prayers
or lists of miracles.
That's not the way Greeks use them.

On the other hand,
I'm not much of a Greek—
a thin eighth of my blood
from a great-grandfather
who reached America in time
to enlist in the Great War
and be drafted for the Crash.
Besides his monthly pension,
he clutched his worry beads
as if they were a handful
of his native soil,
where they hadn't come from
but where the Ottomans
had left them, with belly dancing
and coffee in half-sized cups.

The strand's passed down to me.
I hold it slack, describing
a parenthesis that closes
its Hellenic years, ended
in Illinois, where
I've learned about the ways
bad breaks and misplaced love
call for miracles.
Then I clack the beads,
taking them through an arc
that takes in Turks and Arabs,

the handlers of rosaries,
full-blooded Greeks
and all of worry's deep
and wide fraternity.

LOOKING FOR GOD ON ILLINOIS ROUTE 47

At five miles over the limit
the desire to portray
the shafts of light in the western clouds
is transcended, passed up
like walnuts on a roadside branch.
The hulls shrink in perspective,
and the tree is left behind the earth's curve;
the rearview mirror clears like a conscience.
No hubris ranges wide enough
to put the fields on a canvas,
none high enough
to paint the penile silos large as life.
Photographs would show a quicker failure.

What the drive inspires
is performance for no visible audience,
a recital of names
gathered in the exuberant uselessness
of knowing the created world:
the crown of the road,
corn tassels, the wooden horse,
furrows—field and brow—
and the assemblies of milkweed,
their pods proclaiming floss.
A telephone pole stands
top-heavy with provident insulators—
in its shadow, grooved pavement
and a mound on the shoulder, a past animal,
near a single black shoe, a red plastic lighter.

Cabbage butterflies strike the windshield
steadily, a measure of time,
then fall away to feed the soil,
so deep in this region
that for all anyone can hear
the very stones below may be speaking.
It may be time for them to speak.

THE HUNDREDTH NAME OF GOD

In legend, the camel knows.
In the desert, he spits at his hostler
to proclaim that, again,
the packs are overloaded.
Loose syllables blur
and rumble in his stomachs.

With nothing to trade,
just tape recorders and notebooks,
bands of linguists follow caravans
to recover the sacred word
from its diaspora
among the phonemes.

Software arrives at the rumored name,
the lexicon complete—
a final strip of papier mache
laid over a balloon:

the shell dries,
latex rattles inside,
the noble gas having fled
what it shaped.

A LAND OF SAINTS

No one is practicing his backhand,
nor his serve.

The game of tennis, as game, is frivolous,
its elements suspect:

the lob embodies sloth
and topspin turns to mendacity.

Hands free of racquets weed gardens
against heretic dandelions.

Hands empty of oboes or novels
are filled with good works for the poor.

Existing so that good works may be done,
they take their soup, their block of casserole

and lie down in hostels
to dream the question

of what delight consists in,
where it might be found.

THE ANNOYANCE OF ANGELS

After the terrible year
of the accident and the wrongs in court,
he still feels the hosts hovering,
familiar as toothache or the urge for sex.

With his remaining hand
he swats at the ironic wings that chafe
and bring no earthly help.

He swings again to scatter them,
reaching for consolation
in the perfection of something,
even if it's his abandonment,
the prospect of moving unattended
in the pure, random air.

POLICY

Because Nubians are still enslaved
I walk my dogs twice a day.

Because a child conceived tonight
will inherit addiction
I leave my dogs offerings
of fresh water, with ice cubes.

Because envelopes and marketplaces explode
I hug my dogs and even carry them
where no shrapnel flies.

Because a manatee is sliced
by motorboat blades
and the last wild tiger
has been born,
I keep my dogs' tags and shots
up to date.

Now that any fact can be known
in an instant,
the smallest love is news.
Things touch at a near or far remove:
jays pass raspberry seeds
over fresh fields,
armadillos, burrowed into freight,
widen their range.

Word of my program
will ride the jet stream,
and land like a petal,
or it will bounce, devoutly,
off a satellite.

AFTER SAINT MARTIN

On a park bench,
to eat one orange
and call its segments
the courses of a feast,
having given up the second
as readily as breath,
a round syllable in response
to a stranger on the bench
who asked for money
spent on oranges.

ANGELS

Even the highest, the recorded ones,
have fallen from the radar range of recognition
that passes for grace in our time.
No wings spread and rustle
across the planes of newsprint.
The seraphic names aren't, like gossip, set
with a red brand to every mouth.

Now the air is voiceless, thin
with the absence of spirit.
If a man has visions of a ladder,
it is empty.

The parapsychogists gird their loins,
load their cameras, and bless
every corner with a fisheye mirror.
Front door and back are ajar
with their implicit invitations—
to predict futures of children and oats,
to levitate a living-room sofa
and set it down along another wall—
in short, all the kinds of singing
for a supper of praise
the ethereal need as much
as bread or a sense of worth.

If they perform any good,
it is by omission, the hard holding back
from giving men what they ask for,
as if any nightclub's walls could stand
after one note from Gideon's trumpet,
as if a policeman could find work
after Michael walked a beat.
Who could endure their help?

If they exist for any purpose,
it is to be found
like the second pulse
the wristwatch sets against the vein,
unheard until daylight's machinery, its necessary voices
are stilled and yield
to a rhythm heard by infants and the Seventy Just Men—
a whirring of known wings

which at the same time fan Melchizedek
and the bones Ezekiel clothed with flesh.
Others may join the hosts in time—or not;
their wisdom lies in savoring the wait.

They have all the time in the world. Any world.

V

CHANDLER VARIATIONS

> "A gun bloomed in his hand."
> Raymond Chandler

First, cells bloomed in the sea.
Lunged life bloomed on land;
Knowledge, on a Tree;
The Pyramids in sand.

One genius bloomed in Poe,
Another in Verlaine—
Answered in Rimbaud;
Disease, in Nietszche's brain.

Lust blooms in the eye,
Muscle on the bone.
Stormclouds in the sky,
Interest on the loan.

The lie blooms from the oath.
The law blooms from the case—
Judgment, from them both.
The skull blooms from the face.

COFFEE

If the coffee could see,
if its liquid surface were
the vast pupil it seems,
it might find itself
reflected in the black ink of bottom lines,
magnified in a dark thread through the blood
whereby men violate their bones' wisdom
and shorten their years to fill them
with their works, which flow across America
wide and steadily as the supply of coffee.

For it looks a man straight in the eye
and meets his lips, unresisted.
For it is made of
the same water as the man.
For its blackness strains from deaths
of coffee beans and campesinos.
For its darkness is the depth
where the Rocky Mountain bootlace performs
a minute speleology in the eyelet,
where the Maine potato eye sees its way to growth.

This depth is the kind of sight
whereby Edgar Cayce, in a depth before my birth,
prophesied from the most deathly
depth allowed a living man
in an America full of men drinking coffee.

We know this from trade figures
and from Edward Hopper's *Nighthawks*, 1942.
In a diner walled with plate glass of implausible clarity
every patron's face is paired with a cup.
The man whose face is a small, hard nail
seems welded to his fedora, his countenance
yellowed like coffee-stained teeth.

We can imagine the counterman, at this unknown hour,
keeps his own cup on a lower shelf.
Only an obscured cup, if it is there,
sees the fulcrum of the canvas, the lone man's face.
A space of black oils sets him apart,
and he shows only his rounded back to the viewer.
If we still posit the cup,
if we posit the man's unseen mouth,
we can believe Raymond Chandler who,
through Philip Marlowe's mouth,
called coffee "the lifeblood of tired men."

A block from the Chicago Art Institute, where
the two-lioned entrance guards *Nighthawks*,
three students at the Artist's Snack Shop
coincide with Chandler.
While one dissects the painting for a class,
her boyfriend views it through the Turner Thesis:
the frontiers are fenced, but new trails blaze
through the dark hours when newspaper machines stand
     empty,
when the day's first doughnuts rise
to greet waiting policemen or dwindling milkmen.
Men. The third calls that phrasing—and Chandler's—
     sexist.
A seminarian, she sips and wonders,
stuck on a thorn of theodicy,
how a loving God allows
H-bombs and low prices for the Third World's crops.
The black stream from the waiter's carafe
arches over their views:
the other two are atheists, who, as a group,
make coffee as well as anybody.
Like anybody else, given the means
they'll buy whole beans and grind them.
At best, they brew Jamaican,
named after the mythical Blue Mountain,

harvested in part by real Rastafarians,
an island in an island of statistical Protestants
and agnostics—resistant to counting,
and a reasonable thing to be in Jamaica.
What can be known from an island
unless, like Crusoe, or John at Patmos,
one brings to it a world—or more?

It was as islands, shrines floating on an infidel sea,
that the Crusaders saw the Levant,
though the Caliphs found, in a flurry of faith, riper islands
as their crescent's points bent
to pincer the plums of Byzantium and Granada.
The star in the crescent, five-pointed with daily prayers,
came to shine more brightly with other intoxicants.
The sheen rose from leaves the Rastas call *ganja*,
and from a dozen breeds of berries, whose names escape
me
except for *Caffea arabica*, named for the land,
berry-red with blood, that fathered a faith,
then the sects, the shattered refractions of faith
that shed their particular lights on America.

If the coffee could see,
it might find American faces, by that black sheen,
seeing themselves mirrored—through a now-Brazilian
        crop—
in Brazil itself, *nosso amigo, nossa imagem*
for our failings in race, for our vast waste of forests.
And what is either country
but a confluence of events—
most dissolved from history
like unique grains of sugar
that can never be reproduced, never
imagined as other than they were.
Nor could it help. No one replays time,
and we identify our forefathers as best we can.
Both countries are spawned from

the crescent's failures, at Vienna and Tours,
to close into a wedding band around Europe,
both sprung from the Line of Demarcation
and a day's weather against the Armada,
which allowed the globe-circling girth,
the once-grandeur of our mother countries.
So our rites, grown behind an ocean's shield,
have encompassed a ring of protocol
around cups, china and paper—and styrofoam,
twenty ounces, sold by Ali or Mohammed,
from Syria or Pakistan, at the Seven-Eleven or Circle K.
He wonders how people can drink that much;
rightly so—we are beasts, a beast-nation,
we feed and grow, then feed more.
We take in everything, we swell like goldfish,
as large as our pool permits, and it expands
with hours of business and electric lights.
A new citizen, sworn in on Lincoln's last birthday,
he wonders what it is
that the native-born have, and those arrived as children,
what thing in common threads through their many minds,
what light in the eye, what balances of hand and spine.
What intangible necessities do they hold with such ease?
Are they what his nieces have in Austin,
what drives them to his aisles of wine and beer
and sustains their unveiled passion?
He wonders about what he tries to be, and never will.
His children will have, will be this thing.
They will sift into their suburbs and, passing through
for business or road trips, they will buy their coffee,
twenty ounces, at a Seven-Eleven or Circle K,
from a clerk, Indonesian or Afghan, perhaps,
a drop in the next wave of store owners,
who will seem odd and familiar
for lacking what their father lacks.
Once you name this thing that makes the country, then,
what harder task begins?

This thing shows its sides and sects.
Coffee could brew over the crosses that still burn,
the campfires of hate that flare
after an interval of forgetting, not an end.
We doubt this for peace of mind,
but our doubt is answered
in the makeup of the men
who reason together over a cup.
Cafe au lait pleased the Wehrmacht, like other men,
as they set their gray against Elsa Lund's blue.
The blue of our own city's finest
no less often sets itself against a black face
or a pink mouth opened for backtalk.
Allies in order, guards and bouncers, assist,
herding unto compliance the lines that wait for tickets
to games that slide toward gladiation,
to concerts overcast by the cloud
from a thousand sticks of ganja.
The crowd is carved by bouncers, edgy with caffeine,
light-hearted from the law's lacuna as to their power,
light-hearted for lack of witnesses.
Those who pass by seldom stop
for fear of settling their load between destinations.
The webbing of roads, flights, and wires
can suspend a man safely en route
through the levelling communion of products and news,
but thousands vanish into thin airs,
the culs-de-sac peopled by new identities of
relocated witnesses and alimony rogues.
Those who travel, travel light and travel tired.
Otherwise the journey might grow into a pleasure, a habit
in a land broad with possibilities.
On the road the alternatives shimmer:
what is it like to be a security guard,
or a musician, seeing the highway from his own bus?
Or someone else still?

Among the gulls or the paramecia
the day's labor for two of a kind
is alike as two drops of water,
but man's business meshes
more variously than I know how to say.
Too many hamburgers feed it, or none;
and, constant as the sun's eye,
the circle, the surface of the coffee sees through
the night and the frontiers that stretch or hide
in market share or a million more paths to virtuosity.
A current of coffee connects the land,
a Mississippi dispersed in space but joining minds.
The scripts of TV and movies, joining us more obviously,
string out weak lines, fill hollow airwaves
with offers of coffee, offers we take, recognizing
how the cups stimulate
our efforts to deal and seduce,
to invent a thousand vital and gimcrack things,
to summarize a lifetime of research
or pad a few seconds of dialogue.
For all the coffee sees, we look into it and recognize
the attempt to expend the years better or more bravely.
Sometimes, in America,
it succeeds by the law of averages if nothing else,
as we write our own scripts and reach for lines, as I do,
always trying, trying anything.

AFTERWORD

The inbred infighting of the poetry world in America revolves largely around the question of what kind of poems should be written. Lines are drawn in the (appropriately) metaphorical sand between free-verse bards and New Formalists, performance poets and academics. These lines are themselves intersected by the claims of those whose work asserts the primacy of ethnic, sexual, and political stance over mere esthetics.

These tempests, in their respective teapots, bypass a more vital question, which is less what kind of poetry than why should poetry be written, or read. A poem doesn't turn a wrench or splice a gene. A poem is seldom decorative like an Impressionist painting, seldom purely entertaining like Hollywood film at its best. Why poetry? Why at all?

The defense of poetry enjoys a long tradition, but like all traditions it is fulfilled only when individuals engage, even struggle with it, and make it their own. My struggle with this tradition—admittedly a minor struggle compared with those of the Tibetans and East Timorese—has taken up much of my adult life. As a first-generation college student, and a scholarship student at that, with all the accompanying dislocations, I found my interest in poetry confronted by doubts regarding the utility of poetry compared to the "real world." Escape from more mundane activities and the vain pleasure of seeing my work in print, my initial self-justifications, began to seem morally irresponsible unless they were subsumed within a larger rationale.

I have caught glimpses of this rationale. The first presented itself to me when, as a teaching assistant, I was preparing a first-week lecture for a required literature class. My students could rightly wonder what use was literature when they were preparing for careers in business administration or pharmacy. My undergraduates may not have accepted my explanation, but they did get one. In short, most good and practical things are physically and economically necessary but also —fortunately— replaceable. A community may depend on a bridge in a particular location, but if that bridge falls to calamity or age another can be erected on the same site. The reverse applies to poems and similarly impractical things. The survival and economic prosperity of the human race have little to do with whether a given poem is written, or remains extant. The value of a poem lies precisely in its reflecting a unique perception; meeting our survival needs gives us the means to share that perception. As for the poems that go unwritten, we quite literally don't know what we're missing. The poems that have come into being still occupy a precarious position. The lost works of the ancient Greeks and Romans, the holdings of the library of Alexandria, for instance, haunt us with possibilities precluded for all time. Similarly, if *Paradise Lost* or "To His Coy Mistress" were to vanish from pages, disks, and memories, no crew could appear at a job site and build a replacement. Whatever the demand, the supply would remain nil. Even Borges' Pierre Menard, at the end of his fictional life's work, could only recreate one chapter of *Don Quixote*.

More recently I've begun to wonder what is meant when we discuss usefulness. The term begs the question of exactly to whom, or to what, an activity is useful. Is it useful to shareholders we may never meet, or to the building of an abstract GDP that does not necessarily correlate with human well-being? Or is an activity's usefulness measured by whether it provides us the income to pay for advertising our unreciprocated loyalty to one or another brand?

Determining to whom our activities are useful becomes, as far as I can tell, a way of determining to whom we ourselves are useful. Are we merely means to ends—often decided by others—or are we ends in ourselves? If the latter is true, we are turned back to the issue of how we can realize the possibilities of our individual existences; the philosophers called this the question of the good life before the term was commandeered by advertisers as a euphemism for hedonism and wretched excess.

My possibilities, however limited, involve writing poems. They are never sufficient in quantity or quality, but they represent an attempt to derive the greatest benefit from my consciousness; for human beings all activities, including basic functions such as eating, drinking, and sex, somehow contribute to this end.

Writing poems keeps me off the street; it is one of the more harmless things I do in the course of a week or month. If I am lucky, what I write will be of some value, some use, to others.

for Leo Dangel, Dave Jauss, and Carl Lindner —
my first line of defense, sage and patient readers
whom I spare nothing of what I write

PHILIP DACEY

The Paramour
of the Moving Air

PHILIP DACEY, the author of six previous books of poems, most recently <u>The Deathbed Playboy</u> (Eastern Washington University Press), lives in southwestern Minnesota, where some of the time he teaches at the state university at Marshall and most of the time he writes. His current project is a book-length sequence of poems about Thomas Eakins.

CONTENTS

THE PARAMOUR OF THE MOVING AIR

I Not Noticing We're Naked

INHERITING THE GIFT OF
BLARNEY

My mother kissed the inconvenient stone
by hanging upside down at Blarney Castle.
She went back every summer
and kissed the Irish air.

Her father, a Cork man, recited poetry
to captive relatives at holidays
and once chased his son down the street
for snickering at a solemn line.

I grew up inside the word,
though I did not know it then.
My place was green with vowels,
and waves against the cliffs of Moher

were consonants. Blind to maps,
I wandered the hills and valleys
of a sentence, cooled in the shadow
of a pause like a ravine.

I think of this now because today
I talked a man out of a gun,
with my words pried his fingers loose
from the loaded anger.

Because he was no fool, I even
warned him of my words, their undeniable
design. But I didn't warn him of
my warning, which was, of course,

in words, all honest ones, of course,
yet kissed with something like music
to enchant the will, no force but that
of the tongue, its tender insinuation.

O, may I always hang so upside down,
beside my mother, my lips pressed
to whatever's slab-cold
and a bit of a reach, perfect

precondition for speech, and may
I live out all my days in Blarney,
hometown for the ear, the mouth,
so that when I die I'll translate

wholly into it, a story to tell.
Make me up well, Friends,
and say Death's the biggest
load of blarney there is.

HONEY

Near ninety, wanting to die,
my mother tells me
she calls the Blessed Virgin Mary "Honey."

"But, Mom," I say, "nobody
calls the Blessed Virgin Mary 'Honey.'
She's not some waitress in a cafe.
Why do you do that?"

"Maybe that way I'll get her attention,"
she answers. "Maybe then she'll listen to me
and grant my wish."

"The mother of God may be sweet, Mom,
but she's no Honey. I doubt if anyone
in two thousand years has called her that."

But then I wonder. Maybe the Holy Ghost
at that intimate moment long ago
called Mary "Honey," at that
immaculately sticky conception.

Or maybe the young Joseph,
vainly pressing Mary
at the village well,
stirred her damp hair
with his whispered, "Honey."

So that now, in Heaven, a sound
catches Mary's ear. A word floating up
from far below, raspy, weak,
but golden in all that light,
fanning memories
and softening her will until
a long pour of sorrow
fills her, this Mother of Sorrows,
and she yields to the time-weary
petitioner, pouring back and down
an answer that spreads,
thickly, slowly,
a smothering and final goodness,
over an entire life.

THE ORPHAN

My father's thinking out loud:
"My father died when he was thirty-nine,
already a widower for more than a year.
I was three. I'm ninety-two now.
Let's say I die and go to heaven

and walk along its streets, and there
in front of me is the man I remember.
My one memory of him's the time I broke
my leg and he carried me into
the house. That sad face above and close
to my face. So I go up to him and say,
'Hi, Pa!' But all he sees
is this old guy who's news
to him. He's stayed thirty-nine.
Now, what's he going to think?
And what's he going to feel?
He'll say, 'Joe? Joe?
Is that you?' And maybe
I'll feel like his father, not his son,
because of our ages. It'll be
a confusing moment. Things will be
all turned upside down.
So we walk along those streets
to talk, to leave the confusion
behind us, our arms linked.
But he's also holding onto my arm
with his other hand, because
I'm so old, the way he held me
when I was so young. He's been steady,
I'll say that for him. 'I've been waiting for you,'
he'll say, still taller than I am,
who grew past him but then
stooped as I shrank. The precious pavement
will shine under our feet
as it leads us to a group of women
standing in the distance. All young,
shaded by a great tree. Only one
turns her head to me, and she's so beautiful
I feel as if I've died and gone to heaven.
My father says, as my knees go weird,
'I bet you'll never guess who that is.'
And I think we'll all be naked,
but we won't notice that."

THE LOST ART

Benjamin Eakins was a professor of penmanship
for fifty years and wrote four books on the subject.
—Thomas Eakins

1.
The hand has a vague memory
it cannot sharpen,
perhaps that of a bird,
excited by evening,
swiftly looping back and forth,
or a skater, a kind of
moving light on a surface of light.

2.
Sister Mary Rose leaning over me
from behind was a cave with beads
as she whispered, "Palmer method,"
her mouth close to my ear,
and guided my hand,
her black sleeve dragging
like a broken wing.

3.
Certain muscles in the hand
will never be used again,
little dodo muscles,
passenger pigeon muscles.

4.
The hand, overcome with shame
in its tendons,
in its fine bones,
seeks the retreat of a glove.

5.
Goodbye to the pleasures
of dotting an i, that stab
of precision neither too far left
nor too far right, a balancing
to point the way,

and goodbye to the stain
on the thumb, the forefinger,
that blue or black badge of courage.

6.
The hand climbs up
the cliff-front of
keyboard and screen,
leaving behind whole swathes
of flowers,
those inkiest whorls,
in the valley.

7.
It must have been like love,
the hand moving with just the right
pressure and angle,
following the contours
of a name, a long body of names.

GIVING AWAY BOOKS: A RHAPSODY

Let the ink flow between your fingers,
black silk in which to wrap the world.
All the tightly bound pages deserve a scattering
to the wind of someone else's
excited attention.

Would you insulate your grave with books?
Even now the spines crack like lightning.
And what is the shelf-life of an idea,
of an utterance like thunder?

That wall's a camp choked with shoulder-
to-shoulder refugees from a nightstand.
For dust collects on no voice, only
on its repository.

And since nothing's heavier than a box of books,
save your back and the backs of your children
when you're gone: volume by volume, fly
as you let fly with softcovers, hardcovers,
what matter, any book in one place for too long
grows stagnant, like water,
while to drink from a running book, the cold, clear
words, that is the thing!

To keep all books in perpetual motion, the miraculous
machine dreamed by philosophers,
who inhale the book, then exhale it,
the particles of book circling the globe.
Caesar read the same book you read yesterday.

Because bookless we arrive and bookless depart,
the book holds, a post, against time's drag
only if we let it go, the mother-book,
and wean flesh from the word as solid
as cedar and scented, nose buried dead-center
in the cleavage bound by glue.

The truest library is the library of the skull,
the stacks pulsing heartbeat by heartbeat.

Though the book makes love to the hand,
the covers wings pressing outward,
that bird's feathery explosion into white flight beyond us

thrills even more than tiny bones rolled against fingers.
And what if you are only a book yourself,
opened a little while, pages
the paramour of the moving air,
just waiting to be given away?

AMERICA WITHOUT BASEBALL

When baseball died,
back in the twenty-first century,
Americans were too maddened with grief
even to go to the funeral.
Instead, they raced backwards around the bases
again and again, subtracting a run,
each time a foot hit home plate,
from 1839, the year baseball was invented.
Reaching zero, they fell down and wept,
released from their long slump of denial.

With baseball gone, Americans could see
that the moon had become a towering
fly ball, possibly a home run,
though the line between fair and foul
had been obliterated for all eternity.

Soon, box scores began to look
like Greek or Sanskrit so that someone
chancing upon them in yellowed newspapers
could have been meeting an old flame,
the embers cold, and wondering
what he possibly had seen in her.

The word "fungo" disappeared
from the language except in the dreams
of a few Americans, where it was uttered
by a stranger who came at them

angrily waving a club
or else the word emanated from a rock
seawater had begun to shape into a perfect sphere.

3 and 9 became magical numbers—
all automobile license plates
carried either or both,
as did the logos of some commercial ventures,
though often buried in the design
to work subliminally on customers—
though no one could remember why.

The crack of the bat
travelled the universe
as an ambiguous signal picked up
from deepest space,
and the radio and television announcers'
measured drone as the ball speedily
toured the field in a series of sharp
angles, hand to wood to wall to
hand to glove, sank
to be a hum at the earth's core,
a basso continuo from which seismic activity
got an assist.

Some prophets appeared
speaking of the second coming
of America's favorite pastime,
but passersby left them
stranded on streetcorners
like baserunners on second and third,
the side retired.

Only the flowers showed up
for spring training,
impressing everyone with their knowledge
of the fundamentals, and in mid-summer
the batting averages

of the corn, the stars, and the rivers soared.
In fall, when the World Series once
filled the calendar,
lovers abed
passed the hours
with the best of seven caresses.
And as winter approached, Americans everywhere
listened to their heartbeats
scoring over and over
and felt for the first time
released into free agency.

WHAT FATHER LEAHY DIDN'T SAY

After I entered the confessional,
that upright coffin, morbid voting booth,
letting the black drape fall behind me like
all hope, and gave my name to Father Leahy,
my personal confessor, so that he
could recollect my history of sins
and thereby, placing new transgressions in
the context of old error, rooted habits,
better judge and guide me,
                                        I told that priest,
in a voice that must have sounded self-oppressed,
that I had gotten pleasure from my balls,
I meant from scratching, not just having, them;
that I feared I did not need to scratch them
as much as I did, but chose to do so less
to ease an itch that naturally occurred
than quite deliberately to gratify
the flesh, digging and scratching purely—or not
so purely—for the sake of nails sweetly on skin;
and that I begged forgiveness for my fault,
my grievous fault, knowing how each scratch drove
a nail more deeply into Jesus;

                              but Father
did not say to me in a warm voice brimming
with kindness in the face of virtue warped
by youthful folly in that year of our Lord
1958, "Son, cool it, relax,
give yourself an obviously needed break,
for you're afflicted by what's technically
known as a hyperscrupulous conscience,
which makes into a sin some act that on the great
screen of sinning isn't even a blip,
and which has led you to forget how brief
and threatened on all sides by everything
from numbing boredom to fatal accident
your life is, which life reflects the divine
spirit as it makes a home here on earth
and, more exactly, in your very body,
the ways of which, therefore, merit tolerance,
including at the least a few friendly strokes,
for those two little sacks lodged cozily
between your thighs carry the universe,
past and future so neatly encoded there
the touch of your fingertip is a hello—
which is to say, farewell—to history;
and although it's true man's private parts—equipment,
balls—have led him into serious trouble—
blood spilled, lives ruined, pain indelibly etched—
and desire's a weapon always loaded and aimed
backwards at him who's sighting his object,
I would bet my cincture, my waist-encircling
symbol of the need to gird one's loins,
that Jesus scratched his balls from time to time
and, God knows, would have especially loved to
on the cross,"
                    but only said in a voice
betraying no emotion, "For your penance
say six Hail Marys and six Our Fathers,
and now go in peace," leaving me unaware
of my little adolescent madness,

my deprivation, not depravity,
so that decades passed before I could confess
to myself, as I confess to you, Fr. Reader,
how much I wasted my early years, who now,
with no apology, and with a big grin,
am scratching and scratching down these lines, nails
and fingers digging into language for
just that right spot, that certain syllable
all tenderness and nerve-endings where vowel
and consonant meet in a delicious seam
around which the body of the poem turns.

II A Little Night Music

SKIN SONG

If when you come the first
thing we do is take off our clothes

because it has been so long
in them and apart and because

they are heavy as our touch is light
the clothes clinging as only we have a right to

and if when you come we slip out of
our words and set them beside us

not scattered like clothes at our feet
an archipelago trailing through rooms

but ready to wear like a spur or a bow
when our clothes the thought of them

has faded for good so that our nakedness
goes flounced in volition our dream

the world too shunted away its vain
struggles to move in the folds of a history

all stiffest brocade and dragging train
even the drinks food and news put on hold

then let it be love and our limbs
bear witness as our clothes were blind

as we were blind adoring our clothes
until the day that stripped to its skin

laid itself out as if it were dead
and the limbs of that day first showed us

the way to a bed where we took off
our clothes and discovered our wardrobe

of flesh which we reached to undo
till we fondled the nothing the absence in lieu

of our names and we kissed it
because it was I because it was you.

GAUGUIN: "WOMAN WITH MANGOES" (1896)

On these two brown legs, I will prop my last years.
The black dog is my soul, low-slung, red-eyed, and gaunt,
these words a slaver drawn from the muzzle near
her raised knee, that peak I climb again and again.
The white cloth she clutches to her lap is not
modesty but all the unlearned desires now
returned home. She is the garden she looks out
of toward the unframed world her body also
encloses. Thus heaven decorates her wrist,
a thin blue band, and the red fan at her head's
a pagan halo. I have no browner fate.
As grain braves the gullets of the pecking birds,
I will sail on the unsinkable boats of her feet,
though mangoes, all my bright works, waste on the green.

AMHERST WITH FRIES

When the bored cashier at Burger King
pauses as she takes my order to note
with at least a little wonder

how "Whopper" and "water" "sound alike,"
I want to kiss her, despite her ugliness
and nature so dwarfish she has to stand
on a stool to punch the register, for I'm thinking
of Emily Dickinson, absolute mistress
of the off-rhyme, her deliciously glancing blows
of sound, and know I'm talking to her sister.
If I'd add, "like 'pearl' and 'alcohol,'" I'm sure
she'd nod and go all dizzy, one more Inebriate of Air.
I want to invite her to my poetry workshop
at the local college or even to conduct one
immediately in this place—among the grease
and sickeningly sweet drinks tell her that
William Stafford said all words rhyme,
any two of them sounding more like each other
than either one of them sounds like silence,
that "burger" has an affinity, therefore, with
"Massachusetts," that language is always
and in any state the special of the day,
and that although few people full-rhyme
all people off-rhyme, that any is more at home
with any other, or should be, than either is
with styrofoam cups or a plastic tray.

Of course I don't tell her all that I'm thinking—
some passions are best concealed, or told slant;
I only accept the fact that I'm order number five
and wait down the counter for what started all this
to arrive, thinking that here,
as the last years of the twentieth century
scrape America off the grill, shovelling it
into the stainless steel trenches,
there's cause for hope in this minimum-
wage earner's surprising—even to her, I bet—
regard for what daily commercial use
has reduced to near invisibility: our life-
giving diet of vowel-and-consonant clusters.
And as I'm eating like any other nobody,

I realize I'm enjoying, more than my Whopper,
the thought of this cashier at her post
playing the role of an intelligent ear,
a kind of subversive national weapon,
a uniformed and smiling stealth poet,
listening with great discrimination
as a line forms all day in front of her.

SHOWER SEX ON SUNDAY

It is a small chapel,
a congregation
of modest means.
Glass stained with steam.
A susurrus of piped music.

There's little room
for side-to-side movement.
It's all up or down,
the clearest moral choices.
Here at The Church

of the Holy Showerhead,
we reach up like supplicants
to turn a concentrated
sermon beating on our brows
into a gentle spray

of grace. The handshake
of peace turns soapy
and runs wild, spreading
good news all over
our nearest neighbor.

Even after the service,
we stand and talk, ministering

to ourselves, in no hurry
to get dry as sin and change
out of our Sunday best.

ELECTRIC LOVE
> *"For those of you who don't know the difference*
> *between a lady and a lightbulb—someday you're*
> *going to get shocked."*
> —Airline stewardess on intercom

I'm glad to have the mystery
explained, the electricity
that was too much. I've been falling
in love with lightbulbs, though now,
by studying to be an electrician,

I hope to find a real lady,
one whose sockets
carry only love. How close
I must have come to death
those times in the shower!

I should have known, the way
they burned out, the orgies
of replacement, the thrill at slipping off
their paper covers. It's time to go
to the source, stand out in a storm

of possibilities with a kite
and the key to my future
and wait for the current in flashing
eyes to give me a lift, my filaments
fried, the monster of romance

once more brought to life. And let the
power failures happen, I'll be
my own generator, always ready
with enough juice to read by
in the middle of the night.

HUM

The next morning in the motel room
when he asked me a five-year-old's question,
"Why were you humming last night?"

and his mother and I knew he did indeed remember
what we had hoped he would forget—
that moment hours before when he had startled us

by sitting up in his bed and calling my name across
the space as wide as the nightstand, as wonder,
though she hurried to lay him gently back down—

what could I answer but the truth? that it was more
talking to his mother than humming, and more singing
to her than talking, unless it was all three at once,

so that I imagine one day years from now
he will again think of that night as he hears
coming through his own lips the same old tune

that disturbs all nearby sleepers with news
of a little night music, song without words,
talk before speech was even invented,

or maybe accompaniment to music, to, rather, music's
source, which is also what all music ultimately
empties into, the sea to its long pour,

and as he falls, after his flight, falls
to be caught ever so tenderly,
he will have the satisfaction of knowing

the mystery of at least one sound that issues from
the adult human mouth has been solved,
which is to say, if he is lucky, deepened.

BECAUSE: TWO LITANIES

1. Why He Beat Her
Because the sun was in the sky.
Because the television hissed at him from a corner.
Because the room was hot.
Because his hands, his hands.
Because his hands detached at the wrists.
Because a fist seeks the resistance of bone.
Because his open right hand and her left cheek
    made a most human music.
Because a universe of dust swirling in a shaft of sunlight
    accused him.
Because the ringing of the phone startled him.
Because she knew how he felt about the red shirt.
Because he didn't believe her smile.
Because he saw his voice
    and flames were shooting out around its edges.
Because he was afraid.
Because her look bore into him and
    spun out the other side.
Because her secret kept insulting him.
Because his last word had fallen to the rug
    and died, instantly curling up.
Because he did not have a gun.
Because the shadow of a tree
    lunged through the window
    and swarmed his leg.

Because the space between them was intolerable.
Because a bat brushed against
   the inside of his skull.
Because her tears dampened the room
   to clamminess and threatened to flood.
Because he wanted to break through to
   the silence afterwards.
Because the flowers that blossomed on her skin
   invited his kiss.
Because he knew he would beat her in such a way
   he would never have to beat her again.
Because a cloud passed in front of the sun.
Because she was holding the ropes of his life.
Because just because.
Because—why else?—he loved her.

2. Propositions
Because I lived my life, I didn't write the poem.
Because I wrote the poem, I didn't live my life.

Because the poem wrote me, I lived my life.
Because my life was a poem, I didn't need to write.

Because I needed my life, I lived the poem.
Because I needed the poem, I wrote my life.

Because my life wrote rings around me, the poem took pity.
Because my poem was a ring, I said I do to my life.

Because my poem said because, my life said why.
Because my life said why, my poem said why not.

Because the poem came unannounced, my life was
welcome.
Because my life welcomed the poem, I announced myself.

Because I breathed my poem, my life was air.
Because my life was clay, my poem breathed me.

Because my poem broke into lines, my life went on and on.
Because my life stopped, my poem stiffened into stone.

NOTES OF AN ANCIENT CHINESE POET

1.
When a new emperor
comes to power,
certain old poems quietly
revise themselves.

2.
Shave the head
of your poem
lest it like what it sees
in the mirror
too much.

3.
Who can write a poem about
blossoms falling in the wind
and mean only
blossoms falling in the wind?

4.
Listen to the voice
of each dead poet as if
it were yours.
It is.

5.
To say your poems by heart
is to know how a migratory
bird feels flying home.

6.
Outside, the wind.
What poem can compete?
The one that strips
away dead thoughts.

7.
Tea leaves
in hot water,
words steeped
in silence.

8.
Snow on the mountain,
flowers in the valley,
one landscape.
Compose the poem
with icy detachment,
with a simple heart.

9.
You must learn
to pull the poem
up over your face
as you die.

ON LEARNING THAT DYLAN THOMAS
AND WILLIAM STAFFORD WERE BORN
IN THE SAME YEAR

The force that through the green fuse
drove a deer along the Wilson River Road
drove two poets deep into a time.

As wise men knew that dark was right
and a lizard gripped the desert hard,
the poets took their pens in hand.

Green and golden under the apple boughs,
where the unknown soldier did not die,
their words marched victorious through our town.

For never until the mankind making
animal that drank up sound
heard them did the world break true.

A candle in the thigh warms youth and seed
and Berky learned to love in that dark school,
in which the poets taught and lived their rule:

to see the boys of summer in their ruin,
to say what the river says,
one shot like a star, the other meandered, just as far,

where death shall have no dominion.
Though we live in an occupied country,
a rich year breathed twice on us, and we were free.

ELEGY IN THE PRESENT TENSE

As I read Lynda Hull's words,
in memory of her, shortly after
the accident, and attempt
to resurrect her in my attention
to her attention to language,

I imagine how someday someone
will read mine, just after
my death, picking up one of
my books as a way of marking
the loss, of keeping me present

in the line like a carefully
exhaled breath, and, so imagining,

die into these words you are reading,
the syllables a living elegy,
a sarcophagus waiting

to be filled by the voice
of the dead, the tone
deepening, the pauses more
poignant, the consonants and vowels
in their odd marriage like

that of the living and the dead,
who come together again as I return
to "Little Elegies," by Lynda Hull,
after having set it aside,
because I had died.

THE KILLING POEM

I'll die reading poetry
as I drive.

These rural highways,
so open and straight,
so little travelled,
encourage me to make the most
of my time, left hand
on the bottom of the wheel,
right pressing a slim, opened
volume against the top.
I'm practiced at this,
eyes moving from line
of verse, black on white,
to center line, white on black,
and back again, I know
the clear road I see will last
just so many syllables,

a measure of them,
and that I have the best
of two worlds, speed
and the hard stasis
of memorable speech.

But I also know someday
a line will lead me on
past my limit or a phrase
arrest my heart, my tongue,
in a delicious collision
of adjective and noun—
"sylphish tissues," say,
or "inchoate nougat,"
even "voluminous pistachio"—
and when I look up,
the truck will have just come out
of the blind spot caused
by the setting sun
and be bearing down,
its engine pulsing
with the intense rhythm
of closure.

So you there, you
obviously familiar
with the danger of language,
with the thrill
at the edge of a word,
send me a poem I can read
on my way,
send me a poem so good
it will kill me.

III Bedside Breaths

1. Florence Nightingale in Egypt
   In 1849, the 30-year-old future nurse, her life
   directionless, toured Egypt with friends, five
   years before her apotheosis in the Crimean War.
   —Edward Hall, *A Concise History of Nursing*

> The dead presided everywhere, colossi
> along the banks to observe our coming home.
>   Even the air that made our sails hum
>   seemed the breath of kings rushing to say
>   we were the dead, not they.
> The grand houseboat belonging to the Bey
> shrank as it passed through shadow after shadow
> until I felt our figures turn miniature
> to fit a tomb, and a hand begin to lift us there.

> At stops, I wandered by myself for hours;
> "one more wild ass," a friend joked. Solitude
>   walked beside me. Under the Pyramid
>   of Sakhara, in sinuous chambers,
>   shades offering their store
> approached me like perfect hosts. In that dark, my suitors
> fell away, unreal, and I abandoned them forever,
> emerging with the richer company of ghosts
> I married on the spot, each of my vows desert-blessed.

> Then that day in Cairo, as curious as a dream:
> the morning spent with Roman Catholic
>   nuns devoted to the poor and sick,
>   the afternoon in a hareem.
>   All the Anglican tea-trays
> in my head trembled as the Nile-freshened breeze

boldly fondled those women's skirts and sleeves.
I stretched, dizzy with possibilities,
across a spectrum from stout hearts to languorous eyes:

I watched the reverend mother feed a one-
eyed boy blinded by his mother to cheat
the army out of fodder, called recruits—
whole regiments of one-eyed men
defeated her—and saw
the pasha's favorite wife, in silken yellow
trousers and fur-trimmed pelisse, with slow draws
on a diamond-studded pipe burning ennui,
simply—if marble households are ever simple—be.

So when the Sphinx at Gizeh asked me the Ur-
riddle—"Who are you?"—and I confessed, "An exile,"
a jackal somewhere howled its approval,
and the Nile showed me the way, which was far.
I longed for a cartouche
whose hieroglyphs spelled out my life, its wish
secret even to me. But I only saw a child wash
a basket of clothes in the river, her lowly task
heightened in silhouette by the last pulsing of dusk.

At Ipsamboul I laid my body down
prone on a dune in darkness, sacrifice
to a buried lord, half Ra, half Christ.
Against the sharp cold before dawn,
I was all prostration,
my hands and feet burrowed backwards to a sun
still echoing its wombish warmth to my skin.
Light would be a voice. And was, as a thin wave
quickened the dune's peak: Bid ye rise, whom I will save.

Morning held out to me an heroic lamp
I accepted and mounted on the prow of our boat,
which flew back downriver without
sail or oar, like Ba the winged imp

shuttling between two worlds.
My soul entered the solar currents and rippled
powerfully like water muscled to propel
itself forward solely for its own speed's sake.
I left all camel-travel floundering in my wake.

Thus I passed through Egypt as through a clear solution
that changed me. Old England burned up in the heat,
and I rode free on crests of light,
free to lift my future's burden.
My parents turned to sand
these fingers sifted to the stony floor like grain,
where my sister already lay, writhing, the wand
they'd waved at me now a mere snake, helpless, shy.
Like magic I was Isis, queen of my destiny.

On my last night there, walking the beach alone
at Alexandria among the falcon-faced gods,
I first knew the stars were the body
of Osiris torn to pieces, soon
to be reassembled whole,
the sky my promised land, in which a battle
lit one by one the wounds now mine to heal.
The vast, dark field leaned down so close to me
I felt a bedside breath twine with air from the near sea.

2. Rat
   Florence to Parthenope Nightingale, 22 April 1856

How you would have cheered for your sister last night!
If you didn't faint first. Our parents taught us
Much at Embley Park but not how to kill a
                    Rat. I've been learning.
If you can, surrounded by England's comforts,
Picture me in deepest Crimean dark, save
For my saviour lamp, which is always near by,

Lighting a tent up.
All were sleeping. I on my rounds had come to
Sister Rose's bedside—or cotside, rather.
Sometimes even nurses need nursing, nor can
Rome prevent illness.
Fever held her, maybe from too much praying
God would enter Protestant souls whose bodies
Languished. Our commission's perfectly clear: No
Proselytizing!
I can't count the number of fronts I fight on.
Thus, last night, I relished the time of quiet,
Watching Rose breathe, soothed by the rain's report; that
Is, till I saw him.
("Her" perhaps?) Betrayed by its glowing red eyes,
Like a shard of night displaced there above me,
One whose whiskers trembled so delicately
Clung to a cross pole,
Ministering damned angel shorn of its wings.
I stared, it stared. Rose slept. Though now I joke its
Face was Doctor Hall's (he resents, and threatens,
All my reforming),
Then I felt the rat was this war itself, that
All its filthy challenge had taken shape just
Inches from my nose and flicked a long tail to
Sicken and scare me.
Scared and sick, I did what I could, turn war-like;
No rat-terrier could have matched me. Weapon
Was my one thought. Then I remembered: rain—I'd
Brought my umbrella.
Slowly, lest the beast start, and keeping contact
With those eyes, I slid a foot toward the doorflap,
Toed the wooden handle of Excalibur,
Bloodless too long, and
Dragged it through the dirt of the tent-floor to me.
Rat watched, mesmerized as I bent to grasp his
Death--a Russian rat, you may wish--and froze, an
Animal, crouching.
Wood in hand to swing the steel tip, I plotted

How to do it, angle and force, the spot of
Skull I'd punish, even foresaw the arcing
                    Fall of the body.
All came true. Light cavalry never struck as
Swiftly, deadly. At my feet the thing landed,
Flesh, bone, blood in harmony thudding. Done. No!—
                    Felt my shoes clawed at.
Rain of blows, I crazy to set its soul free,
Which I did, but that didn't stop my swinging,
Arm and hand a life of their own, until I
                    Woke up the patient.
What a shock! Her "Pope" (the nuns' nickname for me)
Stood there like a mad one. Rose blanched. In role, I
Booted out the body, unfurled a boast: "I
                    Killed Martin Luther."
Then—to end mistaking F.N. for an R.
C.—I danced a few savage steps in triumph,
Whooping, too, before she returned to sleep, her
                    Strange dream all over.
Stranger is the thought that has gnawed me all day—
Rat was wholly innocent, nose to tail. Be
Glad I've so much work here to keep me busy.
                    Ever yours, Florence.

3. Death Cocoa
   *Florence Nightingale, who refused a cocoa company's request
    for a testimonial regarding its product's effectiveness in the
    Crimean War, dreams she addresses the nation.*

I drank this cocoa late at night, alone
after my rounds, and stirred it with a bone.
I warmed my hands against it and looked in:
faces rolled up into view, like the drowned,
then turned away, the drowned-in-cocoa, who
were too many to tell, though I will tell you,
for whom they died, for whom this cocoa spilled.

It drained, the blood of twenty thousand killed,
into the Bosporus and changed the tides.
For always pots were brewing more: outside
the flapping door of each Scutari tent,
the future breathed its unmistakeable scent.
And what men lived still burned their lips on it,
but didn't mind, because this chocolate
was all they had. Its steam drove back the night.
Corrupt winds blew to cool the sweetness off,
and froth floated across it like Charon's skiff.
Go tally the cups of tin or smashed clay
dotting the abandoned heights, but let me say
this cocoa gave me strength to look upon
the work of generals, the general ruin,
which ruin was added to the recipe
so that in time the drink darkened, and we
bore its stain, some martial decoration.
I saw a soldier's side, torn by shot, run
with cocoa, his dark brown life, where I,
to drink it all to save him, put my lips
against his wound and drew in, but he went dry,
and dead, before I could catch even a drop.
I saw in piles of amputated arms hand
after hand reach for cocoa and get sand.
The cocoa that they reached for was their own
selves that had been poured out as bitter, thin,
something in the end unpotable. Christ
was no more potable. I think He must
have lifted cocoa in that final room
and bid his men like soldiers do the same,
saying, "Drink this in memory of me,
who am cocoa, for all eternity,
and in time and space," where I saw him walk
among the beds of sick and dying like
a London waiter, a tray full of full
chalices—their gold our only light—bal-
anced miraculously on one hand, no drop
equally miraculously riding up

and over the brim, all, all contained by him,
who'd say, as the other hand in steady rhythm
lifted down to pale lips what each man longed
for, "Careful now, it's hot, don't burn your tongue."
And no one seemed to notice he still bled
from where the thorns had laid seige to his head,
nor that the drops fell like balls from the sky
into the drinks as onto an impotent army,
transubstantiating all to blood or
maybe blood to a tonic, creamy saviour.
In any case, once he'd served the whole tent,
nothing was the same, there was sacrament
everywhere, the very air was chocolate
and all our prayers made a thick, rich foam that,
dried, lined our upper lips. We were holy,
or mad. Doubtless at Sebastopol he
served the Russians as he served us, although
theirs was an Eastern Orthodox cocoa,
not what I'm holding now, its familiar tin
colored for you, England, as brightly as sin,
this offering impossible to refuse
because it swarms with flecks of dream and is
pure tribute to the nation's appetite,
which you'll love, even as you choke on it.

IV Guardian Warriors

UNDER OATH

I raise my right hand,
as if I were about to strike,
and swear to my god, not yours.

You don't fool me
with your talk about truth:
I have seen the face of your god

slip, a mask, revealing behind it
your own face, pale, sick
with longing for exposure.

You invented your god,
but my god invented me.
My god can beat your god any day.

I'm under oath
as under a great sky.
The truth is what I hear

the wind say.
I swear I'm taking back all the power
I ever gave away.

THE PRESIDENT

One day the President remembers the silence.
It was somewhere back home,
and long ago, under a porch, maybe,
he can't remember it well.

A blizzard of talk keeps him cozy now,
white heaped on white, his own
the whitest of all, what he's paid for,
though none of it disappears on the tip
of anyone's outstretched tongue.

Maybe this winter he wills
makes him sleepy, inclined to drift
toward memory's cave, for as he snows
another season won't let go
of the roots of his words,
when it was dark under the porch
and his grandparents rocked slowly

above the boy he was then and his silence,
which like a person or animal
lay stretched out beside him,
breathing, a shadow, and there
was lattice, so the light was all diamonds.

Of course there is light here, too,
he thinks, stirring, or trying to stir,
whole snowbanks of speeches, blinding,
a glacial terrain across which others trek
in every direction, and before which he would raise
his hand, shading his eyes, but his hand
is heavy, as dead and content
as a two-by-four under a porch,

where the old people don't know
he is hiding, or pretend not to,
but only worry the wood of that porch
to complaining, mild, with their motion.

And then he remembers,
remembers exactly, as if he were there,
that what was powerful then

was the summer evening, its light,
failing and horizontal

but wide with forbearance,
and the scent of the ground
touching him the whole length of his body.

COUNSEL TO THE PRESIDENT
After the heart bypass and before the trial of Robert
Altman, Clark Clifford occupied himself by reading the
collected poems of W. B. Yeats.
—Michael R. Beschloss

A sudden blow, the indictment beating still
against my fibrillating heart, that thrilled
so when each year I'd pocket a cool mill.

No greasy fingers fumbled in my till,
but manicured, which set the tone for all
the lawyers who followed me, their courtly slouch

toward Washington to be born this time rich
a terrible beauty draining brains deep
into Potomac corridors beyond reach,

sacrifice of the provinces' prime crop.
Missouri, for instance. I would arise and go
back home to ride with Truman's whistlestop,

like swans forever young at Coole, or throw
the poker game Sir Winnie thought he won
enroute to Fulton for the Iron Curtain speech.

O sage Cuchulain and sage Acheson,
my guardian warriors, one hot and one cold,
tell me I'm not changed utterly, but simply old,

that my good name which ever brightly shone
persuades hearts still, as if it were Maud Gonne.
But spirits fade at the ring of a phone—

it's Lady Bird or Jackie just saying hello.
At the club, few handshakes, and I eat alone.
Who goes with Fergus or with Clifford now?

My famous gesture—the judicious press
of fingertips together topped by my advice,
what journalists called "Clifford's wisdom-tent"—

feels like the merest arrangement of small bones.
Nothing can be whole that has not been rent:
loopholes were my life, through which now dolphins

plunge, ecstatic as their tails mock my hopes
for First American, whose chairmanship
proved I kept only a rag-and-bone shop.

How can you tell a banker from his bank?
Turning and turning in the widening hunt
for smoking paper trails, the banshee-accountants

can so far claim to have transformed my swank
hair—thick, waved, distinguished, a blinding mane
that once made women, and investors, swoon,

as silver as the apples of the moon—
into thin, loose strands as white as a ghost
that lifts and falls like Connemara mist.

Yeats dreamed angels copulated to breed
light; I dreamed money fucked itself for no
reason and spawned a stain like clouded blood.

The consummate insider thrust outside,
I push my floor's number and rise into
the vaulted sky of a New York apartment.

This is my tower at Ballylee. From here,
I see Central Park and Ireland's wild shore,
where a fisherman casts his long lament.

THE BAG

After each of a dozen trips to the former Eastern
European country that broke itself into several warring
nations, the professor of genocide, our college's greatest
authority on evil, presented his findings to the local
community by means of slides, a video, and a lecture.
Trusted by the various antagonists in the war, he had been
able to move among them freely and gather copious
information for a book he was writing, as well as for
possible use in a war crimes tribunal, at which he expected
he might be asked to testify. For years a young scholar of
genocide and student especially of the Holocaust, he had
finally been provided by the currents of history with the
chance to witness the twentieth century's brand of atrocity;
in addition, his training meant he was equipped to
participate in its documentation. Each warring faction's
spokespersons, believing the professor's impartiality
would lead him to corroborate their claims, made
available to him all the horrors of the war as it was
happening. He suffered complete, or virtually complete,
knowledge.
    Accordingly, the presentations to our community became
successively grimmer, the images more shocking, the
lectures more relentlessly a catalogue of man's inhumanity
to man, as well as to women and children. Despite that
fact, the more he descended into the shadowy recesses of
his professional subject, the more vital was the impression

he made on us. His red hair flared; his scholar's pallor flushed. His nerve endings seemed to have been issued a general all-alert, as if he were in the constant presence of danger, terrible but exhilarating, and he delivered each lecture with more animation than the last. Though he had eaten from the tree of genocide, it had not choked him but released certain hitherto untapped energies.

After the third trip, he brought back a knife he had found in an open market. It would have escaped the eyes of other visitors but he had recognized its function by the odd twist at the tip. His studies had prepared him to know it was designed specifically for cutting and pulling out tongues at the root. A glint on the steel leaped into his eye as he placed the weapon on a table off to the side of the lectern and invited us to inspect it later. After the eighth trip, he brought back a business suit belonging to a victim of torture and murder. The professor, who had acquired the suit from a forensic pathologist whose job it was to exhume mass graves, wanted us to notice the rips and holes, the bloodstains. It was a business suit like those which many of us were wearing. He draped it over a seat in the front row. Not until after the twelfth trip did he bring back the bag.

It was canvas, smaller than a duffle bag but larger than a handbag. A leather band trimmed the mouth of the bag, which was pulled shut by a tattered string. He did not refer to it when he brought it into the auditorium and set it down without ceremony on the floor against the wall under a map of the region that had become a kind of second home, or exile from his first. Motionless, a little collapsed upon itself, the bag made an eloquent gesture behind him as he spoke. Before long, in that room where earlier in the day the professors had been arguing at length over the school's emeritus policy, he passed around the bag, insisting that each of us reach in and grasp what it contained.

DISNEY: THE WALL

The proposed Disney American History Theme Park
"would be split into nine 'playlands' with themes
that include. . . the wrenching era of the Vietnam War."
—N. Y. Times, June 15, 1994

I'll never forget the way Snow White
stood out so pretty against the polished black
granite and how I jumped when the sniper's shot

stained her gown with fake blood that looked
so real—you can count on the magic of Disney—
I thought I was going to be sick.

Instead I cheered when, slumped against stone, she
launched a flare and the prince, looking handsome in
fatigues and combat boots, dropped from a Huey

to kill the sniper, who turned out to be the Evil Queen
from Hanoi. And all the dwarves lined along
the top of the wall danced up and down,

even Dopey, who was got up like a Viet Cong
in black silk pajamas I wouldn't mind having a pair of,
when the prince and Snow White exchanged rings

in front of the dates 1959 to 1975
to show us what those war years
were really about—true and undying love.

I cried, but you should have seen the tears
fall when guess who announced that everyone
carved into the wall was now a mouseketeer—

Mickey himself. He even handed out to each veteran
present a pair of the cutest mouse-ears.
I helped one man with one arm put his on.

It's true he and some of the other vets (hair
short, Walt's rule) freaked when Donald Duck
yelled, "Napalm!" as he threw volleys of water

balloons at them, but I don't think
that little cutup meant anything but good.
Anyway, Donald scrammed when the Buddhist monks

set themselves on fire (college kids
zipped into special suits) for the grand finale
and formed a circle to represent the woods

inside which a starlet playing Bambi
(fluffy tail, and the deer's name sewn
on her tank top) struggled on hands and knees

until a pack of Dalmatians with green
berets tied to their heads rushed in and led her out
to safety in a demilitarized zone,

leaving a ranger to proclaim the end of Tet
as the National Park Service's sprinkler system
put out the monks. Some packs of cigarettes

(gifts left for buddies who didn't come home)
got wet, but the overall point was that war,
even a lost one, can become a good dream

when an entire nation wishes upon a star.
I didn't know a simple wall could be such fun,
and I'm proud that we placed our history

in the hands of the Disney Corporation:
it's the most American thing we could have done.

Mexicans love murals so much they even install them where there are no walls. Many murals in Mexico City can be seen hanging in mid-air, paint sustaining itself against gravity by the power of the muralist's imagination and the hope of the people. Sometimes a wind will blow a mural into the middle of the street, and then traffic stops or slows to flow accomodatingly on either side until someone tugs it out of the way, as if the mural were a confused old man or woman who had wandered from home. Walls have occasionally been built to support a mural after it has proven its popularity, but the wall-less mural is in no way considered inferior to the walled variety. In fact, some aestheticians claim that the wall's fixity taints the mural with its first knowledge of death, whereas the wall-less mural bespeaks freedom. Politicians of both left and right persuasions appropriate the phenomenon for their own purposes, erecting cheap versions quickly, with inferior materials, which, like their promises, do not last past the campaign. The idea of the wall-less mural doesn't export well; in fact, wall-less murals in other countries consistently fall down. The Mexican air, especially the thin variety of elevated Mexico City, is presumably closer to dream-air, or else the muralist's art here is so sure of itself it requires the merest breath as substance upon which to consummate its love. The greatest danger to the life of these murals is presented by birds; not infrequently one will fly through a mural, leaving a hole in it. Such destructiveness, though regrettable, does account for the spectacularly colored birds on view in the capital.

Give me a break.
It was bad enough
in middle-age
getting lost in the woods,
but now, an old man
in his hundreds,
trying to catch a few
divine winks, I keep
getting dragged out of bed
to take another walk
through somebody else's
poem. My feet hurt.
I can't see well.
The doctor says
I can't go on this way.
It's not that I mind
being remembered,
God knows, that's
heaven, too, it's just that
I'm running out of
things to say appropriate
to every new time
and place, and Beatrice
is getting touchy—
these calls always seem to come
in the middle of the night,
she keeps waking up and finding
my side of the bed
empty. Anyway,
one man's woods
is another man's
piazza. I figure if
you can call on me for help,
you're not lost enough.
As one who travelled so far down
it turned into up, I know

the getting lost itself
will save you, if you let it.
You don't need me and my
dark woods, especially considering
I come with a leopard, a lion,
and a she-wolf: imagine
the food-bill. No doubt you've got
enough expenses of your own
without taking on
those beasts. So I wish you
well—watch out for
roots and all that—
but let me say, with your permission,
arrivederci. If I leave now,
maybe, with luck, Beatrice
won't even know
I've been gone.

V In the Shadow of a Train

ONCE

A fox walked the border
between my place and the valley.
He flashed red at me in the morning sun
and was gone,

the first fox of my new life here,
the color of fifty years.
Then for months I waited
for another, but none came.

The deer that nibbled the lilacs
in my yard said to me,
"You need only one fox."
And I think now that could be.

SELF-PORTRAITS IN LYND

1.
Because the nearest neighbors are three horses,
he is grateful for the corral of the sky,
the bright herd stunned by their own beauty
into fixity, though the entire fixity
moves, as his heart moves
when he tilts his head back in country night,
no competing lights for miles, victory
by default to those who have raced all this way
to him and whose muzzles in his outstretched hands
are cold enough to burn.

2.
The horses chew and I read, four heads bowed
and browsing in a green world—I think I am ripping
words with my teeth out of some willing ground—

where the cousins evening and autumn reunite to brew
a sweetness on the lifting air apples fall through
at my back—the thud the music of excess—

bruising themselves where bees will mass,
a danger to me gathering day's-end treats,
one of which once, inanimate globe, all rosy

passivity in my hand, impossibly bit me
and which I will pour rolling like perfect vowels
over the fence into the circle of scholars

poring over an indecipherable if digestible
ancient text, every margin thickly overgrown
with a perfume glossing these hours

so well it becomes its own text, the drift
something about a neck as firm against a palm
as the spine of a book, the curve of a flank

repeating, natural wonder, the exact curves
of the twin mounds of that book fallen open,
the tail a mind in restless motion,

the greater wonder that such flimsy pages
together could make such a solid volume,
which the wind will tear at with its teeth.

Because the deer
ate the shrubs,
I hardened my heart
to the shrubs,
though I still love the deer,

who come unasked,
to eat the shrubs, the perennials,
to which I have also
hardened my heart.
I don't care what grows here,
I only care
what eats here.

For years I cared
about the shrubs, the perennials,
planted and cared,
cared and planted.
I wanted the deer
to step majestically
through my yard, impressing
guests, and me,
the man
with deer walking through his yard,
deer
with self-restraint.

The pie pans
hung from the branches
didn't stop the deer,
obscured the shrubs,
prevented pies,
and made me look silly.

You should see now
how they look,

the shrubs and perennials,
for which
I no longer have feeling.

I can do that;
I can say,
I have lost this,
therefore
I do not care about it.

I can do that
because I am not a deer,
though I love the deer
who come through
eating everything.

INTERSTATE
for Stephen Dunn

He came to Minnesota
and it gave him a good metaphor.
For years afterwards, back on the coast,
he carried our state, his idea of it,
in his pocket like a lucky charm
he'd take out and finger with his language,
hold this way and that until
it shone light into one of his poems.
Big sky. Unlocked doors. Weather
that turned everyone into neighbors
and all neighbors neighborly
until things cleared.
On the familiar busy streets,
he could develop a little leverage
against the stone and steel,
make them shift
ever so slightly
if he said Minnesota in the right way.

And he took us with him, we who
didn't travel much off the farm
or far from our world that lacked
strangers and stoplights.
We rode in his pocket, wide-eyed gophers,
peering over the top
at Times Square or pick-up hoops
in a dangerous playground.
If he rode the metaphor,
if he went to town on it,
then we rode him riding it.

It changed my life,
he said, that time there,
three years, which have extended
to twenty-five by now, because he never left,
because we kept him there–that is, here–
against his will. I mean
we turned him into a metaphor,
the outsider
who could see us
as we couldn't see ourselves,
the one who,
while we all stayed inside
naming everything family and good times,
though the light on our faces had a square source,
was out walking alone
near the edge of town, where ghosts
of the harvested ones
impersonated the Northern Lights,
and naming everything night,
in all honesty making up stories
like those of the archer or bear
that shone above him,
though his were about such ordinary things,
our lives, say, how we turned up
the thermostat and thrilled to think
we had wounded the cold,

that we believed them, and him,
who believed in a commerce
so unregulated,
between states
with lines
so porous,
we knew we could depend on it.

THE LAST PICTURE

"This is the last picture of me
standing," my friend says, pointing
into the album during my visit
to his apartment where everything's
within easy reach for someone in a chair,
the center of the floor open
as if for a dance, and all I can do
is nod and stare, caught
in the headlights of those words
as simple as ice on a country road's
curve, as penetrating as the sound of metal
rolling over on itself like tickets
in a thunderous drum of chance.

In the photo he's a lanky twenty,
more than half a life ago, his legs
slightly spread, taking the measure
of the earth, a smile that speaks
the sun at noon, though he does not look down
to see himself shadow-free
in every direction.
Simplified to black-and-white,
Leo isn't looking anywhere that day except
out at me, who's been exposed,
the one sitting by choice.

Afterwards I will imagine other
last pictures, for other lives—
this is the last picture of me
believing in God, this is the last picture
of me making love, this is the last
picture of me writing a poem—
and albums will collect and fill
with last pictures, a great and drifting snow,
while the photographers of last pictures,
those self-renunciatory saints,
work in obscurity and the knowledge
that a last picture's never
a last picture until it's too late.

For now, though, I'm still marvelling at how
the plainest English—quiet, matter-of-fact,
a mild disturbance of sound waves
between pictures of parents and sisters,
farm-scenes—can shrapnel through the air
and make spines anywhere send a blizzard
of electrical information up and down
their long and living strands.

I am afraid to stand up, or try to.
I start taking pictures in my head, fast.
I pose with Leo for a picture
we both know is already developing.

EQUINOX

The horses leave, snows come.
We enter deep winter horseless.
The pasture goes begging for hooves.
Only the light steps of the cold sky
disturb the leaves that circled down
in panic, the half-thoughts of stubble.

And drool, that mute and sticky
declaration of earth's goodness,
exists, if anywhere anymore,
in those far, odorless spaces,
each string or pool, pearl, of it
frozen and sparkling like fire.
Here, though, the fence remains absurdly
at attention, a sentry on duty
long after the palace behind him
has been blown up. Neigh turns to nay
where the sun had romped all summer,
its high vault owed to the hardly
herd's example of impulsive
rocketing and the wish to join,
even lead, such an anarchic
trio, but now goes sick, low
slung, its companions hauled off
to their hay-filled winter quarters.
What we tried to forget
has become painfully obvious:
they were not our horses,
yours and mine, as much as we
led our guests across the lawn
for introductions and bought time
for the stroking of manes and thick
necks with distractions of apples
or tiny perfect blocks
of sugar we palmed to them
incongruous in their great mouths.
They had never been ours. That is why
we look out from sealed houses
and think the first swirls of snow
are the horses returning, or the ghosts
of the horses departed,
whereas the snow is only grief,
the broken pieces of our refusal
to let go of the old season
when it let go of us. For the prophet,

as young as a colt, could not
foretell how the sight of the slow
downward sift of our will's
dispersal would gladden us,
but only hinted that, in this
natural religion of horses,
God would return in a van
backed up to a gate, the top
of her rump the only visible part,
a ramp there to lead her down
to a puddle, its mud reaching
all the way to her fetlocks.

THE GARDEN

1. He Discovers a Gravemarker in the
Flower Garden of His New House

Raking the mulch away as spring began,
I found cement and thought, How tacky! Who'd
pour leftover cement into a garden?
But then I saw the colored stones and the word
they spelled so reverently out, "Foxy."
Dear Foxy! The owner had even worked
the marker's edge into a ruffle, the way
a cook pinches the crust of a pie with a fork.
Was Foxy a dog, a cat? In any case,
she was mine. Or, at least, her remains were.
I had bargained, but not for this—caretaker
for the grave of a pet a perfect stranger to me.
Maybe if the previous owner had told me
what lay under the mulch under the snow,
I would have paid more for the house than I did,
because when I discovered that slab of cement
I went immediately inside and got
a scrub brush, cleanser, and a pail of water

and returned to kneel, a penitential gardener,
before that homemade monument, level
with earth, as good as but no better than,
and scrub and scrub the winter's dirt away.
Oh, Foxy, I made it shine as best I could.
And I felt privileged to work so hard,
that with that acreage came Instant Death,
a ghost to keep me company, without
a long, slow lingering, illness and pain.
You should have seen the shoots of yarrow come
everywhere around your name, translating
your yap or yawp or meow into green tongues
that wagged to greet their Master (Mistress?) Day.
Therefore I pledge allegiance to your grave,
nor will let my cat dig thereabouts, but
will lead all visitors straight to it, saying,
Here is my Foxy, whom I never knew,
mine by virtue of a realtor's closing,
sign for your surprise gift of a dead one.
Oh, Foxy, be my gargoyle, household god,
and guardian angel all rolled into one,
nor let me forget that to buy the right
to live on any portion of this earth
is to rent a cemetery, and that the truest
host welcomes all the local or wandering
lost spirits before the living can be made
at home. So lie easy, or happily
haunt your old haunts: those who loved you best
are gone, but, when the new harsh season comes,
whelming our world, imposing icy denial,
I'll sweep the snows against twice-burial.

2. Perennials
for Carl Lindner ("L'chaim!")

Down on my knees, face in the dirt
almost, I must look almost hurt
to a passerby who sees me here,
glasses laid aside as I peer
up close like someone nearly blind
and getting desperate to find
what now my eyes have focussed on,
a little thing the spring has won
from winter darkness in the ground—
uppity nub, aggressive round
and green insurgency whose head
has pushed hard to disturb this bed
where, a pilgrim inclined to pray,
I've cleared some broken twigs away
and soon will gently pour a first
fitted coat of water, for thirst
but more to wash off all the grime
and better see what, one more time,
has surfaced home, unbidden gift,
to give the heavy sky a lift
and me a reason for a hoot,
fist and arm raised in the salute
defiant troops are famous for,
or players who have changed the score.

How did that old haiku go?
Don't worry, Spiders,
I'm not a very good housekeeper.

He letters it onto paper,
frames it behind glass,
and secures it

high in a corner
of the living room, where the
spiders can read it easily.

Over the years, they bind it
in lines of gratitude,
the bunting of workaday joy,

until he himself is dust
and swept out
in a general housecleaning.

The train came by every day while I lived there,
in that new house I had bought turning fifty.
And some days it came by more than once,
a friendly gesture.

And when I died I went with it,
it had been coming by to prepare me,
friendly gesture. No one for miles
knew why that train stopped that day,

on the top of a hill, between here and there,
the hill I climbed, spreading the lilacs
in my yard at the foot of the hill
with my hands, friendly gesture,

but I knew, slipping through and up—
knew how the train had timed so many
arrivals before to catch me on my knees
in the dirt, my hands going deeper
and deeper, the friendliest gesture,
then waving, goodbye or hello,
I couldn't tell which, and couldn't tell
one gesture from another

as the train shook my house,
they were so close, and I laughed,
as though lucky to live, a shadow,
a friendly, gesturing shadow,

in the shadow of a train.

AFTERWORD

One question that frequently rears its head, as I write or read or teach, always undoes me: What's the relationship of poetry to the personal? I excuse my difficulty with it by calling the question a conundrum and consider any answer I arrive at provisional. My own poetry represents an ongoing negotiation among the various answers. That Yeats could be both friend of the personal, insisting that, "When ever I remake a song...It is myself that I remake," and adversary of the same, saying it "soon rots; it must be packed in ice or salt," provides no help beyond the comfort of company.

Further witnesses, close to one Yeats or the other or somewhere in between, abound. Louise Gluck, taking a cue from Rilke's archaic torso of Apollo, seems sure of herself: "We can change who we are by changing the poem, just as we can change the poem by changing who we are." The badly, or well, written poem as—sobering thought—referendum on our moral character. Whitman did indeed seem to change his life, create a new self, by his invention in verse of "Walt Whitman, an American." And for all of Eliot's talk of "escape from personality," not expression of it, "The Waste Land" is now read less as cultural document than cri de coeur, not to mention the loophole his use of "personality" rather than "personal" creates. We seem to leave our fingerprints on everything we touch.

And yet I confess my ears perk up when in a recent essay Richard Kostelanetz writes that poetry "at its truest could be about" not "communication from writer to reader," but "the creation of structures indigenous to language: no more, no less." How dry! How like a martini, a fine wine, a certain kind of wit! A heterodox idea for sure, even blasphemous, but intoxicating. Thus, according to Kostelanetz, the best poem is the one most thoroughly about itself, albeit furtively so. Even Robert Lowell, arguably personal in his poetry to a dangerous extreme, seems to lean Kostelanetz's way when he claims that poetry is "an event, not the record of an event." Self-protecting rationalization only, or is he staking out some autonomy for the art of poetry á la Stevens when he scolded Robert Frost, if half playfully, for having subject matter?

Just when I begin to be convinced, then, of Verlaine's "Music before everything else," even in place of everything else, I remember Nazim Hikmet's poems from prison to his wife, and wonder if we really are to read them as dissertations on the structure of language. (Get thee behind me, Heartbreak!) Unless they are just that and only that, must we strip the medal of poetry from them? Don't the British World War I poets give the lie to Kostelanetz (as they gave it to the war's cheerleaders)? And relish for their own sakes the moves of William Stafford's language as much as I want, the voice of "Sky," one of his last poems, like that of so many others of his, penetrates me with his opening words, "I like you with nothing. Are you / what I was? What I will be?" and bears down hard through to the end: "You will bring me / everything when the time comes."

So, in keeping with all these conflicting pulls, these days I answer the question, Is poetry personal? with an emphatic yes and an equally emphatic no. (I recall Robert Graves' claim that without the "cool web of language" protecting us we die into madness, but wrapped in it we die into volubility.) For explanation of my Janus-faced position, I fall back on an analogy with roots—the personal—and flowers—poetry. A poem, like any human gesture, must trace to the personal, but it needn't be more than the poem's source. The flower may not exist without the roots, the flower's sine qua non, but we admire the flower, not the roots; the roots serve the flower, not the other way around. Valery perhaps meant something analogous when he said, "Ideas in prose are of a different order from ideas in poetry." That paraphrases to: the personal in poetry is of a different order from the personal elsewhere. In other words, the personal in poetry undergoes more than merely transmogrification; rather, transubstantiation.

Perhaps Yeats said all of this at once and neatly: "with nakedness my only shield." I hear him suggesting we can only successfully alchemize ourselves into the artifact—accomplish a grand letting go of the old life of flesh and blood—when the personal provides the art's profoundest impulse. And his fellow Irishman Oscar Wilde was likely circling the same prey when he cracked that it "is only shallow people who do not judge by appearances." Personal depth best translates into style.

In 1967, poetry came to my rescue, unasked, a hand that reached to me from the blue nowhere and pulled me up and out of a serious slough. More than thirty years later, I am still all amazement, gratitude, and commitment. Yet I find that my strongly felt sense of poetry's sway over the personal has been tempered through time by my appreciation of its independence from the personal as well, its detachment that allows for greater, not less, help, as if my rescuer had been a model Buddhist sage. Or maybe, better, angel.

ON THE WAY TO THE TREASURE

Give me your hand, says the hag, grinning,
Wicked as sin, all sag and wag
And the last path the only way in.
A hank of your hair, she demands, winning
All of my hoard, my bag, my swag;
And fingernail clippings, if you please.
Ah, this game is as clear as gin:
A tooth for a tooth, bone for bone
And a ragtag battle to do one of us in.

ANN GOLDSMITH

No One Is the Same Again

PHOTO: JEANNETTE M. SCHNEIDER

ANN GOLDSMITH, a Buffalo resident since 1976, has published her poems in a number of journals and anthologies and has taught writing classes for the past twenty years in Western New York, Long Island, and the Albany area, where she grew up. For twelve years she served as Western New York Coordinator for ALPS, a statewide poetry-in-the-schools organization. She was a poet in residence for two years in the Chautauqua Institution's summer writing program, and has taught and lectured at a number of colleges as well as at the University of Buffalo, where she is currently teaching. *No One Is the Same Again* is her first full-length collection.

CONTENTS

NO ONE IS THE SAME AGAIN

I

THE MAN IN THE WHITE SHIRT

Here we all are, on the deck of the S. S. Something,
Maryanna, Rosie, Aunt Anna and me,
And the man in the white shirt.
I am wearing my beige striped dress
With the three-quarter sleeves and wide belt.
Left arm around Maryanna's waist,
I puff on one of those French cigarettes
Wrapped in pastel papers:
Maybe the lavender one. Or the pale green.
We're all in a board game, miming ease
On a bucketing pulse midway between continents.
Behind us, a few deck chairs, the high rail,
Some tourists examining a glittery swatch of ocean.
The man in the white shirt could be smiling.

Aunt Anna wears her taupe hat with the Scottish
Brooch, and a sly half-smile.
A month this side of the episode already
Goading her into cryptic pronouncements,
An implacable aversion to Rosie and strange men,
She will come home changed, unable
To assimilate the voices from the deck
Chair, the fountain pen, the Parisian
Sidewalk grating. After the shock treatments
She will sit and smile until we graduate
And she has her stroke, when Maryanna
Comes home to feed her and rub her feet
For two lead-weighted years.
The man in the white shirt may or may not be smiling.

Meanwhile, Rosie, unaware she is the antichrist,
Smiles broadly in her creased pink blouse.
Small, round, gullible and glib, she is the one
Who wrung directions from a dour Swiss farmer

Entirely through sign language
When we were lost in the Alps. Maryanna,
With her blowing black hair, laughs for the stranger
Holding the camera, throws an arm over my shoulder.
Two years into college, we are still almost best friends.
We are in the middle of the Atlantic, depths
Immeasurable all around us, along with the man
In the white shirt, who looks into the camera as if
He wants his picture taken too, as if he wants
Someone to remember this moment, and him in it.

NIGHT PIECE

At 2 a.m. I don't know where I am.
Lamplight circles the room, my book
has fallen to the floor.
Through an open door I see the kitchen
fluorescent, the space heater
pulsing red semaphores over and out.
Why is everything on?

Plucked from sleep, I am still
in the field with the singing horse.
Beyond my window, a hush like snow
defines the continent of night.
One car whines by; a single pair of feet
taps past, hurrying. How far is home?
What place is this?

It was summer in the field: daisies,
early goldenrod. The horse was singing Bach.
Someone said, *We must cut out his heart.*
There were poppies suddenly
under the apple trees.
The orchestra went on playing.
The space heater keeps waving red flags.

Does everything imagine itself elsewhere?
Would the horse be here if it could,

keeping warm, while I search for hearts
in long grass?
Is the heater on a dangerous mission?
Whose heart have I lost?
Someone is keeping the true story from me.

PHYSICAL THERAPY

Richard fields my energies like a magician
handling wilful props.
He rotates a smoking shoulder,
backs the tiger into its cage;
presses the gladiola bulb in my neck,
returns a halved woman whole.
But never does he go where I point.
Flourishing my symptom, I say,
Here is where I need release.
He looks me over, revs up an offstage device.
Today, for example, I am grinding my teeth.
He works long and hard on my back.
Last time, *neck*, I said. *Can't turn my head.*
OK. We'll work on the spleen.
That's the body's filtering system.
But . . . Have you talked to your spleen lately?
Not exactly. Well, there you are.

I am trying to improve my vision
or perhaps my hearing,
but I seem to lack aptitude.
Richard, on the other hand,
siphons energy readings everywhere.
Today he arrives wearing a black leather jacket
and a peculiar fragrance.
Formaldehyde, he reports cheerfully.
He's been working on cadavers
and guess what? The bones buzzed.
I don't know what to make of it.
The life force was missing, of course,
but there was this hum. Isn't that interesting?

Now my teeth seem to be trying to tell me something,
even as the chandelier faintly chimes
in communion with the noon train.
Does Richard hear all this in his fingertips–
the faint far tingle of the dead, for example,
exhaling and vibrating and possibly combusting
right through the quivering skin of, say,
a stiffening patient even now laid out
on his midnight blue collapsible canvas table?
"It's just this muscle here," he says. "Hold still. There."

CHINESE MEDICINE

In accordance with instructions
I swallow them by handfuls:
the tiny dark brown pills
that smell like strong coffee,
the unscented flat pink-petal ones.
Tincture of strange roots
and creeping stems,
they are guaranteed to *core*
convulsions and *parlysis*
of various body parts,
as well as to remove *cold*
and hestic affects.
Best of all, for my purposes,
they promise to *easy pains*
in the joints. I have only
to take *sin tablets*
two or three limes a day
and voila! I am *cored*.
This poem is in praise
of creeping stems and strange
roots and the hands that
gather them from gingery
nests in fog-trellised bogs
and forests so that I,
lumpy with spurs and cellulite,

may kick my heels and bray
at my side of the moon, joyfully
translated this very evening
from its bed of Chinese blue.

NOT DROWNING BUT WAVING

Which is to say the starlings
in the chimney woke me up
and just in time.
Not much in the way of music
but I climbed out of the water
to the tune of their tinfoil chimes,
their tin spoons banging tin plates.

All night the sidewalk was tipping
into the lake, my book bag slipping
like a spoon into a mouth,
the crossing just a few feet to the left
if I could just, if I could

Now a tangle of fishhooks
minces the brightening December
sky into silver minnows and the next
door spruce shivers all over
like a bee-bitten bear. Sparrows
flick in and out all nonchalance
as if the right dance step is all it takes.

But just moments ago, the sidewalk
was tipping into the ocean
and the water was deep and cold
though the crossing, marked by white
lines, was merely

And did I mention the small birds
swarming out of the gulf
on aluminum wings, all
hinges like tongues and doors

just as the starlings began tuning up
and I fell backward into my book bag
embracing a large balding noun?

Well then, this morning I wonder
if chimney songs and wings
graph the abyss, and white lines
guide the dancers' feet,
and is it snowing there now, as here?

SYCAMORE

The 300-year-old sycamore
in front of the Analytical Psychology Society
on Franklin Street is shedding its bark.
Stacks of dried syllables litter the sidewalk.

Its watery designs infringed by patches of dirty white
wrinkled skin, plainly the tree
has been scratching itself on the nearby lamppost.
It is so broad at the base that three people with long arms
can barely surround it. The blackened sign
          —Oldest Tree in Buffalo—
still hooks passersby. And now it is sloughing off its past
just as summer leans back, resting on gilt lawns.
In another city my uncle sits and smokes
in his rump-sprung armchair
with the little stained leaves and flowers,
cocking his head to hear my answer to his last question.
I can read his face better now he confesses
how deaf he has become in the good ear.
The other one has a device he fiddles with,
swollen fingers fumbling the miniature controls.

"Mine and fine lose themselves in my ears,"
he remarks, shrugging off another piece of bark.
When he serves me a blank smile, I know my words
fell behind or before him or mixed themselves up
somewhere in the changing seasons.

I look around at the family portraits, the brass candlesticks,
the drooping dahlias on the mantelpiece.
What's three hundred years?
The gleam in an antique dealer's eye?
A ten-inch slice of sycamore rind?
Never mind, I say to myself, *this is some tree.*

MAN WITH HAT

the small man with the bowler hat
has appeared again this time
he dozes over the wheel of
a dirty grey vehicle the sort of car
that loafs in weedy lots wheels gone
doors sprung but now

it inches up Main Street ahead of me & now
the wizened man in the round black hat
slows for a green light another gone
hope on this morning of ditched deadlines & time
takes its own sweet as this wheezing car
crawls to the foot of

Snail Mountain just before Christmas when of
course it's snowing me late now
I'm stuck behind the cowcatcher's car
& just yesterday he drove a new copper Caddy & the hat
was some sort of plaid with a small brim & every time
I'm in a hurry he turns up between me & where I need to go

& the light or the last chance is gone
home or south or under the porch beyond the clutch of
harried women caught in the traffic jams of time
there he is now
in a pick-up truck & cowboy hat
puffing out from a small street in front of my car
& he's too short to see over the wheel he's a regular car-
toon of a guy a doggone

sackful of laughs in a slouching hat
hogging both lanes at ten miles per on a bloody snowy
        morning of
last minute happy yuletide errands all yapping *now*
& *now* & *now* but so help me this time

I dodge around him into the Jubilee lot one parking space
        left & time
fucks me over again he's backing a blue car
with fins into my place I can't believe it now
I know the angels are gone
from my side to his & meanwhile how many of
him are being fitted this minute with small round hats

on a time line set for infinity the first batch ready to go
as the cars creep into place each of
them blessed by a single small man now grinning & waving
        his hat

THE JOYS OF SEX

Sometimes I worry about my reputation.
Oh, not in some friend's distant look
or the curled lip of a sales clerk in orange spikes
who sees me lingering like a thief
near the black lace and the perfume called *My Sin*.

No, I mean among the ubiquitous lean young men
restlessly shuffling and fiddling with dials
who call me ma'am and look away
as they tinker with my muffler,
read my meter, pump my gas, park my car,
ring up the change for my hormone pills, my face cream.

I mean the cool, polite absences
who seat me with book at a table for two, non-smoking,
who deliver the new mattress, perm my hair,
sell me chocolate bars at midnight.

I mean those Robins and Batmen
who spring up my stairs to check out
the static in my telephone line, the crack in my wall,
the way my furnace, my wiring, my plumbing
backs up, leaks, fizzles, fumes without apparent reason.

Last week, the meter-reader pounded on my door
while I was still in bed.
'LECTRIC! he roared, violating my ears
and the dream of the pink wildebeest.
COMING! I shrilled, dropping my glasses,
kicking a slipper under the dresser,
fumbling my hairbrush and wrestling into my wrapper.

This one was blue-eyed, brush-cut.
I think he had been warned.
You gotta be careful, they told him.
Whooey! Some of the tricks these old girls'll
get up to, all alone at home, nothing to do.

After one electric glance, he bolted.
Before the bathroom mirror, I saw what he'd fled:
cleavage where my red robe gaped,
tousled hair, bare ankles, liver spots.
And this at 8 a.m.
But I was up late! I yelled at the mirror. *Working!*
I'm a busy woman! You can't treat me this way!

I got dressed fast, marched into my books.
How dare they! The call came three days later:
heavy breathing and a lewd suggestion.
Surely no connection, but
the weather was turning cold anyway
so lately I've been wearing turtlenecks,
bulky sweaters, long socks.
I keep my hair combed, stay away from wildebeests,
rise when the morning is still an untouched bride—
and if my earrings dangle down around my jowls,
well, I can't help it if I'm not dead yet.

Just now returned from hunting them
with children on Long Island
I wonder, where does a poem prowl
before it peers through the leaves
at the bottom of the yard?
Some of the children had far to go,
calling and coaxing. Often I too
awaken hungry in a strange place,
behind a cow's eye or climbing a waterspout.

On the bay where I was, town leaks into
town, mall into concupiscent mall.
The same orange convenience store
on this corner as on that.
The same demented azaleas shrieking
their passionpinks and magentas
from bungalow to shuttered bungalow,
while a wind comes heavily off the sea
and in the far pockets of playgrounds
thugs gather at dusk.

It is not so different here in Buffalo,
where the wind off the lake
has a whiskey voice and a squinty eye.
Mills sold out, knives working the bars,
though the leafage is splendid in June.
Our children drag their sticks
and hockey nets into all the small
snarled streets, calling to each other.
Sometimes the pavement trembles
with a lakebed light and catalpa pods
thrash against the rough curbs like startled carp.

Two blocks from home, in their cage
at the zoo, the lions moan,
waking me on some blank shore
just before dawn,
fur in my mouth, the wind rank,

my bed shaking under me.
Nearby, eyes open in the palms of leaves.

THE FOURTH GRADE POETRY CLASS

The stop sigh is as red as blood,
they write, making it new.

The night moo is white as snow.

When I am flying in the sky
I feel as light as a father.

Loud is an adam bomb blowing up.
Loud is a loin's roar.

I was scared to deaf
going up stars in the hunted house.
But later I got home.
Few! Made it at last!

                    Meanwhile
back here in our risky city
where a magnificated sunset
breathes on every window,

all the corners suddenly bristle
with stop sings

so we shut up and listen
to the echoes of our voices
falling down star after star.

II

1. NOVEMBER

Take blue under cottonwoods, those prayersticks
Propping now the green plate, now the blue bowl.
Blue is a worry bead, a small oiled stone.
Age plays the blues on a stick and two bones,
Blue crushing stars into the frost-gnawed lawn.

In November's coffins the sweet airs of summer chafe
        to their blue bones.
Aspirin is not enough in November.
The song of martyrs dwindles to thin rain in November.
By late November, light squeezes between stones,
Its blue juices watering the wintering hills of thought
        in wry November.

2. FEBRUARY

Dragging my red blanket, I was Hiawatha, famous
As a red dress among debutantes, my fine feathers
Wizened cranberries from the Christmas tree, more
Black than red, bitter as death in exile,
Though I imagined them plump, spicier than red hots.

In February, I stood wrapped in my blanket, a red
Coal on February's white breast, the sun
Squatting on the hill like a cooking pot. February
Is the month of waiting. In February
Hiawatha's heart turned blue with cold (in February,
        many coffin-lengths from home).

3. MAY

Now green is what we want, well water
Green by the house, algae smearing the pond.
We want parrots, and little bright green runner vines
        in the woods,
Green-bearded paving stones, chartreuse mists
Wreathing every quick green hill.

In May, old women curl their hair.
Camels make love in the green of May
And May's mad juices drive revolutions. People
Dance around maypoles or hurl red grenades,
Everyone green and uncoffined, uncorked in May.

4. AUGUST
I lose myself in the white . . .
White is a thousand greens gone to seed, a blister coat
the leaves wear,
The white hoods of thunderheads stooping over
Beds of blanching zinnias.
White is the hope of fanatics.

In August, I wish to be not white but dark blue,
A coffin's precise, august shadow.
I walk under pines in August. Last year
Behind the whiteface of August's sad umber groves,
The first leaves drifted loose, all those souvenirs of August
where your face should be.

AFTER THREE WEEKS OF RAIN

Out on the farm, cattle founder in the feeding pens,
Fires mutter and spit, a peevish wind
Whines about wet clothes and gout.
It is the same here in the city, where rain drags the leaves
Down early. Underfoot, they smell of the sea. We
Root irritably in our hutches, sniffling and quarreling.

But uptown, near the park, a fine silver mesh nets the
boxwoods
And telephone poles take the gloss of agates.
Sparklers enter the pools on pavements
Like water striders shaking thin chains from their legs.
A brief phosphorescence pricks my face as leaves overhead
fidget
And all around me soft, secret tongues are lapping.

The sky is sullen, yet the grass in the park is still
Deep green. And so heavy: like a swimmer's hair.
And by the basketball courts
Footprints keep their shape in the softened earth
As if the ground were a great sponge like a woman's heart,
Burdened with more than it can hold in one season.

OCTOBER: THE POND AT JAFFREY

It lies on its back in the forest.
Birch and spruce encircle it, the cold
spring that fed it forty years ago
still bubbles under hemlocks
where moss darkens a hollow
thick with forget-me-nots in May.

Today, the leaf-clotted water
rusts and flakes under silver veneer
and my heels crunch on the thumbnail beach
where a fat old boat with a hole
in the bottom used to loll upside-down
like a tame whale, nudged
by the slippery snouts of floating logs.

This is where I learned to swim, to ride
leviathans, tumbling among clouds,
weeds and treetops, half
waterlogged, half in flight, clumsy
and hopeful and blind, my glasses
left stuffed in my shoe
and the cold pond shimmering
among the ancient, rune-whispering pines.

Now as I peer in this old looking
glass, the surface dissolves
to webs of drowned leaves, each layer
paler than the one above, drawing me down
until, greyed to ghosts, they hang

far below, barely visible
on the bright shield that holds imprint
of sky, tree bones, my changed face

and the two geese that beat southward
through netted branches, baying
across water through whole time zones,
dipping their wings in my hair.

LIKE A PARENT WHOSE CHILD

The dog and I await the return of our family.
Under a quarter moon, the bushes bunch together,
The telephone wire stretches an ounce of silver
Across two lawns and a blackberry patch.
Trees blaze and subside along the road.
The dog turns and turns on the rug and sighs
Heavily, frequently. The black fur
Curling away from his spine in glossy waves
Gleams with little lights from the lamp by my chair.
He rouses and hurries every few minutes to the door
Like a parent whose child has bad dreams.
He does not want stroking.

Tonight is so still
I open my window to listen to crickets,
But their keening charges the air with static
As if this hour were tuned to the wrong station.
The refrigerator whines and the dog
Leaps up, lies down again.

With a hiss like a steam valve,
A breeze escapes, bangs something out back.
I can feel the house tighten around me.
Panting, the dog rolls out his tongue.
The moon has slipped from the left
To the right front window and they are not yet home.

Will it be we two forever, dog and woman,
Panting and peering into night's closets
While some galactic jukebox grinds out the tunes
And even dawn forgets to come home from the dance?
Under a quarter moon we bunch together,
Blazing and subsiding, stretching our love
Thinly across the uncorked, billowing night.

LEAVES

How one thing makes way for another.
All winter the cabin in the woods
Holds still for trysts and photo shoots,
Its secret life set out to hang on the wall
With moose heads and naked coat hooks.
The sky rests its forehead on hills
And shores we never wholly believed in
When the leaves filled this space with their tents.
Old swing-set bones, swathes of yellow grass,
One more high-ribbed deer rubbing its haunches
On dry tree slats: no mystery here.
No hidden quartz quarry or hermitage;
No secret cove where oars feather still water
Under a shielded moon. Now the town dump
Shoves forward its bald tires and stained mattresses,
Its amputee chairs and twisted chrome.
Down chalked-in back roads, junked cars
Brazen it out with collapsing porches, Pepsi
Cans, spent shells, headless dolls.
The equalizing light, coming from so far away,
Burnishes a bent spoon, the edge of a cloud.

FOREST TRAIL

The way the darkness draws one inward
yet with lights along the course,
trunks deeply bedded

in bays of fern, the path
unhurried, discursive
so that there is no thoughtless thrust
but rather a slow dreaming
toward the interior . . .

This is not for everyone.
Entrance looks much like exit
somewhere between two trees; penetration
has no coordinates with conquest
under this flickering grid
of greengage on damson opening
and closing
as the glances of knitting water.

Here are salamander, hermit thrush
and bark canoe, time told
by star clock, indian pipes
cold as toads
witching their pale lunar necks
up from leaf mold millenia thick.
Here tree spiders continually
invent the wheel.

Kindling, gloaming: these beds
are older than moss, these
ligaments of trees
connected with all roots.
This old liver-spotted path
stirs in its sleep
as the moon's white moccasin
steals toward the woodcarver's cabin.

WORKING LOOSE

In New Hampshire they are common as clouds.
Plows trip over them, hoes spring back.
By March, they poke from lawns and furrows
Like giant early peas. To save a crop,

The farmer harvests walls, handset, ungainly,
But practical as denim. They amble round
His fields, tuck his orchards in.

His wife sets out phlox and foxglove, starched
Flames to flare against the stacked oat gray.
The town incises them with names and dates,
Stands them upright, polishes them
To lend some shine to death's dull nullity.
Along roadsides, they set apart one owner's hogs
From another's sheep; this one's Queen Anne's lace
From that one's berry bushes.

All through New Hampshire, knuckles and bunions
Swell up in meadows, clump and meander
Deep in woods, by sudden cliffs,
Through quarries, thickets, gravel pits,
Moss-matted, leaf-layered, gapping and slipping,
Bramble- and grape-hung, still keeping track:
Along this ridge, by this cold spring, someone once
Laid tacit claim: outside-in. Wild and worked.

Before the maples turn each autumn,
Between pine fringe and lap of lilac, bindweed
Trails crimson boas over granite curves,
Working knees and elbows loose, its tough strings
Unlatching hip from pelvic socket.
Forests grow around these bones, a long overhauling
Like water hoarding light in bogs or winter
Trudging toward cornfields out of low mist.

When first sap rises, they overbalance,
Crack and topple, as if they know
You can't hold any line forever. As if,
All settlements aside, they want to be ground small
In mills of wind and water, to fall
As grains of sand through the stems of grasses
Down to the world's floor where they remember
Even now being born.

COUNTRY HOUSES

Country houses crack their knuckles, click their teeth
and fire pistols after dark, snapping shots
from the hall, coat closet, spare
bedroom. The refrigerator hums loudly
to robots stationed behind trees.
Lightbulbs make little kissing sounds
and the kitchen clock takes ragged breaths
as robbers push through stiff grass
outside the open window,
make vehement love under the poplars.

Large moths mate on the screens of these houses
and red ants chew through clapboard and tile
all the way to the bathtub, where they fall in
and gather round the drain, peering down.
Elderly spiders race up their webs
when the cellar door opens
and half a dozen baby garter snakes
bumble up through living room gratings
looking for grass.

After dark, light is hard to remember.
The clock wheezes, the lightbulbs kiss,
The robbers squall and scuffle in the rhododendrons.
All the world's separate things are netted
and dragged to the edge of the knocking heart
as a step is heard on the stairs,
the first shot ricochets off the closet door

CLEANING TREES

Catch a night wind in a white tablecloth between two hills
And let stand three days in an empty room.
On the morning of the first day shake a mixture of sand and salt
Into your palm and blow it, howling lightly, through the keyhole.
On the evening of the second day, lay a white feather and a blue feather
On the doorsill and tell the dream of the four witches and the black fur

Butterfly, omitting the last word and facing the nearest crossing of three
      ways.
Open the door on the third day at the hour when the sated owl
Hunches home to the hollow sycamore
And you will find a dozen brushes, fine-haired, with ebony handles,
Excellent for cleaning and fluffing both leaves and evergreen needles.
Gather them in a brindled cat's cradle about the size of a smoke ring
And when first milk flows in the morning sky, carry them
To the edge of a stand of trees. Begin humming.

Soon the brushes will start to vibrate. Hum
Until the first brush enters a tree. You will notice
How the tree appears to shake itself. Dust, pollen, dried nests,
Moth wings, bits of mold, and cankered nutmeats will fly up in clouds.
Now the other brushes will whirr around the tree
And the air will begin to shine. You will hear the tree singing
And you may glimpse large, transparent bubbles of fire and pearl.
The tree is soon clean, but its song will continue for hours.

As the brushes move on, they will launder a whole forest in one day,
Sometimes jumping small fields, and stirring up a deep thrumming
Like an ocean of guitars or an orchestra of whales.
The air appears to lurch and tremble with fitful lights
And such paths as weave among the bracken may lose themselves,
To be found days later crumpled up like dried snakeskins
Under some gooseberry bush or tangle of vine.
It is dangerous to linger, once the brushes are all aloft,
As the ripple effect compounds quickly, rocking ponds miles away
And setting cows quickstepping in clover. Do not pursue the flaming
      baubles;
They vanish when touched. Hang your cat's cradle
On some thumb of twig or stump and walk briskly away, letting the
      first waves
Gently lengthen your stride and repeating thrice the dream's last word.
Then, until you have passed two hills, keep silence and do not look
      back.

first dark is under the bed that toothy yawn
from another dimension swarming
with soul sucking revelers but before long
the forest marches in with its
gradations of dark covens and ovens its thickly
enlaced shades and narcotic pools
its wolfbreath disappearing paths and hundred
year old bramble stockades hung
with unfortunate young dark devoured princes
born on the wrong day but then
before you know it it runs off down some engorged
river all clouds and rocks riptides
fins and salivating bogs floating heads and dark
tricklings over stone at the same
time welling up in cisterns and cellars bumping
at the lids of wells until it breathes
its endless unfoldings through innumerable hinges
refusing all containers lavishing
itself in thick exhalations over lilies and tar pits
stairwalls trees and merry go rounds
perfectly opaque revery undreaming light thread
by vein until at last one morning
it opens a materializing eye on the lakebed of a pale
blue ordinary room flattening to ash
in the fathomless attentiveness of its moonless look

NO ONE IS THE SAME AGAIN

In some countries the aged
Are put out like old rocking horses

To brood at the edges of forests
And caves. Sometimes

Their hair grows so long it tangles
In the branches of their thoughts.

Their eyes glare through thickets,
They do not sleep, and where their

Hands move over the earth,
Small fires flicker. The ones

Who sweat down to bone bags
And unhoused voices work at night.

Earthquakes slide then along the faults
Of village dreams. The villagers come

Awake as if caught by the heel, and all day
They look behind them, forgetting

The good beer, the geese and stars
Who preen and sparkle, meaning no harm.

They dodge the small brown bird
Dipping over ripe cornstalks

And shun the flapping curtain
Snapping like a dog down the widow's lane.

But worst are the electrical storms.
These are the not-yet-loved,

Tricked out at last in spectral auroras,
Pulsing near wild water: irresistible

As any long-haired stranger who might be
The one selling magic beans or hearts on stalks.

No one is the same again who comes
Near those eyes when the power is on.

The Grand Imperial Imbibers were tanking up
again. "What wuz that last mix?"
muttered one, wiping his mustache
with a foam-flecked wrist.
"Rum an' tequila wiz *pickles*?"
He belched, and a section of asphalt
peeled off Highway 90,
slipping crookedly down a rock face.
"Nah. *Chocolate*,"
grunted another. "Whassa matter?
Los' yr tasebuds?"
He scratched his chest and a bristly valley
in the Ukraine convulsed,
bringing down two small mountains.
All of Nigeria suddenly spoke Hindi.

Just then the third one hauled himself out
from under the table, grabbing at
chair legs and tumbling half
of Bogota on top of the other half.
"Where's m' beer?" he inquired
liquidly, exhaling a tidal wave
the length of the Nile. Painted boats
washed against the pyramids
and bazaars floated out to sea, trailing
belly dancers, clouds of cardamom,
strings of camels tangled in carpets and minarets.

"Bottoms up!" yelled the first one,
sending a shudder through the Amazon
Valley. And they pounded their fists
on the table, causing China's Great Wall
to saraband across the Steppes
as a number of heads of state
ran out of reassurances
and all seven reflecting pools
split their sides to receive the Taj Mahal.

The oak table was strong, but
a knothole fell into Vesuvius,
causing a chain reaction
that sent the moon careening past Jupiter
as the floor buckled, spilling jugs, flagons,
casks, suds and planks, casting it all off.
From the fiery core, the dragon rose, lashing its tail.

III

RED RIDING HOOD: HER STORY

It was not something she could explain.
He tied her up, kept her in a dark place.
After awhile, her soft glades
And hidden dells forgot their shame,
Trampled and invaded as they were.
Like a dog, she learned to cower and obey,
Even to put on a kind of numb display,
A bid for leniency. Home
Was somewhere else, on the far side
Of the moon or the forest, where fields,
Cottages, church bells, the village pond,
The path to the good oak door
And enfolding arms, were sun-drenched
Miniatures, far back in her mind.

When they came for her at last
With glad cries and breaking glass,
She could not seem to put one foot
In front of another. Outdoors,
She had to close her eyes against the sun.
Back between sheets that smelled of
Thyme and wild geranium, the ghost
That would not go away was the child she saw
Reflected in her mother's eyes, a sprite
Foreign to her, except as glimpsed
In snippets torn from some old fabric.
Now in her mind were holes she could
Drop through faster than a hand could reach,
And in every one a wolf was waiting.

The day she was born, she smiled.
I didn't dream it. The midwife saw it too.
At five months, she desired food,
kisses, and my carnelian beads.
I made her first red cape when she was four.
All laps were a comfort to her,
a song, a tale by the fire.

What's done is done, they say in the village.
You can't cry forever.
Some nice young man will make her forget.

Were they standing at my door when I sent her off,
the basket heavy on her arm,
feet dancing anyway in the dust of the path?
Did they take her back, out of the woodsman's arms,
filthy hair matted, pinafore gone,
her great eyes like empty spoons?

Why didn't I send her the long way round,
through open fields?

The neighbors say we're lucky.
She's home again, be glad
he didn't kill her like he planned.

Better to be gobbled up in your bed
like my poor ailing mother
than still a child and scraped out like a gourd,
all skin and echoes.
What death can equal this?

She sits in the corner facing the door
hour after hour, watching. . . .
I build up the fire, light the lamp
while the sun's still high.

But sometimes
I dream she's out there still,
wolves swallowing her up again and again
right here in the circle of my arms.
Then it's all I can do
not to lean back my head and howl.

PAULA'S SUNDAYS

Things recede: voices, shades
of red, slam dunks, the daily gold
snuck out with the neighbors
through some hole in the week
that seals itself
before she can get there.
Her ears are stuffed with silence
and if a bird tunes up,
its meager bell chimes on dead air
outside the garden with no door.
For the bird is a wind-up bird
in a paper tree, and the faithless
street has emptied in the night
like a mirror in a room erased
by snow, the long block
with its bicycles and dogs
having bled away into some canopied
park or painted mall
where people with real lives
are picnicking or watching a movie.
The house fronts with their closed
mouths worn thin, line up
outside the room where the child
sings herself across a crevasse,
snow sweeping the sill,
the bird long since having shut up.

He goes into town reluctantly,
Rusted from a winter spent practicing
The long view from the lighthouse,
Learning the harmonies of grey
And tending small fires.
His bird has died. His dog is old.

The party is a carousel accelerating,
A fireworks display over his head.
No one is interested in the long view
Or the small event. Last evening
He talked with the moon,
His one-eyed friend, a good listener.

They had a little wine together,
Some fresh herring with cream.
The night was clear,
She tossed a glittering scarf
Across the waves to his window.

Now that was more like it,
The bottle open between them,
One hand on old Helmut's head
And the sea lapping quietly
From one rocky coast to the other.

THE SHADE TREE

Trapjaw was tired.
For a long time he had carried the child
through floods and conflagrations,
cyclones and fallings-away,
and he was very tired.
Rust gnawed at his joints,
his heavy feet stubbed themselves
on curbs and roots. Sometimes

he lurched to one knee,
skyscrapers tilting, snow flying upwards.

The little girl nestled in his cold arms
grew no bigger. She had always
needed him and he had always carried her.
But Trapjaw was tired.
He wanted to sit down in a meadow.
Perhaps even iron nostrils
could take in the scent of wild roses.
Spent as he was,
he would stretch out beneath a tree
and watch her venture beyond its shadow,
doubtful feet balancing, quick hands
bringing him acorns and round stones.

Yet she clung to him still, knowing
how tired he was, but afraid.
Not yet. Not yet.
It would always be *not yet* for her,
the ravening world waiting, paring its nails.

Her trust pierced him, her need
inflamed his weariness.
Ordained as he was, he would disintegrate
before he dropped her,
but he was nevertheless very tired,
and a great shade tree grew
in the meadow of his longing.
In his mind, he moved toward it
stepping lightly, almost on air.

THE ROLLER COASTER CHILD

The roller coaster child is still at the fair.
No one told her when to go home.
She thinks her cotton candy has a treat in the middle,
That the dimes in her pocket are true silver.
She thinks her caramel apple

Grew that way on the tree
And the voice that said, *Eat,* was her mother.
She thinks she is going somewhere,
Maybe to heaven.
                    The serpent
On whose back she tilts and slides
Never lets her touch the ground.
It tells her she is a princess and tosses her high
Where the sun glitters her hair.
It reminds her she is alone
And loops her down among shadows that moan
And reach for her hands.
                    She calls her mother
But the world is closed this season.
Everyone has gone to work, to school,
To bed and war, perhaps to heaven.
She cannot get off the roller coaster
Because it loves her so, and because the gate
Is unattended and doesn't take dimes.
The hands of her watch are straight up
Every time she looks.
                    Between epiphany and terror
Everything is blurred.
Somewhere people sweat and bleed,
Carry groceries, muddy their feet.
Somewhere laughter is rich,
People eat together, taking their time.
The roller coaster child fills up on candy
And dreams she is rooted
Like the trees and houses she glimpses
At noon.
                    Only on the lowest loops
Does she notice,
Sidelong, that the serpent is eating its tail
And the view ahead
Is no different from the one behind.

I wish I could have loved you more.
Your beauty was my sorrow,
Who stood ungainly by the door.

As stars upon the river pour
The salts they lightly borrow,
I wish I could have loved you more.

Suppose the brush runs out before
It finds the ink of sorrow:
Who stands ungainly by the door

And watches as the crowds adore
Today and yet tomorrow?
I wish I could have loved you more,

But took an oath. In blood I swore
No graces would I borrow,
Who stood ungainly by the door;

Then darkly laid me in my store
Of unrelinquished sorrow.
I wish I could have loved you more,
Who stood ungainly by the door.

What's the worst thing? I heard in the air
between the osprey and the cliffs,
the lake rumpling and smoothing itself
by my feet, elsewhere shining and still.
Perhaps a bone spoke or the wolf
spider caught in my shirt. *Not counting
cruelty, what scares you blind?
Poverty? Loneliness? Old age?*

A rough basketry of pine and wild grape
had let me through to the beach
but the other night it was pizza, beer
and her voice, singing us far and small:

> *I lay down golden
> and woke up vanishing*

Now, as I walked, head down, by a half-buried
oarlock the red balloon appeared,
wilted pod on a string rooted in sand,
with a sodden bit of card bearing a message
from a school two states away:

> *Please send me a fact.
> Love. Emy.*

I seemed to hold her flushed face in my hands,
child still golden, far east
of where I stood with sand in my shoes.

Back through the woods I took the balloon
and laid it like a plover's egg inside my car,
its shell softened to aged skin
still wrinkled around a child named Emy's breath.
Through fields of mist toward night and home
I tried to think of facts for her:
that people used to write on bark;

that alligators fall asleep
when rolled on their backs; that the gut
strings of a cat can be stroked into music . . .

But that was years ago, and friends
have died since then, my husband
missing, parents skimmed off, thin air
rinsing the stone step, the window panes.

> *I lay down golden*, the singer crooned,
> *and woke up gone*

Emy, this is what scares me: that
every breath rides its fading
farther out to sea, deeper into the mountains,
away, away.

But see how the stars bathe us,
how far you have exhaled your question.
This worn red sac still hoards
its dwindling mana
but you have passed over lakes and cities
and now the galaxies open like fans.

IV

THE PLAGUE

began far away seemed to began to begin in a far a faraway
began they thought elsewhere very far
from here

        that was it you see
someone else someone far very a very
long way
        from here
it was a very long way very far someone else
no one any of us no place we
                no one
no one we could know it was so far
                   from us

you see this is important it was not anyone any of us knew
it was no one we it was so very far and no one we could
it was not possible that we could we couldnt possibly know
        any of them

so it was happening
you see elsewhere
far from nowhere near
another place entirely
        from here
and how could we they
were so there were
so many of them
and what could we be
expected they werent anything
        to do with us
but then
    but
then it began that is it
began to appear this is hard
to be clear about it seemed to begin began it

appeared to begin
                    coming closer
not here but near
                              not
among us exactly
or rather among some of us but not
most of us that is it was just
certain ones of us not
our friends and certainly not our
relations not close not
ourselves or anyone we could possibly
so we still
                    felt   far
but not as much
                         because now
there were well certain signs were appearing to beginning to
appear among us and we looked that is we began to we tried
          not
but we began to begin we did in fact begin we couldnt help
          it
wasn't possible not to look at each other
                                          for signs
and the signs seeping somehow
under or around or perhaps
through or into or out of

                         the signs

all around us
and we   and they   and we couldnt not
because it wasn't
                         far   now
it was no longer somehow it
the somewhere was no
we tried to the elsewhere was not you
see the question is how
to say this it was no longer very a far that
is it was wouldnt wasnt was it
wouldnt was
not was us here there we said it

was us

      and here

and now

ON THE WAY TO THE GALA

It is warm for mid-October
And we ride the bus past sycamores and plane trees
Downtown to a nave of small leaves murmuring
In the square by the Plaza Hotel,
Where a bored fountain slinks into a stone
Basin, and I nearly step on the man

As we round the corner, a young man
Adrift in a box in fearful October
And sick. For bedding, newspaper, stone.
Help me, he cries to the trees
And the legs schussing by as dusk swabs the hotel
With gritty sweeps, muttering

Old mop-wringer murmuring
To herself. A fly in her path is the gesturing man
Pressed to his wailing wall, his flatulent hotel
A pavement room, already half of October
Run off like yesterday's lover through scabbed trees,
Last light oiling the edge of the curbstone.

Somebody help me! A stone
Through the heart's window, rumors
Of death in the street among trees
That know nothing of men
Dying young, of spring mislaid in mid-October.
We step around his outflung arm, the hotel

Wrapped in light now for the gala, fine hotel
With fine windows, glittering stones
Set in ramparts built to counter October's
Thefts; rich rooms laid open to murmurous

Guests posed under chandeliers as women
And men discourse on the Virus—under glass trees

Preening and drinking wine—and the plane trees
Brush the edges of this downtown hotel
With withering fingers as a young man
Works his dying into the flat stone
Centering each evasive eye, while decorous murmurs
Bring to heel the terrors of a mild October

Evening darkening trees and stone
Facades as at the Plaza Hotel, murmuring
Languorously to itself beside a young man vanishing in mid-
     October.

SOMETHING THAT SHROUDS ITSELF

Twelve months ago, on New Year's Eve,
I danced with Carlos.
His sister Maritza smiled, his mother
Carmen kissed us all.

On New Year's Day last week
He lifted like fog from his slag heap
Of limbs, breath
Between breaths, just before dawn.

One year to learn it all: to slow
Dance for months with something
That shrouds itself but
Finds your tongue, handles you all over.

He knows a refrain I'm afraid to learn.
I can see it in the austere
Seam of the mouth where the form
We knew by his name lies waxed

And rouged in the overheated,
Flowery room. A year ago, two-
Stepping with me, he did not
Know this tune. Last year, we touched.

The white shores of a new season
Loom hopeful and terrible.
Their messages fade in from so far
I hear them as ghosts upon the stair.

That night we blew tin horns, wore paper hats,
Spritzed one another with champagne.
We opened the windows and listened
To all of Manhattan coming ashore in the dark.

FAMINE: ETHIOPIA HITS THE TV NEWS AGAIN

Bituminous eyes starestruck,
they stumble out of the crackling hills,
landlocked rafts carrying
their lives on their backs,
those perilous fire balloons
pinned to the ground.
The sun is a rock they cannot pass.

Bellies stretched
around hunger's furnaces,
they turn up here at dinnertime,
river of rags and bones
groping along a boundless sandbar
toward a vanishing sea
past fields of munching cows.

We've seen all this before.
Turn the channel. Now
they're gone

INTERROGATIONS I:
ARGENTINA, TURKEY, TIBET . . .

The Prisoner Is Revived

It is peaceful here in these mountains,
the air so thin it rings like a wine glass,
the sun a fizz of sequins.
In a blue robe, I float on a bed
of blossoms, fragrant as crushed berries.
I have been all day climbing
to this ledge beyond the last prospector's cabin,
where the trail wrinkles away
to a valley I almost remember . . .

Something sweats and sobs, shadows
rummage the grass.
A crow peels from a cliff face,
hoarse wrenched hinge . . .

                    What falling rock
              rams my hip?
                    . . . Why hornets
              stinging my lip, my eyelid. . . ?

Why do dark faces loom from the sky?
What walls are these, bearing down on me?

LIGHT ARMS AROUND YOU

If you were cast adrift as a baby
wrapped closely in the fleecy blanket
your young mother must have knit for you,
if you were laid sleeping
on the venturing current
just as the first cottage flamed,
the wailing began,
if you grew up in a far place
and no one ever told you—

where you are now
would you guess you are
different from these others?

Now the family that calls you theirs
sits in deep chairs drinking
dark red wine,
the baby chews on a flannel tiger,
poker chips pile up
at the lucky uncle's place;
but something is not in place.

The wind fists the windows
barely sheathing a sharp cry
gone before it is wholly heard
and among the feathers of lamplight
stroking the scarred table
a knife carves on the wall
of your breastbone:
I do not belong here.

Light arms are suddenly around you
drawing you out of the circle.

On that day you begin
lifting heavy stones, testing
for the one
that will turn or slide or spring back
as a voice intimately known to you
whispers, *Come*, or, *Welcome,*
here you are at last.

V

SOLITAIRE

It's raining lightly. The oak leaves
Stick together like paste-on stars.
Pink phlox yawns under the crowding lilacs,
A stain spreads in the driveway's open palm.
Between the spangled gloom of the garden
And this room, yellow lit,
Silver salts tremble in emulsion.
The stone birdbath is all pins and needles.

Across from me, my father balances gingerly
Adrift in his old brown chair by the window,
His feet propped,
Ivoried fingers fumbling the slick cards.
His bowline already floats free,
Not quite caught
In the current that tugs and nags,
Teasing him farther from shore.
How well does the stern line hold?
Or is that the one
That lies like a question mark on the water?
Drops slip and smear on the pane.
I touch the table, shuffle my feet on the floor.
Cool touch, sound of wind in the corn.
Stay with us, Daddy, don't go near the water.
My father plays at playing solitaire
Alone in thick weather, the wind rising.

Not long after the infinite weariness
Rose from the ground

He stopped singing. One son
Mowed the field outside his window

But he closed his eyes. Speech
Lay down on his tongue

Except for *No*, to his other son's
Are you afraid?–the question seemed

To surprise him–and *Bless my soul!*
When he was told the new night nurse

Had driven two towns past the house.
Otherwise, every part

Was simply too heavy to lift or open
Or even to hold any longer.

So when the day came to go
He slipped free and flew into the garden

With a flock of swallows and bluebirds
That hung about for two days

Touching the house like lovers
At the windows and under the eaves.

He left his canes behind and his old
Gray jacket with seeds in the pockets,

And he went out, to the rose beds
And the mountain, to the stones and trees

Where chips of light were flying like leaves
And the sky opened wider than ever before.

In my dreams, he appears at parties,
his smile eclipsing every other face.
He doesn't linger here,
where his name has drifted somehow
onto this stone stubbed into loam
beneath a rock maple, a pane of sky.

Some evenings we picnic on this spot
before the summer concerts
next door in the meetinghouse:
wine and pasta, jeans and gypsy skirts.
We watch the sun cutting
orange prisms through the leaves.

It's so unreal: the violins
tuning up behind the stage door,
mosquitos whining high A-flats,
his ashes in a little pouch
thumbed into the wordless ground.

He is not here, who walked in the garden
in the cool of the evening,
who sang me to sleep with the *Gasoline Song*
and brought me tools and tiger kittens.
Not here, who taught me to waltz,
to not cry, to drink like a gentleman.

But when I see that king-sized lantern
kindling the leaves at dusk,
I feel him near, his arm relaxed
along the blueing hills,
the constellations ripe on his tongue,
the sun his best cigar.

Herkimer, Canajoharie, Gloversville, Cooperstown:
I have known forever these aged hamlets dozing near water,
Homes of Beechnut gum, fine ladies' gloves,
The Baseball Hall of Fame. Carved lace
Still frills the tall houses of oak and brick
That commandeer corner lots, cap the round hills
Of this wooded river valley where I follow a county road
Built for tractors, pick-ups, family wagons.

Tonight, the locals can't get through. We travelers
Hog their road, nose to tail, herded into the scenery
By a chemical spill on the Thruway.
We caravan through towns that flow slowly toward
And away from us, in ribbon candy streams.
It is like visiting an old teacher
Who serves the right yearbook with tea and macaroons.
The flowers on her walls nod off, the parlor grand
Has asthma and yellow keys, but her eyes glint,
The tea is strong and sweet, she remembers you well.

A tanker truck overturned
The plans of hundreds of home-bound drivers,
Funneling us past these wreaths on fanlight doors,
These lights like ice chips, red, blue, green,
Deep inside high-ceilinged rooms. At intersections,
Blurred men in dark overcoats wave us on with flashlights,
Penciling shooting stars and crescent moons
On the night air; and out of sight,
Where the land slopes down to the Mohawk River,
Men in masks work to capture and contain
The murderous chemical that fumes over frozen ground
Where the Thruway waits, bare as bone.

When, safely shepherded through the dark,
We surge once more into its channel,
The fast lane claims me by reflex
And in no time I have found the right river town
And the narrow white house
Where three sets of candles bracket a thin tree

Bristling with white sparks in the bay window.
My mother has brought out the old icons for Christmas.

I do not go in right away. My father, two months dead,
Stands beside me. *Isn't she something?* he asks.
I can see him in his long dark coat,
Breathing white vapors, steady as a fence post
On the hill where he patiently watches us shoot our sleds
Down the steepest slope at the public golf course.
The cold is deep out here. Downtown,
The river scabs over, breaks open, black and slick.
In a red dress, my mother appears at the window, waves.

It is the hour when sheep and oxen speak.
Time to go in. Under the electric stars
We will drink wine and break open little cakes,
Hoisting our glasses to my father
Blowing smoke rings in the doorway,
Thinking nothing of the cold.

THE CROSSING

Last night my mother did not die.
I cannot tell how it happened.

We were crossing the road
(I, eldest daughter, helping her)
when my right shoe flew off
and she got away from me,
unsteady on her crutches but
moving faster and faster
to some coded message or melody
I couldn't hear but plainly saw
in her tilted head and reckless oaring;

and I ran after her in my one shoe
but it was already too late:
she was tottering into the fallen
leaves at the far side

where uneven ground tipped over
the lip of a low hill and I couldn't
save her, she went over so fast,
as if a hand were at her back.

But this time she did not die.
I know, because in my one shoe
I stood tensely, listening:
with my ears and eyes, my tongue
and hands, my bare foot
and the small of my back, I arched
out over the ravine, listening

until from the sheaf of her
letters suddenly in my hand
came the soft breathing
and softer still from the small black
recorder in my other hand, but
steady, the breathing.

                    After that
I didn't look for her anymore.

HOW TO SEE YOUR MOTHER THROUGH

Get there. Drive all night
to the hospital in another state
where your brother and sister
are already holding her hands
and a priest touches her lips
with a wafer dipped in wine,
while her eyes roll up in the trick
that kid taught you in first grade
and the pale green oxygen mask
rescues and returns
breath after waterlogged breath
as she sinks and swims toward whatever
shoreline collects itself
behind windows that give no view

beyond this flattened white room
where all your faces keep
opening and closing like doors you remember
that slammed shut, never closed,
swelled tight when it rained.
It is raining in some hospital
room as you read this. The nurses
bring you tea and turn her carefully.

Stay with her. Suppose her eyes
flew open and no one was there?
Bring daffodils, Schubert, scented soap.
Bring poems and read them.
Bring bedsocks, your father's picture,
the London shawl. Rub her feet.
Sing to her.

Above all, go when the call comes.
No matter how far. This
is the last time.
Come in from Miami or Buffalo.
Don't mind the eyes or the small papers
that blow about in her throat.
They have nothing to do with her.
She knows you're here.
Touch her; talk.
Remember the borrowed black dress
she swore was the reason
your father proposed?
The treasure hunts with clues in verse?
The valentines stuffed in shoes and pockets
when you were a child and shy?
With these you are weaving a sling
that may hold her weight.

Of course you can't really see her
through the whirling blades, but
you can stand there waving
and if she doesn't look back
it is probably because
she is hungry and your father

has been waiting so long
with mangoes and pineapples and the torchlit
smile that was always only for her.
Then you might as well go home
and get on with
whatever it was you were doing.

WHERE WE NEVER WERE

When my father died, I smelled cigar
Smoke in the garden three nights in a row.
The wind blew three ways.
There was a knocking on walls.
When my mother died,
I saw through the green eye of a massive wave
The pale beach dead ahead,
Wave and I cresting, moving at terrible
Speed in full sun, no last verse,
No clandestine breast between us and the hissing sand.

When my father died,
He went down in smoke and up in rain
And out through the names of things.
He built a hut of clouds by Orion's third buckle.
My mother left when I wasn't looking,
Through a hole in the sky.
The moon made a space for her.
Some greased thumb sealed the spot without
A trace and my heart gills opened and
Closed helplessly in thin air.

How smaller than a camel's eye is Eden,
Where we never were, whose homemade
Groves we wander still and grieve.
The forms that rise, drown, and rise
Dissolve in the clay bowls of my hands
And a dream of black coats

Flaps up from the pond, wringing its empty sleeves.
Good child that I am, on sleep's
Edge I say my prayers and sign my parents'
Names in salt, on the high forbidden door.

WHITER THAN DOVES:
AT THE JAFFREY BURYING GROUND

Day's end, and tomorrow, a long drive.
I stand among silences gathering shade
Thinking, Why have I come so late?
Beyond a row of brooding druids
The mysterious pines of my mother
Lean in, silver-tipped; the low stone
Wall of my father recedes like a wave.
Some bird I hadn't noticed falls silent.
My watch doles out the widening hour.
As a few spangles rub off the vanishing sun,
The stone I have come to visit flares up
In the last ghost rays: a young shoot,
Barely set in its concrete boot.
From across the grove I watch it:
Whiter than doves, brighter than rain.
The old stones coalesce, the earth rises,
The sky falls, and my parents, newborn,
Look at me with soft eyes.
Absence is presence, they say
As the moon hangs fire and the small
And various lights disentangle themselves
One by one from the arms of the trees.

VI

The image woke up in a cloud of unknowing
wrapped in her colors and textures,
feeling lonely.
She might be a stone or a fish
or a seventh veil,
it was hard to tell.

Meanwhile, the details were busy
building a house
but it was difficult
with only shingles and nails
plus the odd stair
or pane of glass.
They were diligent
but kept going off in all directions.
The house couldn't get a sense of itself
and kept erasing rooms
and demanding new beginnings.

The concept, kicking a bottle top,
had left the office early,
there being nothing but high-rises to design
or more condos.
His head ached with the pressure
of gabled roofs, spires and turrets, hidden
courtyards, sudden views.

When the image burned her way
through the cloud,
some disgruntled details
left their work crew
to settle on her shoulders, in her hair.
The concept, walking by,
was dazzled. What colors,
what textures!

He followed her to the house,
a sorry-looking structure, but suddenly
bristling with possibilities.
Smoothing his beard,
he considered opening lines:
Haven't we. . . ? Has anyone told you. . . ?

The house felt its floors steady,
its angles multiply.
Details attached themselves
to carpets and cabinets,
while at attic level, a captain's walk appeared
with two figures on it.
Later, in a room where thin curtains
capered in a sea breeze,
someone was making love.

MEMOIRS OF A MINIMALIST
Regards to W. S.

Three women spinning
in a cave
are three women spinning
in three caves

Or one woman
spinning
in a green sea cave

Or three hundred women
young and old
spinning in one or three
hundred sounding caves.

This old yarn
will not untangle itself.

Three women
only
spinning in a cave

Will not untangle itself
yet is certain as fate . . .

The women are black-haired
and their calloused fingers
delicately part and weave the strands.
They sit crosslegged.
A wind from the sea
lifts . . . Where was I. . . ?

So the women spin.

The hair of the youngest one . . .
The crone's yellow thumbnail, long and sharp . . .

IN THE GARDEN

She walks among the tigers he named lilies
and their fiery velvets rub off on her skin,
sweet seasoning. Leaves and wings
move like thoughts over the grass
and by the lake a smoky tree
dreams itself into sky water.
Would that be toward heaven or. . . ?
Too many questions, Adam says, shaking his head.
When, newborn, she bent over a stream,
a face appeared, smiling and startled
as she was, risen from where?
She could not bring it up in her hands
though it seemed to invite companionship.

Then that voice, that gong,
from the clouds and stones.
Turn away, it said, *from this false image*
and find your true self in the eyes of Adam.

His artless student, she peers hopefully
at the likeness of a pliant creature mined, he says,
from his flesh and bone.
He is pleased with what he has produced,
and guides her hand to the soft spot
under his breast. *See,* he explains,
how we are one creature,
she, the thought of his heart made flesh,
he, the mold from which she tumbled, twinned,
before she knew herself.

But she does not find in Adam's gaze
the face that smiled at her from the water
as if it already knew her from another place,
like the tree that curves toward its twin
dropped in the lake sky.

Sometimes she dreams she is bending
or rising toward another being she also is,
who waits with poised intent in pollens
and fragrances, shadows and reflections.
Does Adam know this Eve of Eve?
In his arms she feels only his hunger,
prowling the hollow that will not fill again.

NAMING THE MOMENT

A woman sees a man walking, walking
Through snow along the eaves of the world.
He is looking for God.
Down the street the woman is on fire.
All her real estate is burning:
Her hotel, the Victorian house
With a grandmother in it,
The garden and hidden laboratory.

Then a tornado in the form of a mastodon
Slumps down on a field of cattle

While the woman, now naked, waits
In an octagonal room under a kind of sunlamp
For the millstones in the next town
To finish threshing the bodies.
Arms and legs whirl through darkness
And she must name the moment of transformation.

But Transit Road has turned into a closet
And the girl underwater sleeps
As an octopus devours the baby alligator,
Watched by a small stone child.
In a giant underground barn, two
Dapple-gray horses brush their wings
Across their owl eyes and grow fat
In their foul, forgotten stalls.

As a last resort, the woman
Orders the girl into a tree-high
Glass bell filled with flame.
A garden appears. The woman walks
Up and down its paths, thinking.
Someone taps her on the shoulder.
"Eve," says God,
Calling her for the first time by name.

ROSE RED AND THE BEAR

It has been different
since she moved to the hills.
Her saucers fill with birds.
The jeep nuzzles her hand.
The stove with claw feet
breaks daily for the iron quarry,
mad with tribal angst.

So much to keep in check.
She shoos the birds,
feeds the jeep, ties the stove
to a chair. At night

the songs of the trees begin.
Aromatic notes flick from the leaves,
hum at her window.

Wrapped in her grandmother's
old brown shawl,
she crochets a rose, snipping
the crimson thread,
as her shadow slips its leash,
glides under ferns to the hollow
log where the bear stirs, yawning.

AMERICAN GOTHIC

the stars are polysyllabic
the moon is a shaman's word

leaning against the door
she doesn't know how
to say these things to him

opening his coat at 20 below
he is a comet's tail
shaving the rim of zero

this he can't logically
explain to her

their bed is rumpled
more often than not
he sleeps crushing
a pillow doll in his arms
she with her hair
in her mouth

but the house is clean
crocheted doilies in the parlor
chairs at right angles
he mucks out the barn
mondays all weathers

and the years fall around their ears like ninepins
and their children disappear down a tunnel
and the earthmovers grind dangerously close

in a field of vanishing edges
they sweat a language
heavy as stones

but she still licks the moonlight
from her finger
he still bares his chest
to the sun's hooves

and what they know they
cannot tell

FACTS AND FIGURES

Old walls have no truck with figures.
They know themselves built from the ground
Up, that what comes down from the sky
Lacks history. What's real is here
Where foundations state their dense facts,
Let clouds and leaves embroider what they will.

Leaves and clouds weave subplots as they will,
Won't be harried into stone figures
No matter what Medusa stare of fact
Quick-freezes every point. Walls are ground-
ing for the quick-tongued embroidery of here
And now, the madrigals enlacing sky

And wall at once, as if it took some sky
To lick and quicken a wall's will,
Ripening moments as on a tapestry, here
The burdened cherry tree and here, the ritual figures:
Hunters, maiden, unicorn, rising from the ground
Of unembroidered, hard, enduring facts.

All walls, of course, stand on simple fact:
A unicorn, for all its hooves and horn, is sky-
Born, pure embroidery, no ground
In common sense. We all know who will
Offer him her lap, and how those figures
With their longbows and their horns have heard

The snapping trap, in sunlight here
Where a virgin cradles death in her lap, a fact
She may not yet have figured
Out, for look how tenderly the sky
Embroiders shadows on her small white hands, that soon
      will
Seed the garden's brightly woven ground
With dragons' teeth. Already on the castle grounds
The falling fruit splatters ancient walls, while here
Among embroidered fields, truth will
Bury its teeth again in trust, bloody fact
In the heart's wild fictions, nothing under the sky
Exempt, not walls, not one of these figures

Embroidered on the latticed ground as fatal fact,
Though each recurring form blooms here against the same
      old sky,
Springing back fresh, in season, willful and young,
      transfigured.

VII

Just playing, you say, on your heels
in the creek, building a dam.
Nine thousand feet above where I'm from,
coffee roils over fire already fallen
to coals, as curls of new pink light
melt in the water's eyes
and last night's sleeves and stockings
slide down the trees to the forest floor.

Just playing, you grin, the twin
scoops of your hands moving rock,
shoveling sand. The sun still
lurks behind Arapahoe Peak, but already
you are changing the course of things.
The raveling creek slips like skin
in your palms. Last night

I shaped myself to your entire length,
praise rising in me like a hooked rainbow.
This morning I am stupid
and fall silent as I bring you coffee, black.
I want to help, but do not know how
to play this game. The tongues
that transformed me
belong to the language of lilies, salamanders.

Stumbling, putting my boots on the wrong feet,
I am a tree of gold tassels,
a trout dancing, a creek in love.

How then imagine the far November dawn
when I will awaken early in my bed
by a lowland lake, dreaming someone
has spoken, thinking perhaps
it is you, returned from timberline,

holding back the heavy, swaying curtain,
turning my name over
and over in your dissolving hands?

STICKS AND STONES

I. Sticks

On the buffed and burnished library table
The torn branch curves all ways
At once, twice abrupt, four times urbane,
Sloughing old toad scales.
One wall eye ogles the well-bred lady
In the portrait with gilt nameplate.
One cracked cheek
Rests leaf-light on its image.

I could snap it with my hands,
Old knock-kneed spine in ashen rags.
But my elbows sleep
On the glass-waxed tabletop
Where its shadow floats,
A hobbled wave obliquely instructive
In how a line is softened,
A dried branch obliged to flow.

II. Stones

You are gone off up the trail
Where lodgepole pine dwindles
To vast debris of chopped rock,
Fissured ice, rationed breath. Deep
Space swarms dark up there, the wind's
Broad lungs flail at ribs of silence.
In stifled light aged tundra brings forth
Miniatures: stonecrop, forget-me-not.

Back in town, the house snarls
As, bristling with spleen, you stiff-arm me,

I bite your thumb. We bring home trolls,
Grizzlies, goads. We believe in stoning.
Yet over the clang of our brazen tongues
Floats an occasional green thought.
In its gelatinous shade we slide all ways
At once, a pair of peeled twigs.

MALEDICTION

May the man who gave me this ring
And five sons
Before he ran off with his green-eyed
Geography student
To saunter in public parks
And loiter in satin sheets: may this man
Be stabbed by every rose he plucks.
May swans attack him
And honey turn to paint thinner in his mouth.
May he grow a tic and a squint
And a wart on his tongue.
And his other tongue.
May colognes smell of goats and monkeys
Where they touch him
And may he spit when he speaks.
May waiters ignore him
And bums escort him, even to the podium.
May his books be remaindered
While the works of his rivals increase mightily
In the citations of his colleagues.
Yea, may he be a wax fork in love with fire,
A palm with no thumb,
A wave that cannot crest,
And may the witch child tell him so
In the presence of his enemies.
Then may he flee to the Isle of Bitter Echoes,
Where every word of love
Returns as lunatic laughter,
Where clouds ape the shapes of desire
And winds blow the covers from his shame.

There may he howl
Forsaken by all save breath
And thirst, forever and ever
Or until I choose,
Amen.

SOME NIGHTS THE DARK HILL

When, walking in the park at twilight,
I hear footsteps behind me,
I call my silver shepherds, my three
Spirit dogs, and they come,
Padding through the wastes of darkening
Meadow, past the crocodiles in the woods.
Tails low, easy in their stride,
They keep close as they always did,
And the footfalls I thought I heard
Veer aside, onto other paths.

Once, these beasts lolled their blunt heads
Against my thigh, rolled in carrion,
Hunted rabbits and rattlesnakes.
Now I go into the dark with my dogs
And the crocodiles sleep, night simmers,
Black peony on an incense stick.
The frequencies in my spine
Tune to the rustle of silks,
The growls and murmurs under hemlocks.

Some nights, the dark hill of my heart
Shakes out like a rag
And my root system sings electric,
I smell blood on the moon.
Tangled in pink refrains,
I plummet, singing my one lame note,
Down through musk-breathing caverns
To the path by a river veining bone
Where a man my bones know
Walks at evening with his three black dogs.

WHAT ARE WE TO EACH OTHER

Who will go with Fergus now,
And pierce the deep wood's woven shade,
And dance upon the level shore?
W. B. Yeats

The deeps between flakes of snow,
How the eyes of fleeing deer
Swallow the rage of the hunter . . .

Last night, dark things rustled
And yawned in their nests and caves
In a great wooded park.
I ran through black leaves and sharp stars.

Tonight, you reach for me
From your trunk in the attic.
You are the white body risen
To the roof of the sunless lake.

This season I am riding the river
Of our brightening and darkening.
Beneath your stone, under each domed rib
A shadow opens its hand.

I must study how darkness seeks
And collects us. How it needs to be loved.
What are we now to each other
In this pierced and woven shade?

ROOM 420, SISTERS OF MERCY HOSPITAL, JUNE 1985: THE VISITORS

Like a dream fading, they inhabit the room,
A tremor on the air, echo's echo;
And once again, I awaken, turn my head . . .

Sometimes a nurse floats near my pillow,
Watcher with black bulb and armband

Over my loosened grip on a fogged world;
Or a strange doctor, brooding down on me,
Folds back the sheet to lift a corner of gauze
Dressing a wound I cannot see.

But often, the high corner room
Where I lie among long-stemmed white tubes
Opens to my clouded gaze like a mirror
Suddenly drained of hurrying figures,
And I blink back from some brink,
Snagged on a dissolving whisper of silk
—or was it speech I nearly heard?

When half-sleep returns, again
In their wings or robes, they stroll
The banks of dream, soft sibilance
Against the planks of my hearing,
All around me a trembling
Like light on rocking water;
And I, in my small craft, almost see
The shadow of a great sail, can almost tell
The moment when the mirror floods with music.

CHRYSALIS

From her hospital bed one afternoon
she sees the sun come from far
like a view long despaired of, suddenly
iridescent along the window frame,
the dark trees moving their shoulders,
no clouds in sight.
                        Split and pinned
at the body's main hinge,
she loiters, restless and rooted,
watching the wind flick light
in fishtails over the narrow roofs
crowding the street below,
and dreams of butterflies
skewered to clean white sheets.

She longs to feed on the sublime:
nectar of Bach, chocolate nut bars.
But a rusty nail in her hip
snags breath and speech;
the food trays reek; on the huge
hanging tv, sleek women and feline men
claw and beckon interchangeably.

                              Later,
dusk rising from cindered canals
filters through crystal,
gleaming mauve at first, then
lavender, then purple-black
as down the elegant street, lights swerve,
red and gold, roofed in silver.

Some creature of the air
trembling with colors and transparencies
crouches on the ledge of sleep
drying its wings, not quite
invisible, the window now
open to let it out into the night.

SUMMER STORM

Heaviness explodes in the trees
at 9 p.m. Silver ropes.
Song of krumhorns. Flash photos:
corner of porch with bush
and barbecue grill, two apple trees,
chandelier floating over ghost lawn.
Then the cannon with fireball
opening a fiesta in the reticent woods
and the house goes dark.

Stumbling on the stairs, the newlyweds
laugh softly on the way to their front
center room. Next door
the widow falls down a well

where her bed should be,
magenta longings flooding the night.

But everything gleams in the morning,
from brush pile to telephone wire,
and in the garden, two monarchs loll,
each on its own palatial dahlia.
Deeply tranced, wings vaguely fanning,
they are too far gone
to fly from hawk or human.

The newlyweds are off up the mountain
and the widow is transplanting,
hunched over marigolds,
sun smearing light on petals,
knuckles and stones.
As she unravels buried webs and knots,
time keeps unfolding
and someone turns around on the mountain.

The bees, treading their looms,
knead and sing, sing and knead.
By degrees their drone
darkens, deepens, the garden fades.
Only the sound surrounds.
In the center, vibrating,
she is a honeysuckle, a rose mallow,
bee hum now the whole nectarine world.

When the newlyweds return,
the widow is brushing her hair.
Sparks fly from the brush
in a fine squall, the woman
inside the song,
body singing the word.

This is my right hand and this is my left,
said the good Cassio.
I am not drunk.

This is the rose and this is the window.
I am not blind.
Watch me dance to the kitchen radio.
I am alive.

When the children appeared, lost
and tired from climbing,
I invited them in and we sang.
I am not lost.

That was not me you saw
grubbing for hearts in the weeds
by the road. They were rubies and
I was dreaming.

I have a heart. It carries knives
and drinks blood. This is the left
ventricle and this is the right.

Out there on the lawn, a redgold lion
basks on the grass and the stones.
It will soon be dark. Or light.

She is all lightness with her moonwhite
dress and chestnut hair
the girl sitting in sun and shade
with a white parasol
glissandos of sun melting into the trees
as she looks out from under a floppy
black hat embellished apparently
with a large albino soft-shelled crab
and there is more shade than sun
in the woods behind her whereas she
makes of white a delicious froth
not excepting the little white shoe
poking or perhaps peeking out from
the pink-tinged folds of the dress
there actually being as much pink
as white in the gauzy stuff
with its long loose sleeves and yards
of gathered skirt and the bench
where she sits blends the same colors
as the half-hidden sun-stunned trees
with just a little more blue mixed
with the green whereas yellow douses
the air all around as well as the
leaves although spotlit as she is
her lightness is more an ice candle
effect cool with that dusting of
pink and touches of blue in the parasol
leaning against the bench
its long orange tip resting on bare
earth rendered in warm red browns
with veins of orange and yellow
and amidst all this she looks
straight out from under level
rather thick dark brows her lips
a little red bow the sleeping hands
lapped over each other like ivory
fish the ring on one finger quite
plainly the eye of the top fish and
some sort of decorative lace or fancy

needlework rising and falling in two
parallel curves down her bodice
above which the rounded chin is level
so the gaze may meet eyes looking back
and the crescent of one ear shows
through the redgold hair which
escapes its pins on the side away
from us while a china doll blush
lightly glazes the porcelain cheeks
the blood rising there and she looks
at ease sitting upright on the blue
green and white bench daubed with soft
black lines relaxed but alert
the gaze straight out attentive perhaps
hopeful a little challenging
and one can see she is ready for anything
and will one day soon take the arm
of a gentleman under the trees
and under the dress the flesh that is
soft and slightly pink trembles
as the flower on her hat
acknowledges one breeze or another
and it hardly matters which gentleman
for by autumn she will be shaken out
like the half-visible receding trees
in this infinitely unfolding park
where a white dress shimmers in the sun
dark and light overtaking each other
in the woody depths behind her
and it is never again as at this moment
although this one instant extends
into all its consequences.

Who will remember me after I'm dead?
I, an old woman
who struggles head bent
over tree roots
hauling my swollen heart
like a carcass
toward some child's line
drawing of horizon?

Who will wash me and fold my hands?
Wear my rings?
Pack up my shoes and poems?
In that last moment
will I gasp out a name
no one can recall?
Why weep today
for the blue soldier doll,
the garnet beads,
the hairs on a man's forearm?

When the forest and the small room
run together, who will
sing me out from under the trees?
Open the river and let me in?
Ah well, the questions
of an old woman
trouble no one but herself
and one or two scrubby hills
more rock than grass.

HAVING DROWNED EMBRACING THE MOON
IN THE RIVER, LI PO EXPLAINS

So we were drunk that night, it was glorious.
Everything doubled: stars, faces, the words
Of the uncaged water. I was just out of prison,
On my way home. I never thought
I would see a star again, or a woman.

All my life I was dodging some snare or other,
Whether the emperor's eunuch or anarchist plots.
Temple brawler, brewer of bastards,
I was king of the wine shops, guest of goatherds
And mandarins, prince of provinces.

When the prison spat me out, the world
Took me in again. It was autumn,
Leaves thick on the riverbanks, cinnamon-scented,
White herons flaring, and that night,
Dancing girls, barrels of wine.

I was past all caution when the Sky Lotus
Set her bare foot to the shivering water.
Her silver robe slid to the river floor
And we rocked between shore and shore,
Phosphorescent as whales.

They will tell you I drowned in illusion,
I, an old poet drunk and at loose in the universe.
But I only fell into the poem
That had harried me down every road, one half of me
Clasping a star, the other half walking on water.

Afterword

One of my favorite meditations on the writing of poetry is by the Frenchman Paul Valéry, who says in *Aesthetics*, "When the poets repair to the forest of language, it is with the express purpose of getting lost; far gone in bewilderment, they seek crossroads of meaning, unexpected echoes, strange encounters; they fear neither detours, surprises, nor darkness. But the huntsman who ventures into this forest in hot pursuit of the 'truth,' who sticks to a single continuous path, from which he cannot deviate for a moment on pain of losing the scent or imperiling the progress he has already made, runs the risk of capturing nothing but his shadow. Sometimes the shadow is enormous, but a shadow it remains."

When I began writing poems, I hoarded images and built little houses around them to keep them safe. Unfortunately, they were too self-enclosed for much life to breathe through them, and though I didn't realize it at first, I was emulating Valéry's hunter, looking for truths I could put in cages and capturing only shadow creatures. I began to sense that something was missing, no matter how many beautiful specimens I collected; but it wasn't until I read Robert Bly's *Leaping Poetry* and Richard Hugo's *Triggering Town*, that I began to see what was wrong with my poems: they thought they were arrows, when they needed to be trees or balloons or panthers. The mysterious emanations rising from the work of such poets as Emily Dickinson, Anna Achmatova, Ted Hughes, William Stafford, began to beckon towards the interior.

I developed the habit of opening Pablo Neruda's *Residence on Earth* (in translation) when I was at an impasse, and reading around in it. That continually foliating imagination of his would finally charm awake some new thought, some underground connection, which would be just the vital element missing from my poem. I still use this method when I'm stuck, nosing around in one book of poems after another, until my mind catches on some word or phrase that hooks itself onto a memory or question that I suddenly see is the further dimension my poem has been waiting for. Then if I'm attentive, the poem itself flaps up from the bottom of the pool or peers out of a thicket—and I realize there are two of us here, or maybe more—and that we're standing on hallowed ground, wherever we are.

Whenever I get the chance, I repair to the forest of language, where, if I'm lucky, I get deeply lost for days at a time, exploring new detours and meeting the inhabitants. What comes back with me then has some other life clinging to it, touching and continuing to teach me.

RICHARD SEWELL

The Mischief at Rimul

PHOTO: SUSAN STERLING

RICHARD SEWELL grew up in rural Maine. He was a founder and for years a director of the Theater at Monmouth, Maine's classical repertory theater where he directed or produced a wide selection of the canon of theater from Shakespeare, Marlowe and Decker to Shaw, Wilde and Synge. His own plays have had productions at the Spoleto Festival Fringe, in Los Angeles, in New York, at university campuses and elsewhere. He directs at Colby College, where his rhymed translation of Calderon's *Phantom Lady* was recently staged.

THE MISCHIEF AT RIMUL

*A tale of those who saw the first millennium,
for those who see the second.*

CAST OF CHARACTERS

THORA: ("TOH-ruh") *of Rimul, the poetess, first seen as an old*
NUN then as thirty-eight or nine.

HAAKON: ("HAWK-un") *the Earl, master of Norway in the*
absence of a king; firm ruler but infamous womanizer.
HAAKON is seen first as THE WANDERER (himself old,
shaggily altered enough to be mistaken for KARKER) then
at mid-forty. The same actor plays ODIN (THORA'S notion
of the god ODIN.)

KARKER: *Earl HAAKON'sthrall (like HAAKONin height.) He*
has a great mane of untidy blond hair, except when we see
him as the god LOKI (THORA'S notion of LOKI.)

KARI *a serving girl on THORA'S farm, and a crypto-Christian.*
In THORA'S dreams she appears as SIGYN, LOKI'S wife.

OLAF: *Christianized claimant to the throne of Norway,*
returned from exile. A large, vigorous, handsome fellow,
he also plays the CHRISTUS (THORA'S notion of that deity.)

ERA: *Certain late summer nights, afternoons and mornings, era of*
those who saw the year one thousand.

SCENE: *A nunnery built on the site of THORA'S old farm at*
Rimul; then in and around the farmhouse itself.
The set is murky. Behind black upstage scrim, which
either flies or parts, is a central scaffold topped with a
crucifix. CHRISTUS stands on a shelf up there and descends to
stage level via a black ladder. The scaffold base is a platform
where SIGYN stands and LOKI lies under black cloth from under
which he appears.
Up left and up right hang dark, patterned drapes. Behind
one is a platform altar to Frey and Freya; its top surface is a
trap door, hinged on its upstage edge. Through the other drape
is the passage to THORA'S bed.
A bench, a low table and a chest, all in dark wood, are the
furnishings of THORA'S house at Rimul. Downstage to one side, a
doorway is at times suggested by sound and a sharp rectangle of
light.
A gobo of leaf-dapple suggests exterior as needed.

ACT I

(*Loud knocking. Its echoes hint the door shuts in a huge space. An old* NUN *opens the door.* [*She mimes; there is a creak and a rectangle of moonlight.*] *With a grunt, she confronts a white-headed* WANDERER *in a wolfskin cloak.*)

NUN: Eh. Come. There's barley soup. Our rule is, you may stay a night, no more. (*She leads the* WANDERER *up into the gloom where a crucifix hangs, crude and life size, glimmering high up against gold leaf. The cross is rimmed with twined snake bodies; their heads agape hang downward. Below and to one side is a Mater Dolorosa or a Magdeline.*) One night, and use the privy pit and no where else. My eyes are bad, but I can smell. Understood? There's the Lord here. Thank him.

WANDERER: (*He stares up at the* CHRISTUS *for a long moment.*) Small thanks. I am Odin, don't you know?

NUN: What?

WANDERER: Odin Wanderer. The god.

NUN: As gross a liar at least. (*She peers at him.*) Great Odin had only one eye.

WANDERER: (*He holds up the stump of a right wrist.*) I have only one hand.

NUN: (*She recoils, crossing herself.*) You! (*Plaintive with the revulsion flesh feels for disembodied spirit.*) Are you a ghost?

WANDERER: So it is yourself under the headcloth, beautiful old woman? You're still pretty with your mouth open. They told me it was you here; I had to see.

NUN: We heard you'd died, you. . . slinking cur.

WANDERER: Your teeth are drawn now, nun-mother. So are mine.

NUN: Yours were always rotten! (*Peers closer*) In the end dogs look like their masters. I could have mistaken you for Haakon. (*He is amused.*) Don't you grin at me! (*Shaken*) I have been seeing such dreams lately, talking gods and ghosts; old sinew shouldn't have to carry such seething dreams. Was I just foreknowing *you*, afoot on the road? I half thought my talents were coming back to tease me.

WANDERER: You don't make ballads any more? No sagas for your nun-girls? (*She nods upward at the crucifix.*) He hears what people say, I guess?

NUN: We've no time here for talk of berserk blood-brags and love knots.

WANDERER: Only your Bible? Word is, Lady Thora has a book and writes out the old tales, nun or not. In all the North there was no better teller of tales than you. That's the word of Haakon the Earl.

NUN: Hush!

WANDERER: The past wasn't that bad to tell. Only the part about being trapped in a pit with a friend for my mortal enemy.

NUN: You. . . walk in on a body who's up to her eyes in sleep, you scrape up everything that's smashed in your one hand—and scour an old heart raw with the grit! What have you come for?

WANDERER: The story how Haakon and his man came to Rimul and a bad end.

NUN: Are you drunk?

WANDERER: (*Touches his flask.*) Nothing here but water. Do you women brew?

NUN: Someone else will tend to you. In the kitchen. One night, then you go.

WANDERER: You can't refuse me!

NUN: Can't I! I need sleep before midnight mass. This way.

(*They move off into the shadows. Fluctuating dream-light. The hanging CHRISTUS turns his mask-head to look after them. Slowly he moves his arms: they ache. He crouches in his void and climbs down to floor level. In the descent [we don't see how] the mask and painted quality is gone. He raises three pronged fingers and stares at that trinity sign of digits, then crams two of the fingers in his mouth and whistles. *)

ODIN: (*Returns. This is HAAKON again, but different. The ragged wolfskin cloak is now a blue linen one, theatrically ragged, the flowing hair a more silvery mane. He has two hands and one eye. It's ODIN, Wagner's Wotan. *) Me? (*Amused*) You can't refuse anyone.

CHRISTUS: Can't I! Don't start her talking poison-cups and love-rings. She's mine now; she doesn't need the gory... (*Hunts for the word*) claptrap.

ODIN: "Crap," you mean. If you don't like gore, get your own hands healed, Greekling.

CHRISTUS: I am a Jew.

ODIN: (*Shrugs*) Greek to me.

CHRISTUS: (*Points to the wounds in his hands*) What I am, I earned.

ODIN: I too! (*He points to his eye and chants with passionate arrogance.*)

> I was nine nights hanged   on the knot-gnarled tree,
> Spear-wounded, strangled,   myself to myself.
> Below by the world's roots,   I bartered an eye,
> In swap for wisdom. . . (*Simply*) What life is is sufferings;

you can't awe me overmuch with yours.

CHRISTUS: Don't blaspheme.

ODIN: (*Sharply annoyed*)   If anything is blasphemous, it's thinking we're vulnerable to insult!   Can a grub insult a God, for God's sake?

CHRISTUS: (*Loftily*) God, *and* human.

ODIN: So let mortals babble. It's what they were made good at.

CHRISTUS: (*Sighs*) You're right. Peace.

ODIN: And don't be that humble, either.

CHRISTUS: A soft answer turns away wrath.

ODIN: Maybe playing meek *is* blasphemy. Eh? (*Winks*) Is it against your religion to laugh?

CHRISTUS: I never laughed. (*Ruefully*) About blaspheming, you should hear Allah. Allah's a god they've got now out beyond Byzantium.

ODIN: I came to talk to Thora. Your nun.

CHRISTUS: She's sleeping.

ODIN: It's all one. She's listening.

CHRISTUS: Odin, I want peace for her.

ODIN: Peace! Church bells beating up the Sundays, christenings, Christian burials, Christmas, and your name the only curseword worth mouth-spit! I sleep in alleys and people look the other way. You're the *winner*!

CHRISTUS: I haven't *won*! She still dreams. I win no one. The things they do to each other! And won't do! I thirst.
ODIN: (*Offers a flask*) There's nothing in the flask but water. . .
CHRISTUS: (*Drinks*) Thank you.
ODIN: Better than vinegar, eh?
CHRISTUS: Much. (*Returns it*)
ODIN: (*Tastes*) Wine? (*Grins*) Oh, I heard of your conjure trick. You rascals! Jews, Greeklings A-rabs, smacking figs and spiced wines. On the quiet, is it true you people cut off a piece of your manhood to make it small enough to fit? (*CHRISTUS stares him down with superbly disgusted indifference, then looks away. ODIN shrugs.*) Race hate. . . it's just envy. (*He savors the wine.*) All I thirsted for was good fighters for an army. When the Twilight came, I didn't even have that. Your sort thirsts for a whole, good humankind and it's not to be had. Here or there a wise one or a brave or kindly, but all at once is too much to ask!
CHRISTUS: (*Takes a pull at ODIN's flask*) "Too much" is what we are! The egregious, goading the mundane flock.
ODIN: (*Warily*) You're saying "we"?
CHRISTUS: Yes, I call for a love feast. Thou and I.
ODIN: The South excuses a lot, but up here, men just don't.
CHRISTUS: I'm not talking Sodomite, you vile, mocking devil! Satan!
ODIN: One of your soft answers, is this?
CHRISTUS: I should burn the heretics and the burners of heretics in a fire of fire, break their lecherous spines, the crawling, cruel snakes! Trample them like grapes! (*ODIN nods.*) I come to bring not peace but a berserk sword!
ODIN: (*Applauds*) That's the spirit!
CHRISTUS: (*Conscious of ODIN's stare*) Yes. It is. And the flesh. (*He sighs and crouches.*) It's humiliating to be human too. Fits well up on me like tides, damnings, rages.
ODIN: Tides drown men, remember? But I was admiring you.
(Simultaneous)

CHRISTUS: You would!   ODIN: So, your health for the wine.
ODIN: (*Nods to him and rises to go*) I just glimpsed why old Thora ended up with you. I'm off. I was afraid the meek were going to inherit the earth, but no. Shalom.

CHRISTUS: (*He seizes ODIN*) I will not let you go, except I bless you! You're the worldly wise one. Understand me! They paint me in Byzantium, mad, mosaic eyes. . . coming in thunder with Thou Shalt Nots enough to harrow Hell. (*Lightning aloft draws our eye during the moment it takes for ODIN to be gone from his cloak and hat, empty cloth with which CHRISTUS still wrestles.*) I loved my fellow villagers so much I want to smite them, smite 'em for their inveterate, intractable, intolerable unloveliness, and I will have your secret up out of the fire-pit of you! Why does she love you? Why? (*Suddenly he is shaking only an old patched cloak. He turns it inside out and peers around.*) Mountebank wizard. Shifty. . . flighty, always, with your trap doors and holes under earth and tricks of vanishing. Your boast is nine nights on the tree, is it? I can go it longer than that. (*Painfully he crawls back up the crucifix and hangs there. Below him LOKI rolls out of the dark where he has lain, bound. LOKI has close-cropped, flame-red hair. KARKER will have a straw blond shag, like the WANDERER's white locks.*) So, you're back.

LOKI: No. It's Loki.

CHRISTUS: Dogs come to look like their masters.

LOKI: I'm the other one. Less grand, more fun. I laugh. It's a great comforter.

CHRISTUS: Get thee behind me. I recite Torah. That's comfort. "And Joktan begat Almodad, and Sheleph, and Hazarmaveth, and Jerah, and Hadoram. . ."

LOKI: Oh, stories? I've a woman tells me mine. Sigyn! One more saga, love. (*SIGYN stands, with a bowl. She was the statue at the cross foot, she has whipped aside the veil which made her face look like carver's work*)

SIGYN: Ask Thora. (*Sighs*) Well. Once there was. . . a Queen in Sweden, vain and lustful, Haughty Sigrid. She set her heart on a ring she'd heard of, out of another woman's house.

CHRISTUS: (*Exasperated*) Why. . .

LOKI: (*Grinning*) Who knows why she wanted it? Why do hearts want anything? Just listen. That's what stories are for.

SIGYN: Now, some crafty heroes had a mind to fetch that ring to her. . .

CHRISTUS: Is it a parable?

LOKI: There's a nun trying to persuade herself it's to your greater glory to write it down.

CHRISTUS: Yes. She still dreams.

LOKI: Comfort. . . I lie blinking where adders dribble on me. (*The serpent decor of the cross is dripping.*)

SIGYN: (*She lifts the bowl.*) I hold this to keep the venom from his eyes. I am the woman. Every time I go empty the bowl, he shakes till the earth quakes. Another story. He's chained because there was a beautiful young God of loving happiness, a peaceful prince. One spring day Loki managed to have him killed with a. . . wooden thing. Hell might have given him back to life, if everything would have wept.

CHRISTUS: What wouldn't weep?

LOKI: I wouldn't.

CHRISTUS: You'd rather lie with venom dripping on you?

LOKI: You choose to hang there on nails.

CHRISTUS: I think I must hang bloody on the tree till you start weeping.

LOKI: I think I must lie tearless in the earth till you stop hanging.

SIGYN: I think. . . my bowl is full. (*She darts away. LOKI writhes; there is rumbling earth-quake and darkness. LOKI fades out. The NUN is here.*)

CHRISTUS: And unto Enoch was born Irad; and Irad begat Mehujael, and Mehujael begat Methusael. . .and Seth. . .and Seth and Enos and. . . (*A sound of knocking on a door emerges from the quake rumble.*) Mother Thora, you are dreaming it again. If you keep dreaming him, he'll keep coming back. Over and over. . . the same knocking. All those years. . . (*He fades.*)

(*THORA's farm at Rimul. A summer afternoon, 995 A.D. Loud knocking. THORA, twenty-six hard years younger, opens the door [a rectangle of light]. HAAKON in a shaggy wolfskin, has knocked and turned to look back over his shoulder. The wolfskin head is over his hair like a hood. THORA has a spinner's stick [a distaff] in her hand and strikes the side of his head with it. With a roar of pain he spins and grabs her wrist.*)

THORA: Haakon! You! In that wolf's hide, I thought you were Karker. (*Silence. HAAKON holds her and stares.*) Now I'd almost think you were. . .

HAAKON: A ghost? I almost am.

THORA: A stranger. (*Clamping down on a nervous chuckle*) You look like a drowned otter.

HAAKON: You looked beautiful there, with your mouth open.

THORA: You startled ten years out of me.

HAAKON: Good. You knocked some twenty into me.

THORA: I've been having such dreams: I thought the gods were up in arms about some business, and it was *you* on the way here! I don't know why I laughed, except that you needn't look so ashamed to drop by. You always used to look so spruce when you came. Walk in, Haakon. Whatever ceremony you must stand on isn't at this threshold. (*He enters heavily, looks about and sits.*)

HAAKON: Dark in here.

THORA: You still know where the bench is. Did you feel the earth, how it shook this afternoon?

HAAKON: I was on horseback.

THORA: Just a tremor. A twitch. (*She begins to explain him to herself.*) So, there's a hunting party.

HAAKON: Yes.

THORA: You've ridden some poor horse to death, or nearly.

HAAKON: Nearly.

THORA: It's very far to my pastures—or it has been, this long time. (*She is getting a drinking horn.*) My household is away reaping, down beyond. I didn't go out; I was finishing a poem. It's just a flimsy twist of luck that I should be here. You almost make me believe in luck again.

HAAKON: Have you been luckless too?

THORA: I am here.

HAAKON: I could believe in luck—finding you this way.

THORA: (*She smiles, going out to get him a drink and continuing to talk from within. He peers about, hurriedly.*) You mean alone? Or just not murderous? (*She brings him the filled horn.*) The bounty of your humblest farm, Earl of Norway.

HAAKON: (*Calls*) Karker! In. (*KARKER enters in a fine blue cloak.*) Give me that back before she staves my skull in. (*He and KARKER exchange fur for linen, then KARKER bows curtly toward THORA who holds out the horn to HAAKON.*) Taste it. (*KARKER savors it and gives it back.*)

THORA: What kind of trick is that?

KARKER: Will I die?

    Thirsty and thankful's   the thrall with the horn,
    the lady allows him her   liquor and life.

HAAKON: Shut up. (*To empty space*) I am Earl of Norway.

THORA: (*She blazes.*) Shame! If you fear death so much, how mean your life must be! Did you come so far to fling one last insult it took your wits these years to think of?

HAAKON: Your tongue has not rusted, Thora. Whose whetstone have you had to grind it on since my days?

THORA: You were enough, Earl Haakon. The blade hasn't lost its temper. . . (*There are tears in her voice which she turns away furiously to shelter.*) till this moment. (*She looks at the drinking horn.*) It *is* poisoned, now! (*She seizes the horn and drains it.*) Let them bury us under the one mound! (*She turns on her heel and carries the horn from the room.*)

KARKER: (*He chants again, with a sing-song bravado*)

    Wrath rots the rafters   where flown love once roosted.

HAAKON: She doesn't like verse from you. (*Quietly*) And, no more talk of Queen Sigrid, either, not under this roof. (*He opens a drape and peers in where two gods stand on an altar. These are Frey and Freya; to a modern eye they would look like Giocometti statues; gaunt, anthropomorphic sticks.*)

KARKER: No cross there.

HAAKON: No ring. (*He frowns then calls to THORA.*) So you have missed our quarrels. I have. (*She's returned, wiping her hands, and gives him a scornful stare.*) That was stupid to say.

THORA: It was.

HAAKON: Get out, Karker.

THORA: (*As KARKER goes*) Thank you. Odin's Eye! I always hated that one! He came in your cloak last time, too.

HAAKON: It never hurts to be seen in one place when you are in another.

THORA: Can you wonder I struck you?

HAAKON: You poets are so jealous. Can't you bear that the gods send him a verse now and then?

THORA: (*With disdain*) If you really think he has gifts that way, it's unspeakable of you not to free him, Haakon.

HAAKON: I couldn't do without Karker. He can find a woman as a hound can find a grouse. . . anywhere! His nose alone is worth the trouble. Tall grass, dew, across water, dead frost. Oh come on, smile, I'm teasing. (*Nods toward the altar*) There used to be an Odin among your house-gods. Your father hung an offering-ring on it.

THORA: It came to me one day I didn't like that one. Too shifty. I threw him out.

HAAKON: Not lucky.

THORA: Who's to say? I had promised him a gift, if you should come that day and ah! there was the hoofbeat of your stallion galloping up to the yard—and it was Karker, in a cloak I'd sewed for you, sent to say you had other business. (*Grimly*) Odin made kindling.

HAAKON: But (*Nods toward the drape*) you kept the love gods.

THORA: I've no quarrel with them.

HAAKON: You *have* missed our quarrels.

THORA: Missed? The quarrels have never gone away. They are here. Three of them yonder by the bed, a dozen out in the yard, one by the pigsty. There's hardly elbow room around here. One on the roof. . .

HAAKON: (*Shakes his head, looking up.*) I did patch your roof once.

THORA: Shouting the name of a new mistress from my ridgepole! I pulled down your ladder.

HAAKON: Spiteful shrew! You swore you'd burn your house beneath me.

THORA: You bragged that you could piss it out.

HAAKON: (*Abruptly wearied of word-sparring, he tilts the horn.*) Well, no woman in the Northlands brews better ale.

THORA: Yes. You used to say I did two things to perfection. *Brewing* was one. (*Pause*) Haakon, we are talking again as if you'd been away. . . oh, a whole week or two long days, *hours* maybe! We should be strangers; I should ask how you have gotten on, inquire circumspectly about the latest bastards. . .

HAAKON: None lately. . .

THORA: And other signs of health, and you should lie that I
look younger than I did, and then (*Her mood darkening*) we'd
come to the gap of nothing left to say. Instead, we fly at each
other's throats like two ferrets. And that proves true a horrid
thing I lie nights, arguing with the dark, to believe is false!
That when we turned backs on each other, time began to balk.
It has not budged. There have been no years! Haakon, it is a
crime not named on your lawstones, to grow this much grayer
and not to have had those years! Those springs and winter
nights, squeezed flat as a toad in a wheel rut. I've felt it; not
like time to feel things, it has all been one shout in me, like a
shout in a well, sound and echoes at once, and the shout has
been "I'm not alive now! I'm a woman's image dangling in a
puddle no deeper than my toe." I think we have been
bewitched. Time won't budge! (*They're silent for an eerie pause
while time doesn't budge.*)
HAAKON: (*He finally shrugs in a savage, private gloom.*) It has for
me.
THORA: (*Quickly*) Then it has for me too! All I said just
now—it was lies, to flatter you a little! I'm content enough.
HAAKON: Help me, Thora. (*This directness surprises her.*) I have
come to you. . .
THORA: You really have. I've never spun myself more than a
miserly moment's thread of hope of your coming, even while I
knew you would. Now, I'm holding shut the gates that herds of
happiness are shouldering at, afraid I'll be trampled. Look,
here's something foolish. (*Holds up the distaff*)
HAAKON: A spinning distaff? To hit me with.
THORA: You threw this at me once. And I have used it as a
spell. Really. I sit to work and the household thinks the
mistress is tame for a while, I look innocent as a girl—how
innocent are girls, really?—but I've a spell-song that I have said
over and over till all the garments on the place have the words
in their weave.
HAAKON: What words?
THORA: No great poem.
HAAKON: What words?
THORA: Flaxen thread,   turn Haakon's head.

Thread of flax,	draw Haakon back.
Thread I spin,	reel Haakon in.
Flaxen thread,	alive or dead.

HAAKON: It sounds like a spell. (*He suddenly cocks a head at her.*) Is that why I'm here? A cloak you sent and your witch-craft? (*He fingers his cloak.*)

THORA: You must know why you're here. You're not afraid of spells. (*She shrugs.*) When we are young we all think we have powers. (*She tosses the distaff aside.*) Then, we put away childish things.

HAAKON: (*Sharply*) Where did you hear that?

THORA: I didn't hear it, I thought it.

HAAKON: No, you heard it said. Have your people here turned Christian, Thora?

THORA: (*Scornfully*) No! Oh, there was a priest here for a time last winter. He talked wonders. I sent him trudging, guest or no guest, after a while.

HAAKON: Sniffing out your father's lore and treasure rings? That would give them something to convert, the sly spoilers!

THORA: No. It was me he wanted for convert. You never noticed, but I am a poetess; I have my fame.

HAAKON: Yes. All the way in Sweden they're quoting your love poems—about me. At the court there.

THORA: (*Pleased*) How do you know? (*HAAKON tilts his head and taps his lips.*) The Christ's priest thought me worth the trouble of hunting down.

HAAKON: Did he bag you?

THORA: Pah! He shaved his head and was as smug about sleeping alone as you ever were about always sleeping double. *Then* he had a night with one of the women. Next day he made her think *she'd* seduced him and would burn! A Christ-priest's bread goes moldy like anyone's. But their wine is sweet. (*She goes to refill the horn.*)

HAAKON: How sweet?

THORA: Oh, it tempts! To chuck the bloody old gods into the coals and opt for one who loves the world. But, Christus-people don't love the world either.

HAAKON: Who could?

THORA: One girl, Kari, keeps a cross hidden away somewhere, but she knows I won't have it. A god that can't even put up with other gods will never stand for mere humans! We're too rank for him. Don't talk to me about the Christians!

HAAKON: What you said about children putting their toys away, was like a thing I heard from them.

THORA: Word goes they say their saying pretty freely in the town now. You will cast them out of the country one day.

HAAKON: Yes.

THORA: Till you do, come over to Rimul when you're sick of hearing them. If coming needs a reason. There are better ones you could find.

HAAKON: You are a witchwoman.

THORA: "Witch" or "bitch" they call us; both names end with the same itch.

HAAKON: (*Darkly*) I came this way with death's wings gliding behind my shoulder blades; I get here and suddenly we are in the midst of a lovesong.

THORA: I never said a word of love!

HAAKON: One of your lovesongs (*He takes her in his arms.*) and a truce, you bitch.

THORA: I never said. . .

HAAKON: You're right about the five years never happening.

THORA: Seven!

HAAKON: I could break out in mouths all over me and bite you from one end to the other at once, you with your spells and your voice that purrs in every sound I hear, you. . . Ow! (*She has bitten him bloodily in the neck.*)

THORA: I never said a word of love! (*She tastes the blood.*) Salty. Why did you break off wooing me?

HAAKON: I had an inkling, even then, you were a cannibal.

THORA: You are stronger than I am, you idiot! You would have had me on the floor in a minute. My teeth were all the weapon you left free. Why did you leave me?

HAAKON: I told you, Thora, then, told you blunt as lead: you loved the helm of Norway and not me.

THORA: The lamed, crazy, old excuse! You think you want a meek doll to fling on a bed or prop in a chair and count on to be very still when you're away.

HAAKON: Whoever prospered who shared power with a willful wife? Better a toy.

THORA: When you get yourself one, you stifle in yawns by the third morning. You've not remarried, not for years, though there've been plenty to pick, slack, limp and simple, even pretty when they catch a glint of you in their lack-luster eyes, prettier than I am, surely, and a few of them weren't even married! But here am I, the milk-maid of Rimul, and the Earl of Norway is afraid of me! I tell you, god of my soul, it makes no sense to say I love the helm, not you. You *are* the helm of Norway!

HAAKON: (*He turns away in passionate despair.*) If you weren't sun-blind with daydream, you would see it.

THORA: I see all I want to see when I see you.

HAAKON: Feed me, Thora. I'm hungry.

THORA: (*She gets bread.*) Not so slim of waist as once. Too many women feed you at command. Hungry troll! You boast that you've made love to half the women of Norway. . .

HAAKON: I boast nothing. . .

THORA: Karker boasts for you. And it's so near true there's no point counting, and you think its your hard sinew and a bear's hug that wins your victories in the bed chamber. It's not even that you never can meet a woman young or old without telling her how pretty she is. Huh! If that were all, some wench would have had her brothers kill you years ago.

HAAKON: (*Nods darkly.*) Yes. (*He eats, then looks up.*) What did make me love-lucky? You would know.

THORA: It is as plain as sunlight. You *talk* with a woman! Most men stare and nod and flatter us and all the while they're thinking about our breasts. But you *like* the women: when we speak, you hear us. You *listen*, Haakon. Any woman might throw herself down the pit of that kind of interest.

HAAKON: (*Nods*) Much wisdom among women!

THORA: (*Touching on a deep annoyance*) *Why* do you say so with such regret? (*He grunts.*) The riddle is easily answered. You are as greedy for wisdom as for gold. . .

HAAKON: I am not gold-greedy.

THORA: And for the same reason.

HAAKON: What's that?

THORA: Wisdom and gold are powers. You are no *miser*; you don't love gold for its own, and you are no *muser*; you don't love wisdom for its own. But you love whatever gives you mastery. You're so greedy for mastery that you forgot being Haakon.

HAAKON: Wrong, Thora!

(Simultaneous)

THORA: You shout against truth!   HAAKON: Wrong every way!

HAAKON: I am not greedy. When can they say I have not given my handfuls of gold at feasts? I'd give wisdom, too, if it were in my gift. But few are takers. Who can say I have misgoverned or been dangerous to any but my enemies?

THORA: Here is a new story!

HAAKON: Any but enemies! I schemed against those who schemed against me, no others.

THORA: Many the dead and gone might give witness against that, Haakon.

HAAKON: No ruler waits for the wolf to show him its back teeth. But when I've picked quarrels they were ripe. You understand these things. Your father here was almost fey with cleverness, and quick to strike, and he died old, rich, feared and honored. Life's much the same for a well-off farmer wizard and for an Earl. *(Grins)* And greed? Puh! *He* was the one singed his beard to fetch a goddess's gold ring from a burning temple, story has it.

THORA: But Father died laughing at the fox tricks he'd lived to play. Laughing, not brooding. Something's changed in you, Haakon. I never thought I would hear you weaving and twisting words to justify your ways! There's danger in such thinking. I have heard you say—and rejoiced to hear it—"I do what I do; my will is my way."

HAAKON: A boy's brag. Where's the. . .

THORA: Those were the first words I ever heard from your lips, Haakon, when your lips went naked of a beard, right at that gate, haranguing Father and twenty other homesteaders who griped over your cattle tax. *(She has opened a chest to exchange her heavy apron for a fine, tabard-like overdress.)* You were nineteen and I was. . . as old as I was, and seeing grand Earl Haakon for the first time with the sun frowning in the ice of your eyes. When you half turned your horse and looked at me, my heart gave a great bang against my ribs like a child when it quickens. And you stared so long that someone laughed. Thor and Freya, what things you dared in those days! No weighing then of rights and wrongs. Love and hate were your banners.

HAAKON: (*Flirtatious*) With the women, yes. (*He fingers her garment.*) You dress so fine. You fuddle us. Where's the ring now?

THORA: (*Ruefully*) Curious, isn't it? We're content to see our man dressed plain, or bare as a birch log,—though your sex is homely, isn't it, dangling there like a bit of ruptured gut? But the men look longest at girls when we're dyed and braided, smeared with colored grease and lacquer and wrapped to our ears in squanderous needlework. So who is the more frivolous?

HAAKON: (*Earnest again*) All I said was I've not been idly greedy. And I haven't.

THORA: You've not been idle. All *I said* was, don't begin now to tell yourself you've done no wrongs. Look your fact in the eye, for the sake of your own pride. . . and your life's sake, too.

HAAKON: My life?

THORA: Pretend you have been what you have not, and you lose your way in the forked paths. You will not know your friends when you need them! That's what these Christians do. They are so anxious to have done no wrongs, they lie in themselves till they lose all track. I have seen and scorn it. Here, you've ripped that, tidy man. (*She takes his cloak to sew up a small tear in it.*)

HAAKON: (*He rises.*) I don't pretend to have been better than I was! But, love affairs aside, women aside, name the man I have injured without cause.

THORA: Women aside! Lay women down or up but you can't lay us aside! Still, very well, suppose I name poor, good Olaf Trigvusson?

HAAKON: Olaf! (*He goes to the door and stares out. She sews.*)

THORA: Was I stepping on such a great corn in your toe, Haakon? (*She lifts the cloak to her nose and sniffs.*) You've been to the coast. Bedded down with some sea-maid in the kelp?

HAAKON: You know of Olaf?

THORA: (*Sewing*) The boy had prospects, and goods. You drove him into exile.

HAAKON: He went into England. . . I never hounded him.

THORA: You would have killed him, Haakon.

HAAKON: People lie.

THORA: Killed him as the tom-cat kills the tom-kitten—for looking at you. And you'd have been wise to, so he was wise to go.

HAAKON: It's a hearth story told to fan up ill will against me, Thora. You knew the boy; he may have been your lover for all I'll ever know. . .

THORA: You would have cared? I remember wondering that, for a few weeks; then I realized all your malice was just at his blood lines and an old claim to the throne. I wasn't in the business at all.

HAAKON: There were a dozen feuds against his household. *You* at least could do better by me than believe ill whispers.

THORA: He used to visit here just so the folk would know my father was his ally.

HAAKON: You'll say now he came just for that?

THORA: That and my stories. I am a poet.

HAAKON: Am I to be blamed if he took fright and sailed? You should know better. (*He stares out the door again.*)

THORA: I know well enough. It was I who warned him to leave Norway. (*HAAKON wheels and freezes. Her attention is on her sewing.*) In those days I knew your mind. Don't be jealous. What is Olaf to me now? Or to you? If the ill-will of grumblers in chimney-nooks has troubled you, think how much louder *the* noise would be if you had set sword to his neck! I *helped* you, Haakon! More often than you know. (*A dry, deadly laugh escapes him; still he does not move.*) I did! And in more ways! If you had used brains and married me, how much more still I would have helped you! You'd have prospered with *this* willful wife! You wouldn't be wandering back to old flames, dark with gloom and cold in the prime of your life, muttering about death coming up behind your back, and bitter gossip buzzing from farm to farm like the bot fly. Let's not talk of this. (*Done sewing, she turns to him.*) Thread of flax, bring Haakon back. Even if the threads are gray! You've come to

Rimul and as long as you stay, be it hour, week or a winter, when I set arms around you, I hold all Norway and mortal Earth. (*She moves to embrace him.*)

HAAKON: You hold nothing, Thora. The landholders have rebelled, to the last man. They're hunting me down like a rogue boar. Olaf Trigvusson has come back for his lands. (*With biting irony*) Oh, you helped. . . Make one of your sagas of that! It's a good twist for a story!

THORA: And you. . . lied this half hour. . !

HAAKON: Anger, Thora?

THORA: . . .talking as if nothing were wrong! Lied to me! You false cur!

HAAKON: I wondered if the fugitive would be as welcome as the Earl. Now you know something new about your heart, how it fries. I'm not alone in loving power, am I? Nothing fails like a failing man. I never lied to you. . .

THORA: But you didn't *tell*. . !

HAAKON: . . .and you were so busy filling my horn with wisdom you'd stored for me, you never heard a thing I wanted to say! Any man can be love-lucky with a crown on. Well, when Olaf comes tonight on my trail, sleep with him for me, will you? Pen him up for a few hours.

THORA: (*She almost shrieks.*) Haakon! Hold your tongue, before you say more than you can ever take back. Yes, I was angry—stunned you hadn't told when you first came in. That you would not have trusted me. . . Having Karker taste for poison was no mere malice. You meant it!

HAAKON: Trusted the woman they'll call "Thora Olaf's-Rescue"?

THORA: You tricked me into telling that!

HAAKON: Did not! (*He studies her.*) I am trusting you at last. Will you help me?

THORA: Like your own hand, your own eye.

HAAKON: Should I trust what I saw in your eye when I told you I was a fugitive? Karker told me be wary.

THORA: You saw pain ! What would you have wanted, glee?

HAAKON: It may be. If you love me all you say, you would be thinking: "Here at last is the man helpless, and I can help him!" That would be a kind of glee, maybe.

THORA: (*A pause*) Yes, it could be.

HAAKON: Instead of recoiling from me as from a broken snake because suddenly I am weak.

THORA: Stop it!

HAAKON: Yes, I had better.

THORA: In all your life did you ever trust anyone, whole-heart?

HAAKON: Myself. . . at times. And Karker.

THORA: And your shadow, Karker! Because he's so low he looks up at you even when you're sprawled flat. Didn't you ever dare hope someone might be loyal whether you were weak or strong, sick or hale, ruler or outlaw? You might have more pride than to settle for a lying sneak that crawls the ground. And speaks ill against me!

HAAKON: Crawl the ground is what shadows do. Why trouble to hate him so? You thought him great for joke once. A thrall can't choose for himself, neither can nor has to, not as we do. We have our wills, Thora, and our great names. A Karker has just his master.

THORA: Yes. Half the women are like that. Women with no honor in themselves at all, only in their men.

HAAKON: And you ask why I didn't trust you. . .

THORA: (*Driving through his words*) And they grow into sneaks and liars too, such women, having no claim on their own wills. It's the old quarrel between us: you think you want a thrall, or a broken mare. But it is me you come back to, desperate.

HAAKON: (*With grim humor*) Any harbor in storm.

THORA: I am glad you dare insult me!

HAAKON: (*Nods*) You wouldn't want me to come cringing.

THORA: No. (*They kiss.*) You are here. (*Suddenly practical*) Your son. Is Egil safe out of this?

HAAKON: (*Masked*) Safe out. You never spoke of him. Ever. Oh, once, I guess, you said "pale pig" or some such . . .

THORA: You gave him the wrong mother, Haakon. No matter now.

HAAKON: No, no matter.

THORA: As long as they have no hostage. . . you're safe here. (*She kisses him again.*)

HAAKON: The boy is dead. Back by the sea. Where Olaf landed.

THORA: Oh. That's a dark thing. May gods make welcome for kin of Haakon.

HAAKON: You do feel glee, spider!

THORA: Careful, Haakon, not to drive me mad. (*HAAKON goes again to look out the door.*) Where are you going?

HAAKON: Out to where I can watch the road up the dale. Karker must eat too. Fill his belly. It's been two days and nights of over crag and down for us. We're headed to Sweden. (*He goes.*)

THORA: Trust in me. (*She opens a curtain upon the statues of Frey and Freya, She pours ale into a trough before them.*)

Frey and Freya   feast full with offerings
     Glad be the hearts of the gods on high.
Strong be the snare   and sound the love-knot
     Deep the horn of the headstrong mead.
Sweet be your bed   and softly strewn
     Long be the love-sleep and late come morning,
Heavy the thigh   that heaves over thigh;
     Frey and Freya, feast of the offering.

(*Outside,* KARKER, *with one bare foot, has stolen an egg, and eats it raw with the relish of hunger.* KARI *steals up on him, grinning.*)

KARI: Whoo! (*She laughs at* KARKER's *alert wheel toward her.*)

KARKER: Come here. I haven't touched a woman in three months.

KARI: So?

KARKER: Keep out of sight. They think everyone's down haying.

KARI: I happened back.

KARKER: Me too. I thank Frey. I thank Freya.

KARI: You stole an egg of us.

KARKER: I can reach under a hen so soft she'll never cluck. (*He winks.*) Or knit herbs to make the cattle breed off season.

KARI: (*She considers this and nods slowly.*) Some are handy with beasts. Come see. There's piglets. New.

KARKER: I want the sow herself.

KARI: (*Fending him off*) Filthy. Someone will see us.

KARKER: They're at their own games, inside.

KARI: Earl Haakon's in there? He made you come so far hungry? (*KARKER nods.*) He is crazy, isn't he, with his gadding up and down ?

KARKER: (*Jauntily*) Yes, he's crazy. Your lady's the same. They're all nit-witted as gnats in a thaw. Know why? Because of us! We find their food; we make camp so they'll sleep snug. Get 'em rich enough, grand and hapless enough and they lose all track of how life gets by. Like little pink fingered babies, little fubsy lambs that suck your finger for a teat when you dip it in milk. (*She smiles; he charms her with his talk.*) The mutton-heads think: "Poor simple Karker, how he sweats and frets for bread and ox-hide." They've their more swaggering things to comb their brains about. Piggyback of our other jobs, we have to clown for them. (*He makes a face, she giggles.*) "Oh my Master! Oh my, oh my!" If they didn't laugh now and again, they'd never notice anything. They'd run so high-and-helpless mad we couldn't get their bacon asses from saddle to bed and back!

KARI: (*Gaily*) You talk terrible. . . (*More seriously, with a shrug*) You want them to cook porridge for you and dig turf? They run things.

KARKER: Don't they just!—more the pity, eh? Being boss is wormwood. It sweet-rots their pretty heads. Everyone knows it, deep down. That's why all this ache to put some god in charge, instead of people.

KARI: (*Pulls back and crosses herself.*) That's bad talk. That's wicked talk. That's shame.

KARKER: (*He points to his mouth and kisses the tip of his finger.*) Stop my mouth.

KARI: Someone will be angry.

KARKER: You've got a man now? (*KARI smiles wistfully.*) Who?

KARI: I just had to say hello to you. Seeing you here, alone.

KARKER: Like three years ago.

KARI: Longer.

KARKER: You haven't forgotten it. Come down into the cave. It was hereabouts.

KARI: It's under the sty now. The stone trough lies over its mouth.

KARKER: The better to keep secrets.

KARI: It's welcome to them. It was a bad place.

KARKER: You were good to me. I was good to you.

KARI: I was bad. You've walked that boot to pieces. Your poor foot will be in sad shape before you're home.

KARKER: (*He peers at her, head to one side, mouth a bit open; perhaps he is near-sighted.*) You do have a man. I can smell him. Next time I come by, he and I'll fight. Today there's no time.

KARI: Shh! You think it's a man, but it isn't. He's a god. (*From her bodice she draws a crucifix and shows it.*) See. It's a god; it's even three gods.

KARKER: You're lying? (*KARI shakes her head.*) You're teasing me? (*She shakes her head.*) You're crazy.

KARI: He can hear us. He hears everything everyone says.

KARKER: (*Without irony*) Tiresome for him.

KARI: He suffers a lot.

KARKER: Why?

KARI: I don't know. Just touch. He is very strong.

KARKER: Away south, he has half the women of the towns. He could spare me you. (*KARI pulls off her headcloth; her hair is cropped.*) What have they done to your hair?

KARI: I cut it myself—for him. So the men wouldn't like me anymore that way.

KARKER: Does he like you, cropped like that?

KARI: (*She bites her lip and looks at the crucifix.*) I hope he does. He does.

KARKER: (*He wraps the crucifix in her headcloth, then sets it gingerly on the ground.*) Now I think he can't hear so well, I bet. (*He touches her hair.*) It's too bad. Too bad. And they built a sty over our little snug-hole! (*He suddenly grows shrewd.*) Oho! Is the mistress here bowing to this Christus now?

KARI: No.

KARKER: (*Disappointed*) So much the better for her.

KARI: There was a great priest snowed in with us last winter; she made much of him for a whole month, and listened; we had hopes for her. But they had a row and it was my fault, I was bad. She liked his talk and could have been saved. But in the end she mocked him till he cursed her and left us. (*Dreamy greed*) I haven't eaten god once since.

KARKER: Eh? Oh, that. It's just a bit of bread they give you.

KARI: Oh, but the priest lays a spell on it and. . . it tastes so good! So good!

KARKER: I guess you turned Christian for the God's bread?

KARI: It's cause enough, if you only knew. But that wasn't why.

KARKER: (*He touches her lips.*) Little greedy red mouth. . .

KARI: You asked once how I came by the scar. . . there? (*She touches her breast.*) I wouldn't tell. Now I will. The Death Mother cut me.

KARKER: (*Awed, he grunts.*) Hu! (*Mystified*) But, didn't kill you?

KARI: It was when the old man died here. They had a real burial, Odin's feast and all. The Death Mother who lives up beyond Hymirsdale was sent for and came. We cast lots on her cloak, and it was me who was to go down under with the old man. All day they tried to make me drunk enough to go quiet, but at nightfall when she came to me with her knife I cried and cried, and gave such a leap back when she slashed at me, she missed my throat and only took me in the breast. Then the mistress stopped her.

KARKER: Thora did? You're sure she's no Christian? I'd a feel she'd turn one day. (*He taps his forehead.*) It comes to me to know.

KARI: Sure as sure? I pray and pray she'll turn, that's my dear wish. But her heart's so hard, you see. She only stopped the Death Mother because she didn't like my screaming.

KARKER: (*Nods*) Some call it unlucky when the goer screams too much. Up our way, all the people shout till the one who has to go is gone, so nobody hears.

KARI: Thora said the old man would find enough women down in Hella's Hall, and they were to let me go. I still cry at sundown, often as not—until I pray and Christ says it's all right. I cried all that summer. (*She laughs plaintively.*)

KARKER: (*Shrugs*) It has to be somebody. Many a sickness gives a worse death.

KARI: They don't cut you men's throats.

KARKER: Killing is killing. They hang us.

KARI: Only once in a great while.

KARKER: It only takes once! (*Grins*) Still, who knows but there's some fun, dying with a hard-on.

KARI: Shame on your foul mouth! When I found out Jesus takes no sacrifices, (*She unwraps the crucifix.*) I turned Christian.

KARKER: None?

KARI: "Thou shalt not kill." They don't sacrifice people, even beasts; fish not even. Just bread and a little drink.

KARKER: I think. . . what's your name, woman?

KARI: Kari. You forgot?

KARKER: You only told me one time. Kari, I think they lied to you. No gods don't take sacrifice. It's what a god is. Look at the piglets there. They think we're never going to eat them. They think we slop them and build sty for them for nothing. For love. Because we scratch the sow by the ear and call them names, we're just like gods to them.

KARI: That's wicked talk! You're smart but that's all twisted wrong. You know about dumb beasts, but you don't know anything about Jesus.

KARKER: I know he's trouble. There's an army raising to bring him into Norway and to drive out Haakon. Wives and mothers are pressing their crosses on the fighters' spears for blessing-luck, and none are saying "Thou shalt not kill." A Christian will knock me dead as soon as another man.

KARI: Warring is different.

KARKER: I'll say different. Some talk as though they liked it. Me, I'd rather run, or swim, or dig, or anything.

KARI: You've run your boot off.

KARKER: So she buried all the old man's goods with him? His holy things?

KARI: She kept it all, in the barred chest. All he took down with him was a yoke of oxen and a cauldron and. . . he was to take me.

KARKER: Kari, dear little Kari. Would you steal a ring out of that chest for me? If it was for my life?

KARI: I can't steal gold!

HAAKON'S VOICE: Hi! Karker! (*The call is pitched low, not to carry far.*)

KARKER: Oh, for shit! Now hide. If he knows you're around, that will be bad.

KARI: That's the Earl?

KARKER: Don't you go running off to tell. Listen. If you do, I'll die. And come haunt you and your Christus too. If you don't, I'll come back and you'll be my wife one day. Is that a bargain?

KARI: Why stick by Haakon? If the folk have risen against him, his luck is over.

KARKER: No. The High Ones owe him one more victory. A week ago, on Tronder Isle, we were trapped, surrounded, and in the night a bright one came that told me Haakon had to send his son to Odin. Haakon sent him. A man who'd do that won't be beaten, will he? A blind fog and a low tide came. We got off Tronder walking through the midst of them.

HAAKON'S VOICE: Karker! Troll take you!

KARKER: I'll be back. Don't tell on us; swear on your Jesus' cross, to give us a day's start. Queen Sigrid is in Sweden. She'll help us.

KARI: (*She nods.*) And don't tell I saw you. You swear too!

KARKER: By Thor's Hammer. (*He starts to go, then looks back, quizzically.*) We're each laying our life on the other's God.

KARI: (*Mournfully*) It's no good. Thor is false!

KARKER: Here's a leaf: chew it and all day you can't die. It works, but only once. (*Chewing the leaf, KARI picks up his torn boot.*) Now listen. In the chest. . .

HAAKON'S VOICE: Karker!

KARI: (*She pulls the leaf from her mouth and holds it out to KARKER.*) You need it most.

KARKER: I gave it to you.

KARI: Jesus protect you for it! (*She offers him her cross.*) This works too.

KARKER: I'm not proud, if it gets me away. (*KARI flees. KARKER tucks the cross in his tunic.*)

HAAKON'S VOICE: You crow bait! Where..?

KARKER: A fellow can step around the wall to make water, can't he?

HAAKON: (*Enters*) For half an hour?

KARKER: I see Queen Sigrid   smiling our welcome.
                 Gold I see going   from grasp to grasp
                 Sigrid the Haughty   hungry for hoard-metal.
                 Let the poetess lend   a last line to the verse.

HAAKON: What does that mean?

KARKER: The good gold ring the old man here got out of the fire when Njord's temple burnt. Thora has it in a chest. I know now. (*He taps his forehead.*) It came to me to know it. (*HAAKON seizes KARKER and drags him off. KARI slips into view and stares after them, then down at the ruined boot which she is still holding.*)

KARI: Is it wrong, Lord, when it's man and wife? He would be good to me, I think, if the Earl was gone. Sometimes I can't help what I think, Ourfatherwhoartinheaven, sometimes I can't. (*She goes.*)

(*Inside the house, THORA lays food on the table and calls curtly.*)

THORA: Karker. Eat.

KARKER: (*Enters*) I'll take it outside.

THORA: Sit to the table. Your master wants to be alone for a bit. (*When KARKER glances up at this, THORA flares.*) Don't you dare grin with your pig's eyes at me, Karker Haakonsthrall! It's not me he's taken sick of, it's himself. (*KARKER eats. THORA watches him.*) I wonder if I have to thank you, Karker?

KARKER: (*He grins.*) For not telling about the last time I was here? (*With a mouthful*) Life is sweet.

THORA: Hold your tongue!

KARKER: I'm good at that.

THORA: Do I thank you for his coming? Did he turn to Rimul of his own?

KARKER: I just follow. (*THORA waits. KARKER eats.*)

THORA: Are they far behind? (*KARKER shrugs.*) Answer me.

KARKER: We led them fox-wise

THORA: How so? (*She sits opposite him.*)

KARKER: At Hlidderend yesterday morning we took horses. They belong to a landholder, over behind Raven's Ridge.

THORA: Mord Coldfoot's matched mares! I can't imagine him giving Haakon help!

KARKER: I didn't say he gave, I said we took. Olaf and all are following with dogs. Down ten mile or so the way forks. The trees hang thick and we swung into the branches. Those mares know the road to their own yard.

THORA: I'd give coined silver to see Olaf's coming to Mord's farm.

KARKER: It's a good fetch. If it works.

THORA: If? (*Smiles*) Then it wasn't you who thought of it.

KARKER: Not me who thought to do it near this gate.

THORA: (*She rises.*) Who else can help Haakon as I can? Who would?

KARKER: His legs. (*This next is a plea.*) We can be half over into Sweden by dawn.

THORA: Haakon stays tonight! (*KARKER throws down the bone he's been gnawing, stubborn and disapproving.*)

KARKER: You have too many people here. You want to save him, but will you bet his life on their closed mouths?

THORA: You might understand loyalty.

KARKER: They're Christians, some! With Haakon's head in trade, they'll buy their way out of the Hell they talk such dread of! They think . . . (*KARKER rummages fiercely for how to make this plain.*) they get forgiven anything they'll do. . . so, they'll do anything!

THORA: It's true enough. A God's a very great matter, but religion brings folk to mischief. We can't live up to it; we get it wrong and nasty.

KARKER: You say so; I've seen so. Master and I will jog. (*He peers with a crooked smile.*) You leave it to me to see he never starves in the wide world.

THORA: My people won't know you're here.

KARKER: (*Grunts*) Not if we leave right off. (*He rises.*) Thanks for the pork, woman. If you were rich, you'd give him travel gifts, I guess. But a woman alone, I think, is right to be thrifty-mean . . .

THORA: Mean! Take care. I will be your master's housewife yet — not early, but late. He has not forgotten me.

KARKER: I guess you took care to be in his mind, this month. (*He starts to go.*)

THORA: How so?

KARKER: Gudrun of Lundar gave him your message.

THORA: I sent no message. Stop talking riddles, Karker.

KARKER: She told him what you wanted her to say.

THORA: I never laid eyes on Gudrun of Lundar. Is she his latest?

KARKER: Ask *him*.

THORA: I will. I'll say you were joking about Gudrun. Now, tell.

KARKER: He saw her at the midsummer assembly. So, he sent a band of us to their place, to bring Gudrun away to him.

THORA: Harpers call her the sunlight of Lundar. She's grown up beautiful as word says?

KARKER: Word says she has.

THORA: You've seen her.

KARKER: I'm nearsighted, around freeborn women. Do you see a thrall?

THORA: A dead one. So what happened at Gudrun's house?

KARKER: While they fed us her husband sent out to the households all around. When we were done drinking, the dooryard was full of armed men. They drove us off, and the last Gudrun said was, "Say if Earl Haakon wants me, he must send Thora of Rimul to ask for me."

THORA: Glib-tongued bitch! (*She chuckles.*) They will be laughing at that in all corners of Norway. Haakon was in a great rage when I called him love-lucky. Did you put it in his mind *I* told her to say that?

KARKER: I put nothing in his mind. He never stands for a word against you, now or ever. (*Head on one side.*) I guess you are good to him as you can afford to be.

THORA: Is this revolt for Gudrun of Lundar?

KARKER: She was the spark that burned the house.

THORA: The better hope then! A pretty woman is a battle banner that soon fades.

KARKER: It will keep the dye long enough to do in Haakon. I've had bad dreams. And I dream true.

THORA: What dreams?

KARKER: Litters of them. (*He glares into space.*) Haakon has hold of a thread's chance at life, if he gets far fast. (*He starts to the door, then suddenly turns.*) "I have a chance at life if he stays here," you say.

THORA: (*Startled*) I didn't say that!

KARKER: (*He tugs his ear and winks.*) But I heard. You said it in heart.

THORA: Get out of here. Weasel or wizard. Go!

KARKER: I've been asking for that. We've eaten; we'll set off. (*He turns with the odd, bright, cringing smile he used before.*) Haakon will come to the Swedes poor as a vole, but he'll come there. . . thanks to you or no.

THORA: Thrall, what is it you want me to give?

HAAKON: (*He enters, smug.*) They have passed us by! The sunset's glinting on their spears way over on Raven Ridge!

THORA: You still have a falcon's eyes. So, I'm saved a trouble. I won't have to sleep with Olaf for you.

HAAKON: Thor's Thunder, witch!

THORA: You are merry, my Earl.

HAAKON: (*He slaps KARKER's back.*) Clever fox!

THORA: Many a thief's trick under that moldy thatch.

HAAKON: Name your wish!

KARKER: Us to be off and away.

HAAKON: Put bread in a sack, Thora. Enough so we needn't to stop under a roof till we are in Sweden.

THORA: See? He tells you when to come and go. Always. You sought me for safety and I will keep you safe! Or is Karker master and Haakon the thrall?

KARKER: Do you want him dead?

THORA: I spoke to Haakon, not to you, old man.

HAAKON: Old? Karker and I were born in the one night.

KARKER: And neither to live long past the other.

THORA: It makes you a good living to have him believe that!

HAAKON: Twilight already falls early: we'll travel the safer at dusk.

THORA: Go stand your guard outside.

KARKER: It's too warm here. This room smells of bed. (*To HAAKON*) May you get what you came for. (*He goes.*)

THORA: (*After a pause*) You came to me. Nothing else is any great matter. (*She touches his hands.*) I wish it were spring. I'd strew the floor all white with apple petals, starry quince, mayflowers, nectar-wet that drag the nuzzler bees from hive-drowse. . .

HAAKON: (*With a throaty laugh like a growl*) Ah, here's my ripe, full Queen. My cup of curds!

THORA: (*She opens the drape on her gods.*) Frey and Freya, feast full of offerings. (*Looks up.*) Can we still make that roofbeam shake, do you think?

HAAKON: If we are any older, so is it. You dress . . . (*Lifting the tabard off her slowly, ceremonially.*) . . . so fine. It's wading through a gem-smith's treasure, to get at you. Put aside the gold and wire-work. (*Loosening her hair*) Find the gold in gold. . .

THORA: (*She drops his heavy belt and sword to the floor.*) It's blundering through an iron smithy by night, to get at you.

HAAKON: (*Caressing*) Careful, the iron's hot. (*He chuckles.*) Karker works fast.

THORA: (*Suddenly ice-bound*) What does that mean?

HAAKON: Fennel and a woodcock feather. He threw a breeding spell across us. Feel the gust? High flood and river spate. . . (*She recoils.*)

THORA: Then damn your river!

HAAKON: Thor — a!

THORA: No!

HAAKON: Thora!

THORA: No! I don't fall into rut because that breeze-fly buzzed at me! No!

HAAKON: Why, you cantankerous, lip-blistering she-weasel! (*He whirls to the mute gods, pointing at THORA.*) May she be set to suckling leeches under Hell's eaves seven summers, and up to her crotch in wasps! She mocks you!

THORA: There's a cow in the tie-up if you're all that frantic.

HAAKON: You want me!

THORA: Karker turns you loose on me so you'll have your fill and set off sooner!

HAAKON: That's not . . .

THORA: And if you think it, it's just as hateful to me as if it's true! (*In ironic fury she shakes a fist at the altar.*) Some god make me numb enough to be a Christian, and shut safe away from you all!

HAAKON: What is this venom you're so swelled with against Karker? Time was you used to laugh and call him Loki.

THORA: Hear a tale. When time was young, Odin thought malice and trouble were the salt and mint of life. He swore brothers with Loki. Then when the Great Twilight falls, Loki betrays Odin. Karker is your Loki.

HAAKON: He's just a thrall.

THORA: You believe his spells. It makes you a great excuse for falling into every bed you come across, doesn't it? Fagh! He's your shifty shadow, Haakon! Three years ago, when I asked you to come and you sent Karker. I sank low. I almost. . . (*No words come.*)

HAAKON: Did away with him? So he said.

THORA: I didn't do you that favor. You know, over and over I dream of the two of you fallen into a pit with a tide roaring in, I call "Kill him, Haakon, or he kills you!" And I see he has poured beeswax in your ears.

HAAKON: Do you dream true, Thora? Karker does, always.

THORA: No one does; not so you can count on it. We want too much and we hate too much to dream true, and the shapes juggle and blur in us till there's no knowing. I dream you. Oh, some nights I see gods stride the rainbridge or walk up out of post holes or some daft place and I hear them wrangle . . . it made a poetess of me, but not a prophetess. Prophets can't keep from lying; ask a so-called wizard's daughter. They end up boasting they can cast spells and pass through walls. And fools believe.

HAAKON: Karker dreams true. I'm alive to tell you so.

THORA: Karker! Driving you from woman to woman, up and down Norway like the district bull, all so that no one, no one but him, shall really have hold on you! Even that first morning, years back, in the dooryard, it was Karker, by your stirrup among the farmers: he nudged your shin and nodded toward me — and you looked.

THORA: I saw ! You didn't   HAAKON: He never did!
even know it, but he did.

HAAKON: Is *that* your maggot? Thora, I'd have had my
women, all and each, if there'd never been a Karker. (*He
points to the Frey and Freya.*) There's them!

THORA: But they are two! Didn't you ever notice? Not Frey
and a dozen Freyas or a hundred. Two.

HAAKON: You always liked me bold. A man's eye ranges and
flesh follows if it dares. The plain truth is that the man who
settles for one woman is just too much a coward to seek more.

THORA: No, Haakon. A man who settles for a rout of women is
just too cowardly to keep with one.

HAAKON: "Cowardly"?

THORA: He fears one woman knows him, he shies off to the
next. Father had a saying: "Ranger is a great hound, but Long-
Gripper is greater." (*Levelly.*) In real love, you're still a virgin!
Bone-deep, lifetime lovers aren't fishing towns you burn
through once on a Viking raid, Haakon, they are each other's
kingdoms, to claim and hold!

HAAKON: Not wise to talk to me of kingdoms, Thora. Not
today. I'm fresh out of them. (*Walks away.*)

THORA: (*Watching him with chill compassion.*) Your people
thought it a lucky thing to raise you with a thrall at your side,
and he shared with you all the tricks of the houseless cur, and
now (*She weighs whether to say this, then does.*) you're hated so
for stealing wives . . . you've lost your realm.

HAAKON: Thora, no need to chew at me; it's been done for you.
(*Suddenly he is alert.*) Quiet! There's hoofbeats. Sorry, Thora,
there'll be blood in your clean house!

THORA: I will hide you! I will. I thank Frey, I thank Freya!
No one will ever call me Thora "Olaf's-Rescue" but they'll one
day call me "Haakon's-Rescue"!

HAAKON: I knew I loved you for good reason, girl! (*About to
take her in his arms, he halts.*) Listen! (*Puzzled*) That's not willful
riding.

THORA: Stand in the shadow. (*She opens the door and looks out.*)
A riderless mare. It's walking up to Karker. (*A whinny is
heard.*) Coldfoot's mare!

HAAKON: There was never a beast but loved Karker. But she has made a trail to us.

THORA: So Karker's wins! (*Bitterly*) He called it somehow.

HAAKON: (*He looks out and gasps, staggered.*) Troll take me!

THORA: What is it? What Haakon? (*No response.*) Speak.

HAAKON: Egil.

THORA: Who?

HAAKON: The boy. Just now . . . just then, I saw him. Leading the mare.

THORA: (*After a horrified pause, THORA helps HAAKON to sit.*) It could be a luck-sight. It could!

HAAKON: Not luck. We were trapped, Thora, in a hole in the sea rocks, Olaf's crew camped all around us. Certain to be captured, and knowing what they'd do. I gave him a death. And he didn't take it . . . well. He's brought the mare on my trail.

THORA: Oh Haakon! You did him kindness.

HAAKON: But, we *weren't* captured. Yes, it's a dark thing.

THORA: My love. My love. Now I think this world has done it's worst to you. I grieve. Now you must go.

HAAKON: Soon. We'll breathe a few deep breaths. Put your arms around me for a while and say good-bye.

THORA: (*Stricken.*) Oh hush! (*Tearful.*) That's what life is, that wise beasts know: arms around a while and then good-bye.

HAAKON: Wild beasts don't cry and laugh. Why do we?

THORA: Because on this earth we're outlanders, Haakon.

HAAKON: Outlanders?

THORA: From away somewhere , we come with a sense for what's right and what isn't, and in a world that doesn't care about that, we're anxious, and we cry. We come with a sense for what's reasonable and what isn't, but in a life that gives no reasons, we feel absurd, and we laugh.

HAAKON: Where did we pick up this outland itch to have things be fair, or to make sense? Among gods?

THORA: Who knows. (*Pause.*) The bed's still there behind the hangings.

HAAKON: If I'm a virgin, I'll ask a great love-gift of you; I warn you fairly.

THORA: You give me that virginity I spoke of, and ask whatever! Come.

CHRISTUS glimmers into view. THORA and HAAKON pause at their exit, not noticing him.

CHRISTUS: Let someone sinless shy the first rock! (*He closes his eyes and chants.*) And Abimelech begat Amoni and Amoni begat sons, Bildah and Mog, and Mog upon Ruache begat . . . be . . . This is too long. I thirst.

ACT II

(*LOKI and the CHRISTUS, each at his own pains. SIGYN attends to the drip of venom.*)

(*Simultaneous*)

LOKI: . . . and Nifflheim spawned Aurgelmir, whence Ymir and the cow Audhumla, whence came Buri, whose son Borr, with Bestla, daughter of Bolthorn, fathered Odin, Vili and Ve. Birgelmir, who survived the flood of Ymir's blood . . .

CHRISTUS: . . Phares and Zara and Tharmar; and Phares begat Ezrom; and Ezrom begat Salmon, and Salmon begat Booz of Rachab and Booz begat Obed of Ruth whom he found gleaning. And Obed begat Jesse and Jesse begat Daud the King, and Daud . . . Quiet!

LOKI: It was working.

CHRISTUS: Hear that noise? Like surf.

LOKI: Is that. . . your Judgment Day?

CHRISTUS: I judge not. (*LOKI cocks his head and peers up to see if this was wordplay on CHRISTUS' part. It wasn't.*) Is it earthquake again?

LOKI: Not. . . my fault. (*He chuckles and glances again to see if CHRISTUS appreciates wordplay from others. He doesn't.*)

SIGYN: (*As the roar rises and becomes more distinct*) Men's cries.

LOKI: Battle.

CHRISTUS: Again?

SIGYN: It is your armies, Lord. All yours now.

LOKI: Trampling the vineyards. One whiff of us and they're like dogs in heat. Scent of a god gets them so riled and frantic they start killing. Worse for them than women or beer, aren't we? (*SIGYN and LOKI vanish at an angry gesture from CHRISTUS.*)

CHRISTUS: (*Anguished*) ". . .and he was clothed in a vesture dipped in blood, and his name is called the Word of God. And the armies of Heaven followed him upon white horses. . . and out of his mouth goeth a sword that with it he should smite the nations. Fowls that fly, come gather unto the supper of God, that ye may eat the flesh of kings, the flesh of captains. . ."

(*Wearily*) I thirst. (*His light begins to dim.*) We are just where
we were.

(*We are as we were at the end of the First Act.*)
THORA: The bed is still there behind the hangings.
HAAKON: (*Chuckles*) If I'm the virgin you called me, I'll ask a
great love-gift of you; I warn you fairly.
THORA: Give me that virginity I spoke of, and ask whatever.
Come. (*She throws open the bedchamber door drape, and discovers
KARI standing terrified, a pair of boots in hand.*) What are you
doing there, you calf-brained sneak?
HAAKON: (*Deadly*) You said the house was empty.
(Simultaneous)

THORA: It was! It should have been.   KARI: I only wanted. . .
THORA: What? To spy for your Christians? (*THORA pulls her
into the light.*)
KARI: I only wanted. . .
HAAKON: (*Calls at the outer door*) Karker! A throat here needs
cutting. (*KARKER strides in; HAAKON points.*) Work for you.
(*KARI drops what she has stolen.*)
THORA: You have been in father's strong-chest!
HAAKON: The *chest*, has she! (*With a reach of hand he stops
KARKER.*)
THORA: Father's boots!
KARI: I wanted them for. . .
THORA: For Haakon?
KARI: For Karker. To get away far in.
THORA: No boots on the whole farm, but you must filtch from
Father's chest?
KARI: He knew the witchcraft, Karker. In these he went to
places, through boards, over water, at will.
THORA: (*Caught by this, she almost laughs, despite her outrage.*)
That they still think?
KARI: (*Quietly*) Lady, we know.
THORA: What?
KARI: He had demons at call. I saw it once. He put on the boots
and stood praying to. . . them there. (*She indicates Frey and
Freya.*) I was by the doorway, hackling flax, then. . . crack!
There was a noise, I looked and he was gone and the gods were

shaking. The house was empty. After a span a cat might eat a sparrow in, there he was walking, out beyond the pigsty. The mud on the boots was yellow. There's no yellow mud hereabout till you come to the River Rang and that's nine miles.

HAAKON: (*Picks up the boots*) If a man knew the knack to make them walk. . !

KARI: They were for Karker. . . he'll know. (*THORA exasperates.*)

HAAKON: (*After a bit, he grins.*) She's an ally. (*Tosses the boots to KARKER.*) Take your love gifts, thrall. I like women who risk to give grandly.

THORA: (*With shrewd malice*) How did you know Karker needed boots? Kari?

KARI: His foot's bloody. He asked for. . . what I can't give any more. I couldn't refuse him footgear.

THORA: You told him you were Christian? (*KARI nods.*) Haakon's wiser now about his Karker's loyalty! A Christian, half-wit talked here with your thrall, he knew what she was, and risked your death.

(*Simultaneous*)

KARI: I didn't mean he. . .   HAAKON: Don't, Thora!

KARKER: She won't betray. . .

THORA: (*Her voice rises over all of them.*) You were ready to kill one of my people as coolly as you'd slaughter a calf . I'll give little Kari a knife and tell her (*Points at KARKER*) there's a throat there wants cutting.

HAAKON: Troll take you, Karker! And you too, Thora! You want my last friend turned enemy!

KARKER: It can be settled quick. (*With knife drawn he steps toward KARI, who opens her mouth but no sound comes.*)

THORA: (*Between KARKER and KARI.*) Drop your busy knife! Drop it. (*KARKER looks at HAAKON, who nods. He drops his knife.*) Now Kari knows something about her lover too. (*To her*) Twice I've spared you, I can't think why.

KARKER: (*To HAAKON*) I'll silence her. Just say. . .

HAAKON: (*Angrily*) I know you would. (*He takes KARI's face in his hand.*) Good! Thora's still not afraid to have pretty girls around. (*He grins at THORA.*)

THORA: (*In ironic, weary command*) Let it alone, Haakon.

HAAKON: Just take her out to a shed and stop up her mouth one pleasant way or another. No harm to her. (*KARKER leads KARI out.*) Thora. I need to trust him. Don't take that away. I've little else.

THORA: (*With towering pride*) You have the love of the poetess, Thora Einarsdaughter, Earl Haakon, and you've her word to turn aside Olaf Trigvusson's sword from your meaty neck, which, (*Indicating the gods*) by these great workers, I swear I can contrive to do!—. . .Are you so soaked in gall you can turn a bleak eye on me and say that you've so little? (*She picks up KARKER's knife, speaking with grand scorn.*) Fools and their iron! (*She dumps it in front of the idols, and pulls shut the drape.*)

(*Outside, in a leafy gobo, KARI stumbles across the yard, followed by KARKER.*)
KARI: You had your knife at me! You would have!
KARKER: Kari, Kari. The knife was just show. I gave you my bogwort leaf.
KARI: So?
KARKER: So something had to turn out. And something did. You aren't hurt.
KARI: I am. (*She shudders, catching her breath as he nuzzles. She turns to him.*) Let's run! There's mountains where nobody comes, they tell, up north.
KARKER: (*Shakes his head*) Wolves up there.
KARI: The wolves here are wickeder. He sent his own gotten son to Odin. That was werewolf work.
KARKER: You don't know! You don't. Where Olaf was coming to land, some of the old wizard men got together to warp up a storm against his boats. Still, Olaf got his crew ashore in the surf. He had our old men bound, out on the skerries where the tide would rise. "Now sing to the weather, you witches," Olaf told them. It's a slow, cold half a day to be drowned by a rising tide. The howling went on. They had worse ready to do to us, men and boy. We spared Egil that.
KARI: (*Unconverted*) Spared! It was a son.
KARKER: Your God did the same with his son, they tell it.

KARI: Just like the paupers, the rich are—with no time to care for a child, day to day. The nurse or the fosterer does the watching and the washing. They think they love their child, in their hustles and leisure's. . . but caring, caring comes from the hours and the irks. . . and the little hands. Rich folks don't care.

KARKER: (*He tilts his head and shrugs.*) There aren't any, I guess.

KARI: Any what?

KARKER: Any rich folks. I've seen Haakon stare at his silver cup that would buy and sell six of you and me, and say, "Karker, as Earls go, I'm poor as a vole." Nobody seems rich to himself.

KARI: Who 's the bigger fool then? Him, or you to follow him?

KARKER: (*Grins, imitating her*) "That's wicked talk. That's bad talk, that's shame." I like it. (*Shrugs*) But we have small choice.

KARI: You and I could run. The Christus would help; already has, maybe. (*She points at the boots KARKER carries. He peers at her, foxily.*) Thora's bent on having the Earl. She gets her way and things will go hard for you then. Someday, somehow, in some way, she will make the Earl kill you. You'll see. Why does she hate you so bad?

KARKER: She is a crazy whore.

KARI: Don't you say that!

KARKER: You don't know or you'd say the same. She's crazy. She's a whore.

KARI: Are things. . . the way she thinks? That's it's you that keep Haakon roving?

KARKER: Me? I just keep him alive. Well, (*Head to one side*) it's funny, Kari. When we are up to mischief, out and risking wild, him in my cloak maybe, to fool folk; we laugh. Not thrall and Earl, just two, riding the one joke, and I feel free. Scared near to piss-britches sometimes, but. . . how often does a thrall feel free? Maybe I egg him on a bit. Maybe.

KARI: You'd feel free if we ran. Try the boots.

KARKER: (*Studies the boots again, then her*) Ah, Kari. Pretty Kari. I'll have to hold you in my arms, to run. I'll show you. (*He peers about.*) Not here in the open. No. We'll need some cobweb. And. . . the shadow of a cow. Come to the cowshed. (*He leads her off.*)

(*THORA and HAAKON are as we left them.*)

HAAKON: So. How would you. . . turn Olaf's sword?

THORA: They call women "peace-weavers." Christians are very great on peace. And Olaf will be shrewd. You'd be better ally than enemy.

HAAKON: Except for the wife-stealing and the daughter-stealing, most of Norway would rather bow to me than to him. He might know that.

THORA: I can find terms you and he could come to.

HAAKON: Would he trust me? Ever?

THORA: He would. He will. Once you have married me. (*HAAKON stares, then exhales a whistling whinny.*) But you must rid yourself of your shadow.

HAAKON: Karker? Huh. Get me safe to Sweden, and, if you manage such a peace, I will come back.

THORA: And marry me.

HAAKON: And marry you. I will. So, exchange a faith-ring with me. Here's a hair. (*He pulls one from his head and looks at it.*) Hell! Not a grey one. (*Pulls another*) Here. (*He ties it about her finger.*) Nothing to show for brag, but till I come again, this stands for a ring. What will you give me? (*She pulls off a ring, he laughs, holding up a little finger.*) That wouldn't jam onto this little outrider. Do better, Thora.

THORA: You will come among the Swedes so rich that they might want to kill you. Here. (*She steps into the bed chamber. He wheels and flashes a fist gesture of grateful triumph at the gods. She returns with a huge gold ring.*) It is the Njordaring. "Don't send me into the mound with it," Father said, " Down there, Hella would cheat me of it. Buy with it. . . what you like," he said.

HAAKON: I'm what you like, eh, pretty Thora? (*Grinning*) He thought Njord would want it back?

THORA: He didn't know about gods, any more than I do. He knew about life.

HAAKON: (*Nods toward the idols*) You're not a believer?

THORA: If there is such a thing as sinning against a god, it's when we suppose we can know, or even have words to tell about them.

HAAKON: (*Grins*) I thought you'd been bargaining for me with them.

THORA: (*Shrugs*) We all believe in Gods, when hard pressed. We're made that way. But I won't insult truth by claiming I know truths about them.

HAAKON: I'd think you'd know your own mind.

THORA: But not the gods' minds. . . I know what all the poets know: that the tree of the world is all around, live and dense with leaves and forkings till we cannot make out root from topmost bough; that we must breathe deep in blossom time and endure the bleak wind and the worm. Gods, for all I know are shapes of sun-spill through the leaves, or true things glimpsed by a twig-scarred eye, or just the heart's fist, knocking to come out. I listen, talk to them. . . what not? But I don't know. I've honesty of gut to endure not knowing.

HAAKON: Karker sees it the same.

THORA: (*Arrogantly scornful*) Karker's a user, like Father! He pretends it's magic. That, I think, really is sin! Don't dare compare him to me!

HAAKON: I won't. I won't. Are you going to give me the ring?

THORA: (*She slips it on his finger.*) They forged it to fit a statue, not a human hand. I give ancient gold, you give me good faith. Don't lose it. We are bound. (*KARI hurries in.*) You again!

KARI: (*Tearfully heroic*) Karker says I must lie with him. He says I owe him, and I do: he spared my life. But I promised Jesus I never would. I won't scream, I'll die and be a saint with light all the way around my face. I see now, I was meant to.

THORA: What you don't see, you crazy child, is that you begin to bore me. (*KARKER has followed KARI in and turned back toward the door.*)

HAAKON: Why bar that door, Karker? (*Grinning at KARKER's new boots.*) If she runs, you can walk through the wall with those, can't you? (*KARKER does not grin back.*) We'll thank the girls and go. (*But KARKER is shaking his head, and puts a finger to his lip. There are hoofbeats.*)

KARKER: Listen.

HAAKON: Who. . .

KARKER: Yes. We've outstayed welcome. (*At a knock, HAAKON and KARKER retreat to the idols.*)

HAAKON: Troll take them!

THORA: Open it, Kari.

KARI: (*Softly*) Karker, show them the cross.

HAAKON: (*To THORA*) Arms around, and then good-bye. (*KARI moves to open the door. She hesitates, then pushes. There is light. OLAF stands there, gleaming.*)

OLAF: The house door at Rimul, barred before nightfall? (*THORA comes forward. We hardly see how the drape before the idols is drawn shut, hiding HAAKON and KARKER.*) I'm still welcome here? (*OLAF bows then kisses THORA's hand; she looks at it doubtfully.*)

THORA: I'd have washed my hand if I'd guessed you would do a thing like that.

OLAF: Rimul is only a farmstead, but you are the Lady here. That's how one greets a lady in Byzantium.

THORA: You have been so far?

OLAF: I've looked at the world.

THORA: And I imagine it has looked at you.

OLAF: Somewhat. Praise the Lord.

THORA: Byzantium. . .

OLAF: It's south, like everything. Even I can't say how far in days of sail.

THORA: Even you. . .

OLAF: (*Excited to recall*) You journey overland. Past Danes, past the Rhine, past the deep Danube. . .

THORA: It was an idle question, if I asked.

OLAF: A good question, Thora. It's good to meet again. And you always want to know everything!

(*Simultaneous*)

THORA: And you want to tell.   OLAF: After nine weeks riding. . .

OLAF: . . .you realize the world is too big for our old Gods to have measured.

THORA: They'd get saddle sores? Bring an ale horn, Kari. Kari. He's tall and all that, but you needn't stare so. (*KARI goes. As she does, THORA smoothly takes the tabard HAAKON*) *removed and drops it over the sword on the floor.*) You could still snap finger on thumb and have any girl, Olaf.

OLAF: I am not like some, praise God.

THORA: Lets not begin by talking about gods.

OLAF: Not in plural, no. Never any more. (*She shakes her head.*) Plural's a word they use in foreign tongues. . . when you are learning.

THORA: Even Thora of Rimul has heard of it.

OLAF: I wasn't showing off. . .

THORA: Oh, a bit. You still blush beautifully. A touch of brag adds color to a man.

OLAF: Not "brag." It's. . . You can't quite say it in Norwegian. Romans call it "Urbanitas." (*KARI returning, proffers a horn.*) It means having lived in cities.

THORA: And you're clever to leave the what-ever-its-ass overseas, since men here won't value it. "Brag" is a good enough word for Norway.

OLAF: (*Bows*) I deserved that.

THORA: Don't be meek, either. No one here will respect turned cheeks. (*She notices that he has not accepted the ale-horn, smiles knowingly and takes it.*) Yes. I drink first. (*He takes a small square of linen out of his sleeve, wipes the brim for her.*) Better and better! (*She drinks, then purses her lips while he drinks.*) Don't speak for a moment. Let me look. To look at you is as good as a deep drink.

OLAF: I look older?

THORA: (*Head on one side*) Younger, really.

OLAF: You actually see that? Yes. I am a five year old child. (*THORA raises her brows.*) I was reborn, in Christus. You're dipped naked in the water and come up new, feeling what you could be: flesh incorruptible.

THORA: A man should know the good of a bath.

OLAF: Don't be blasphemous.

THORA: (*She studies him fondly.*) You always were brimming full of yourself. At sixteen it was wonderfully charming. And all the huge world hasn't drained you: you still brim!

OLAF: But with something other than myself, Thora! In so far as I'm worthy, it is the Lord that is in me, not just self.

THORA: Our gods are always ourselves, in a way, Olaf.

OLAF: Don't, Thora. Old, wry wisdom out of earth won't serve any longer. You talk wonderfully, but I have been granted the way and the truth, better than all hearth-talk.

THORA: Oh, I spent most of a winter having the good news proclaimed to me, under these rafters. It all but took me, bewitching-sweet like honey. That a god would take all griefs and cover the world's muck like a white snowfall. But the bearers of the tale are the same as the rest of us; and their lie is they believe they're different. Arrogant!

OLAF: The "tale," as you call it, is overcoming the whole width of earth! The thousand years are up, and the world must change; and I am to change Norway.

THORA: You really are a new man.

OLAF: You see.

THORA: (*Fingering his collar*) You'll want to go back out into your wide world, your "ur-ban. . ." whatever. Olaf, I see that. You won't be content to give us your sunlight here for long.

OLAF: Not long. (*He peers at her.*) Does that still make you sad?

THORA: Once you've settled things, you'll hunger again for travels . . .

OLAF: If God wills. At your time of life a wise woman should put lusts away.

THORA: (*Vexed many ways at once*) My time! . . and what lusts?

OLAF: You'll find me very blunt now, but we always were frank. Let's be.

THORA: Get out of here, Kari.

OLAF: Thank you.

KARI: (*Frightened but stubborn, KARI moves in front of the drape hiding the gods and sits, speaking really to OLAF.*) I'm Christian. My place is here.

OLAF: Sister then! Don't scold the girl! A decent woman in Byzantium is never alone with a strange man, however upright. It's wrong to give scandal a toe in the door.

THORA: I'll be upright with you. (*She moves to the drape.*)

OLAF: Will your Father be here?

THORA: I doubt it. It is all right. Get up, Kari, you don't have to defend Lord Olaf from the wickedness behind the drape. He has seen them before. (*She opens the drape; the gods are alone.* *KARI crosses herself and recoils.*) Kari was just telling a folk tale for my collection, all about father's seven-league boots. Shabby, pagan witchcraft to you. Now she's shamed to talk of it.

OLAF: Yes, I'm not here for stories now, Thora, (*Looks about*) though I learned a great deal under this roof. Satan braids much wisdom in amongst his lies. I don't forget: I'm beholden to you, and your father, for deep talks in those days.

THORA: They were a joy to me too, Olaf. But, you're on great business now.

OLAF: You hear of that?

THORA: Thwack a beehive with your walking stick, and you needn't wonder much how the bees come to hear of it. We've talked of many things since you came through that door, but the oddest is what you haven't asked me.

OLAF: It's an embarrassment. If I asked that thing, I know I couldn't trust your answer.

(*Simultaneous*)

THORA: That really is very   OLAF: We're old friends.
          fine of you, Olaf. . .

THORA: No one ever called me liar with greater delicacy. Still, you've circled Rimul with armed men, no doubt.

OLAF: Could I do less? (*With drawn sword he throws back the curtain to the bedchamber. Silence.*)

THORA: I'll set you easy. Haakon has come and gone. How far by now, those two (*Gestures toward Frey and Freya*) know better than mortals.

KARI: They. . .

THORA: Kari, don't embarrass yourself. Kari helped him on his way. Which I suppose must shame her. (*KARI looks in distress at OLAF and falls silent. THORA smiles at them both.*) Forgive her. Haakon always had a way with women.

OLAF: To his downfall.

THORA: Yes. But understand, dear man, he has not fallen all the way down. So, we must talk. Sit and talk. (*They do.*) As once. I'm as afraid right now for you as for Haakon, Olaf. I like my friends alive, you know I do. I weave my bit of peace. Be careful. Be wise. That he is hated will not make you loved.

You come back to us rich with your "urbanitas." I can see it at a glance; but, with all you've gained, you've lost a touch with our shagginess. We're simpletons beside you now, in our way, but every day here you must think how simpletons can be ridden with sudden rages in their simpleness: at civil wit, at charm. Sharp wit can't foresee them, only a dog's instinct might feel them coming. You could provoke, by your sheer. . . breadth. I salute what you've become, but I'm frightened for you too. You will need us who still know old Norway by heart.

OLAF: (*Smiles*) Praise the Lord for your caring, Thora. You see very lovingly I'm not what I was. . . Now see what I've become! I'm the Lord's key, Thora. In His hand. He turns me in the lock, and opens Norway.

THORA: You were a brilliant charmer, with as many minds as a spider has eyes; no one ever made me talk as well as you did, or feel as wise. You're even right that I lusted for you a little, though my heart had set its teeth into other meat and wasn't to let go. You gleamed. And dipping you in water won't have made a fool of you. You know well that being Christian doesn't mean you can be witless.

OLAF: What is it you think my wits should do?

THORA: Be thinking where Haakon is arriving now, and what he'll do.

OLAF: Would you really tell me? (*He looks questioningly at KARI.*) Really?

THORA: Yes. He's gone. . .

KARI: (*Low*) To Sweden.

THORA: You'll believe her.

KARI: To Queen Sigrid.

OLAF: So!

THORA: So. You went out into the world and found your allies. Now Haakon will. And there can be no peace for you, Olaf. Feuds and schemes and trouble without end, it means.

OLAF: Do you care?

THORA: You've no cause to doubt it! But alliance between King and Earl . . . What does a king have earls *for*? You for folk to trust and him for them to fear. There would be the peace your faith so craves! It's in me to arrange it.

OLAF: How?

THORA: I have his word.

OLAF: Not notoriously sound coinage, his word.

THORA: And mine. Haakon will help you have back your ancestral lands. . .

OLAF: To lie in?

THORA: To stand on and live long on. And his pledge of good behavior. . .

OLAF: That I'm curious to hear.

THORA: He will marry me. There will be no more forays among the wives of the half-earls, that I pledge you, my dear. (*She has laid her hands on his across the table. He stares at her, then suddenly looks down, withdraws his hand and rises.*) Oh, Olaf. Good, fine Olaf, you don't, surely you don't still feel that way for me? You've seen a dozen worlds—and I was your mother's age. I'm sorry. But if that dear foolish ardor is still there in your heart, I'll speak to it. I wish I were twenty years later born — I'd adore you! But I'm old, snake-shrewd and. . . the kind that mates for life. Haakon used to choose to talk as though I had as many wicked lovers as he did; it was only talk. Use me, now, Olaf. Let me make truce between you and Earl Haakon. Use me. You owe me a thing. (*OLAF is immobile.*) I saved you once.

OLAF: When did I need saving?

THORA: I told you when to go abroad. That was. . . friendly of me, at least.

OLAF: (*Irked*) This about my "ardor" and your "saving" me? You tell some story *I* never knew! I gather that you have come to think I loved you, also that I traveled at your advising. I stopped coming to your father's farm because it was plain you had begun to love me and I didn't want to dishonor your father by leading on an. . . older, unwed woman I would surely never marry.

(Simultaneous)

THORA: That wasn't how!   OLAF: Deep and wise though
                                            she was!

OLAF: I said I had grown blunt.

THORA: (*She shoots a quick glance toward the idols.*) Liar! You heart-liar! I warned you off!

OLAF: I was in the Lord's hand, drawn abroad that I should be saved—from the snares of the next world, not of this one. Neither you nor I had to do with it. God hews our fates to build his temples in this world.

THORA: I begged you to go and be safe! You can't have forgotten that!

OLAF: (*He smiles loftily.*) But, you can't imagine me fearful enough to go because a woman was fretful.

THORA: Olaf! You . . . sneer, you insult me, when I'm offering you peace in Norway! And a great and bold Earl to leave in charge when you are drawn abroad. Don't you want the peace on earth your Christus wants? Or are you just another wolf in your lamb-of-God's clothing?

OLAF: I'm not mild. Purgatory will burn me a while for that. But there's nothing in my life that wasn't caused by God.

THORA: (*She controls her sarcasm.*) Your God brought you here to me this evening?

OLAF: But not to arrange your wedding. (*With disgust.*) Did you know that out on Tronder Rocks, Haakon hanged his own son?

THORA: A wolf in a trap will gnaw its paw off. Or its cub's paw.

OLAF: What men do who talk of Gods in the plural.

KARI: It's so. They'd heard the warlocks howling on the reefs.

THORA: (*To KARI*) What warlocks on what reef?

OLAF: Witches that I drowned. The coven were raising weather spells against me. To mere enemies you'll find few more merciful than I will be, but the Bible tells us don't let witches live. (*He walks sternly toward the idols.*)

THORA: What men do who talk of their god in the singular. (*Slowly*) I think. . . it will not be lucky for you here in my father's house.

OLAF: (*Off balance for the first time, he turns to THORA.*) May God forgive me! I should have guessed! Your father. . .

THORA: Father was of that coven that stood against you on the beach. Yes.

OLAF: Thora, this is the first thing that I've regretted since I came to Norway. It must be I was meant to look you in the eyes and tell you, Thora. God's will be done.

THORA: Odin's manslaughterers. Christus' manslaughterers. Pots calling the kettles sooty. It's good to see your wits run dry for a moment. Will you offer me blood money for the old man? (*Holds out her hand*)

OLAF: No. (*He backs away a bit.*) What vengeance were you spreading for me when you offered me a truce?

THORA: Ah, your wits flow again. I ought to leave your writhing. I said I like to see you blush. (*She laughs.*) Father died in his own bed, a year ago. Chuckled, and died. (*KARI nods to the truth of this.*) Still, you would have killed him? If he'd lived to be there on Tronder beach?

OLAF: I would have. God spared me that.

THORA: And whatever Gods there are know I was spreading no net, for you or Haakon, offering a way to a treaty between you. (*To the idols*) Hear me, you two there. This Olaf thinks you are dead sticks, but I know you have living ears!

OLAF: Hush, Thora. (*He glowers at the gods, then turns from them.*) So, Haakon's going to Queen Sigrid. Beliel will laugh.

THORA: Beliel?

OLAF: The fallen angel of lust. That. (*He points at Frey and Freya.*) Did you clear Haakon's way to her with your father's idol ring?

THORA: Why should. . . what does that mean?

OLAF: Just vile gossip. (*He lays finger to lip.*) Speak no evil.

THORA: Oh, give scandal a toe in the door. Can we talk if I don't know what you're talking about?

OLAF: They're saying Queen Sigrid the Haughty has let word travel she'd be pleased to meet this Frey of Norway, this bedsman Haakon. But she makes conditions. Ballad singers have it that some farm woman, Thora the poet, is Haakon's real love. And, they say, a great ring out of a burnt temple came into the hands of this Thora. Haakon should not come to Sweden, says the Queen, unless he brings her that ring. (*OLAF grins frankly.*) I couldn't help but wonder. You want me to risk my life on a peace with him, so I have to know. Did you trust him? Enough to give him that ring?

THORA: (*Speaking low*) I trusted him. . . I trusted him!

OLAF: But?

THORA: I doubt your gossip.

KARI: It's true, Lady. Karker tried to make me lie with him, and boasted Haakon would do the same with you, and take your ring. Karker had talked Sigrid, Sigrid, Sigrid to Haakon for days.

THORA: (*Releasing one flash of her great rage*) Oh, shut your face, girl! (*Icy again*) Karker was very wrong to boast. Evil will come to him for it. (*Proudly*) Yes, I gave the Njordaring. Haakon needed it. Should I fear Sigrid the Haughty?

OLAF: Neither should I. Thora, as you say, I have to be wise. We have set a bounty on Haakon. A collar of red gold to the man who does away with him.

THORA: And his Karker? What bounty on him?

KARI: He's wearing a cross.

THORA: The sly ferret!

OLAF: Haakon will be as bad luck to Sigrid as to everyone. He didn't kill his boy to spare him, Thora. He *offered* him, hanged to Odin!

THORA: No!

OLAF: This (*Slaps his sword*) cut the body down, Thora. I know an offering when I see one.

THORA: No.

KARI: (*Nods softly*) Karker told. A devil talked to Karker in the night and bargained. They traded the boy for a fog to get away in. They'd heard how the warlocks died.

THORA: (*Shudders.*) Karker. . . and his Odin!

OLAF: Still want to worship such a devil? And wed one?

THORA: (*Loudly, to the idols.*) You there! Hear me! High one, deep in your darkness. Hear! There's a death-bounty for any faith-shifty sneak who'll put a knife in Haakon's back, and whom can Haakon trust? False Karker made him send his son to Odin, but carries a cross under his shirt. Think, there, and be quick now to save Haakon. Be sudden. Frey and Freya, feast full with offerings. (*Turns back to OLAF.*) I offend you, I know, but I had my prayers to make. These gods have their interest in Haakon's life. You understand.

OLAF: They're deaf and blind, your gods, maggots in the dung now. Christ has shamed the old devils. He has put down the mighty from their seats. (*To KARI, who has begun to sob*) No harm, little handmaiden. Heathen prayer means nothing anymore.

THORA: It has its powers.

KARI: (*Crossing herself.*) Karker's a dead man! You have killed him, for sure, for sure, Thora. I warned you would. (*She rises, drawing back from the idols.*)

THORA: Shut up, girl. Him and his boots are far away!

KARI: No, I understand.

THORA: Hold your tongue!

KARI: Too late for Karker. I have to tell! You've been in danger, King. Awful danger. There is . . .

OLAF: . . . a crawlway hole under the idols. One of the old wizard's fox-tricks here. What fool did you take me for? Did you think I didn't guess? (*With a sweeping blow he knocks over the idols and leaps back, sword at the ready, for their tilting back has opened a trap door.*) False and foul!

THORA: Haakon! (*Snatching HAAKON's sword she drives at OLAF's back.*) Now! Quick, now! (*OLAF parries her lunge with a sideswipe that strikes her weapon down. He steps on it and is again at the ready.*)

OLAF: Yes. Better it be now! Out, Haakon, and meet the Lord! Earl Haakon!

KARKER: (*After a pause, he emerges from the hole. He is covered with yellowish dirt, and hunches into his cloak as though wounded, but he holds out his left hand. In it is a severed, white, right hand on which the vast gold ring gleams mutely.*) Earl Haakon is dead, Olaf Trigvusson. Karker, his thrall, killed him in a hole. (*He looks at THORA with a mournful shrug.*) He would have cut my throat, Lady. You put it in his mind to. But you had taken away his sword, remember? (*He lays the hand at OLAF's feet and turns away.*)

THORA: (*Stares long at him*) Luckless. Luckless. (*Stricken, she sits slowly on the bench.*)

OLAF: Comfort your mistress, sister.

KARI: (*Approaches her mistress without fear.*) Lady, learn a thing now. I'm simple, I'm ignorant, but I know. They've fallen. Only great Christus is standing. You can't guess what peace it is when you take all your sadnesses, all hatefulness you wish you'd never done, and bundle them at the cross foot with the other bundles and . . . just give up yourself. What good was it anyway, yourself? All the tears are His, and it doesn't have to make sense, it just is, and oh, Lady Thora, the bread at mass is so sweet . . .

THORA: (*She has heard nothing of that.*) I must haul the body out . . . Kari, you have to help.

KARKER: The earth buried us dark for you. Your father's rotting weasel holes fell in. I brought away all of him I could. You won't find more till you dig the whole house down.

THORA: Sills and broad shingles   to serve for a grave-ship
        Rafters and rooftree   to rot in the mound
        Rimul abandoned   shall be for a barrow.
        Gaunt grow the cattle   that ever graze here!

(*To* OLAF) But that dog there bit his own master. Have him put down.

OLAF: (*Stiffly*) I'm a Christian King, Thora . . .

THORA: No one in your army will endure having a thrall kill an earl and live! Call in your men and see.

OLAF: (*Wryly*) What men?

THORA: The men . . . (*Almost realizing what he means*) outside.

OLAF: I came alone, Thora. Except for Christus.

THORA: Haakon would never have hidden from you, if. . .

KARKER: . . .if he'd known it was man to man!

OLAF: No, though he'd have been wise to. (*He picks up the hand.*) Why does it irk me so that you've been thinking me a fool? I am an instrument of Christ's coming here in the Northlands! It was Providence! Because you thought we were flanked around with armed men, we could talk like civil creatures, and you're one in this crude wilderness I'd care to talk to: for the rest of them I'm just the fellow with the long sword. But, to you I was still the boy you could flatter and wheedle with tales. I don't look so silly now? (*He takes the ring from the hand.*) I'll take the trinket. I go to Sweden next. The Lord's work can always use gold. (*A pause*) My captains will be in a grim lather for me. I must get back to Mord Coldfoot's farm. (*With scorn he tucks the ring safely in his groin.*) It comes to mind, I'm King of Norway. Thora, you warned me I wouldn't understand my people. As my lawful subject, pay the thrall, woman, see to it as is fitting. It is becoming for women to obey.

My part is done in the ugly business; I wash my hands. (*He glows.*) God bless you. (*He goes out.*)

KARKER: (*After OLAF has gone, he slowly bends over and sinks to the bench.*) Kari. Kari. I'm hurting. (*KARI hurries to him.*)

THORA: For a start. Only for a start. Come, Haakon, teach me about hurting. (*She picks up theaword.*)

KARI: Oh, Christ's Mercy cover us! Look! The hand. . . (*She holds up the stump of KARKER's right wrist.*) He lost his own hand too! (*The light is fading.*)

KARKER: I couldn't take the one and not give the other, could I? Wouldn't have been fair bargain. . . with the Gods down there.

THORA: Gods! (*She seizes the gaunt statues of Frey and Freya and breaks them, one after the other as the light changes.*)

(*They are all still, SIGYN and LOKI huddle where KARI and KARKER were, changed but the same. SIGYN has her cup. THORA watches from the edge of the scene, donning her nun's wimple, and with it her age.*)

LOKI: There's another story for you!

SIGYN: There's another cupful.

CHRISTUS: (*He glimmers into view, but this time it is HAAKON who embodies him up there, loin-clouted, thorn-crowned.*) Odin ?

LOKI: Loki again. Sleight . . . of hand.

CHRISTUS: Who could tell you apart in your dark?

LOKI: Not bright?

ODIN: (*He emerges from the shadows. The broad hat, patched blue cloak and grey fell of beard are familiar, but this is he who was OLAF.*) I'm not the old blood-king, shape-shifter, hanged with robbers. You are. . . (*He gathers the fragments of the idols.*) And these are kindling.

CHRISTUS: Poor old Thora—can't tell us apart.

LOKI: What is truth? (*Vague with pain and humor*) We swore brothers, Odin and I. But in the end, call it muddle-earth. Worm-ringed, ring-wormed. It craved quick doing down here in the stifle.

SIGYN: Shh. . .shh. . . Lie easy. I'll tell any story you like.

LOKI: What version will you make of us, poetess?

THORA: (*Bitterly*) I can make nothing of you, you well know. Eaters of blood!

LOKI: Can't be without stories. (*THORA goes.*) I broke her for you, Nazarene, like a mare in a horse corral. When she thinks that I could cut a hateful hand for him, and the earth could fall on him, she's yours.

CHRISTUS: (*ODIN wanders off, CHRISTUS fades.*) These poets make bad converts. They pray, but they won't stop dreaming.

LOKI: Mash them up like grapes.

SIGYN: You'll spill my cup again. Tiresome invalid.

LOKI: Has the even come? The millennium twilight?

SIGYN: Shh. They come and go.

LOKI: In posts and pillars of your houses they carve grinning demon gutterspouts and knots of snakes raise Cain. You did not corner the world's murk. It. . . conquered ourselves, we did!

SIGYN: Shh. Why make him angry? That's just venom babble.

LOKI: Girl. . . I'm the clown. Die laughing is what I do. For a living. (*He rolls back into darkness. The hanging CHRISTUS is just a piece of ninth century art again.*)

SIGYN: (*Referring to LOKI*) He comes and goes. . . by spells. So do I. (*She looks into the cup.*) This has to be emptied. (*She raises the cup as a soft chant of nun's voices begins.*) It's just vinegar. I don't really empty it, I go drink it. I am the woman, Sigyn, Loki's wife. Lord, I never thought I'd run away from you. When we took veils your convent seemed like what a dream could hunger for: quiet, the food, praying between work and work, especially the quiet. Even after she got made Mother Superior over us, (*Mischievously*) because you or King Olaf couldn't think what to do with her, some of the clever sisters said, even then I couldn't guess that one day Karker would knock and. . . I'd run off to him and live in the wet woods and pray again to the trees. Why is it that it's so usually what we can't imagine that happens? I thought I'd be a saint. But I don't have to ask you to forgive me now. I'm Loki's wife. You're not one of my trees. (*She walks away.*)

(*The WANDERER and the NUN, THORA, by the door of the convent, squint at dawn. We are again twenty-one years past*

*the year One Thousand, twenty-six years since we last saw
the poet and the Earl.*)

WANDERER: You couldn't keep from seeing me off, could you?

THORA: (*She shakes her head.*) I'm not here for any love of the
old long since. I just have nightmares to unravel, watching you
go.

WANDERER: I knew a knack for fending off the nightmare, long
since. Tell, (*He glances about.*) before your white hens come to
see what keeps you at the door. Back when you made so sure
that we heard Olaf's death-bounty, down in the hole under
Rimul—why was that, that turn of hate in you against us?
You'd set your heart on saving us, then you pitted us against
each other.

THORA: Why do you say "us"? I only hated *you*.

WANDERER: (*Flatly*) Me?

THORA: Did you ever *really* think otherwise? I was saying at
heart, "Now Haakon will kill Karker, and we will be rid of
him!" Before Christ, it never crossed my mind it could turn out
the other way! Go. No, I have to know something too. Now
that it doesn't matter. Did you tell Haakon about the time..?
(*He looks blank.*) When I. . . (*She is baffled to find she can
hardly say this.*) Sweet Christ, I've confessed it to a prurient
old priest, can't I bring myself to speak of it to you? (*She lays
word upon word with effort.*) Nothing in my life makes my face
burn but that. I'd unbent to *beg* Haakon to come to me that fall
and he. . . sent you! (*With self-revulsion*) and I . . .

WANDERER: You. . . asked the thrall into the bed with you!

THORA: (*She gasps at the work of having said this, and does not look
at the WANDERER.*) I doubt I'd have hated you any sharper—if
you had crawled in! (*The WANDERER laughs.*) It was to spite
him! If you had touched that coverlet, I'd have had you killed.
Now is there a way to win you just to tell one truth? Did
Haakon ever know? Was it for that that he wouldn't just *ask* for
the old ring? I'm a fool to want to know.

WANDERER: (*Not unkindly*) Haakon never knew. . . Woman!
Thora! Thora! (*He roars with laughter.*) It's morning! I'm gone
in the teeth, sagged in the belly and hoarse as a raven, but
don't you *know* me? (*He pushes back matted white hair.*)

Thor's thunder, woman, I'm still Haakon! (*There is a long pause.*) You look beautiful, with your mouth open.

THORA: You liar! (*Seizing him*) Haakon! You hateful, louse-tattered, lovely liar! All the years. . . I have been left to think I killed. . . The years! Christ's blood, let me beat you! (*She pummels him.*) I let them build the abbey here where Rimul stood because your bones lay under it! (*Wrathfully*) Karker mocks me still!

HAAKON: (*Half amused*) Should Karker have told? He owed you small that day!

THORA: But you! You could have sent word, come by night. . .

HAAKON: Coming to you helpless did not turn out well. I wouldn't come again.

THORA: (*She holds the wrist stump.*) Because of this! Proud. You couldn't bear to be anything in front of me but whole and swaggering. As if I'd care. Was it Karker's crazy thought, or yours, to lop it off?

HAAKON: You still don't understand? He cut off his *own* hand; his *own* hand he gave Olaf! The far end of the hole at the pigsty was blocked; there was no digging out with an army standing around the farm. Not while they knew I was alive. "I'll just go have my joke on Olaf now," Karker muttered. The way he would. And he set his wrist against a stone and struck it off.

THORA: That takes. . . thinking out. (*Pause*) You've been much loved, Haakon.

HAAKON: You might have believed that.

THORA: *You* might have. You had my heart, and (*A grim smile*) Karker's hand.

HAAKON: (*Looking at his stump*) I see how you mistook. This I didn't part with till a couple winters back. I saw time was up with me as a fighter. Karker's grave is in the mountains. I went up there and paid him my debt.

THORA: Stupid! (*Sighs*) I might be glad you like things fair, but not. . . that way!

HAAKON: Fair. (*Laughs*) You should have had old Karker into the bed, to make things fair between you and me. I mightn't have felt so outdone by your steadfastness, with all evener between us.

THORA: But, you'd have killed him, you know. And then held both the bed and his death against me all your days.

HAAKON: Probably. Things turn on me. The sleight of hand did. Olaf's word that I was buried was more deadly than a price on my head. When I came to Sweden, they told me Haakon was dead and I was an impostor.

THORA: You were. Aren't we cross-grained, contentless creatures, all!

HAAKON: You hated Karker. You loved me. Now you couldn't tell us apart.

THORA: Well. You know now at least he was a liar about you and he sharing the one death hour.

HAAKON: When the Haakon in a man outlives the Karker in him, it's not all that much a life.

THORA: So. (*She looks at the sunrise for a bit.*) Larks. Good-bye, Haakon.

HAAKON: Just that? No.

THORA: You said you came for a story retold. Here's one, for your roads. It may earn a supper, but choose where you tell it. Olaf, splendid Olaf, whom neither life nor mortal ever had said "No" to, took my ring that the goddess Njord had worn in the old days, father's talisman, my dowry and the object of your shameless scheming once and oh, so many things. . . Olaf took it to Queen Sigrid and ah, Norway and Sweden would be one realm, he thought, he'd bestride the wicked giantess and have her and both crowns of the north. I know his heart heard the Lord promise him all that! It happened a Lettish gold merchant was at her court that fall; no man wiser than he in secrets of metal. She took Olaf's gift-ring gladly at supper in front of all her Swedes; but over night she gave it to the Lettish man to finger and weigh and scratch inside the band. Next morning, with all people looking , she lifted her long fingers and crimsoned nails—and slapped Olaf so the blood ran from nose and ear. That, she said, would teach the outlander not to come to Queens with gifts of brass dipped in a little gilt. It was a whack to split Norway and Sweden past ever mending. (*THORA pauses.*) Olaf tells the world that *he* slapped her, but he says he had Karker's throat cut too, he says he never cared for me. Be smug that the man slapped was Olaf, not you, you over-proud old ruin. So. Good road to you.

HAAKON: Not too proud now. Bundle up your things. Better begging and the woods with me than mouldering here, old woman.

THORA: No.

HAAKON: No?

THORA: Kari went, when Karker came. Thora won't.

HAAKON: Why not? (*Gestures at the crucifix.*) Him? You don't believe in him!

THORA: Believe in him? I do. He's a pack of dreams, of course; so are we all. Religion makes some mean and smug to scorn and kill over key-hole glimpses into their one closet of heaven. (*She is distracted into wry contemplation: she is old.*) On another hand, one sees the godless mean and murderous too. (*She turns again to HAAKON, she is luminous with a perceived truth.*) But I loved someone once, and he was not hateful to me, or mean, as I saw him. He was you. . . a possible you. I'd have settled and loved the solid you with all your deadly sins, like any good wife, if you had let me. But you didn't. I have had to love my possible, grand god. Now I am an old nun and I like loving it. We would not even imagine gods if they were not possible in us. Possible. To be found. To be hunted for. Thora of Rimul owes you thanks for the imagining. (*She goes in. A door closes.*)

END

OF MYSELF

I grew up in rural Maine among craftspersons—a beautiful, solitary, out-of-sync anti-world; at times I still feel like a visitor from parts unknown. This slight obliquity to things has been benign. I've had opportunity to share in founding a union classical rep theater and there to direct most of my favorite plays from the past. *The Mischief* has not been staged. I write and rewrite continuously: poems, plays, novels. I love language and hope to die a better speller than I am.

My best is in having a gifted, heart-warm partner wife, actress Kim Gordon, and kind, fascinating son and daughter. I teach college youngsters who now and then seem to hear something I say or say to me something that shines and startles. Of course I crave more, I chafe and fear loss—few are the blessed who don't. Summing up, I find I am so lucky it seems a perilous boast.

OF WRITING *THE MISCHIEF AT RIMUL*

Some twentyodd books made up the library corner of one of the two rooms of my first eight school years. Always the same books. Two were, I thought, about vikings. (Recalled, they were retellings of Wagner's *Ring Cycle*, complete with hieroglyphs that were notation of leit motivs.) No one else opened those red and blue covers. They were mine, and magic.

So I talked of vikings. The most genial of the bird hunters from New York (come each fall to be guided by my father who had trained their dogs) one Christmas sent two grown-up books: *The Poetic Edda* and *Norse Mythology*. I have them still.

> I remember yet   the giants of yore
> Who gave me bread   in the days gone by;
> Nine worlds I knew   the nine in the tree
> With mighty roots   beneath the mould. . .

It irks me yet to spell mold without that eerie U.

Longfellow's *Song of Olaf* was another puzzle piece, met with as a highschool freshman, still, by bent, a book-viking not a teenager.

> *"Thora of Rimol, hide me, hide me!*
> *Danger and shame and death betide me,*
> *For Olaf the King is hunting me down. . ."*
> *Thus cried Jarl Hakon to Thora the fairest of women.*

Skinny, bully-haunted, I knew what Jarl Hakon meant. So. In one sense this play is private thanks-tribute, paid at the mound of certain foster dreams that fed boyhood.

The scene of Haakon's arrival at Rimul wrote itself unasked over thirty-five years ago. Then the plot dead-ended; its climax needed to play underground in cramped black between two who could not risk a whisper. Still, the characters continued to feel alive. Many plays later I unearthed the scene fragment, and found Haakon was not the heart of the story at all; Thora was. Nor was I obliged to tell what the saga tells. History is passionate fiction: if it is to come at anything like a truth it must invent.

Also I no longer only dreamed. I had begun, very tentatively, to believe a few things.

My plays have taken place in Feudal Japan, in Victorian era Florence, contemporary Boston and Patagonia, Maine of 1776, Kent in 1381. I write what I know. What I know is that locale is trivial. Birthright is trivial. Race, ethnicity, religion, nationality . . . these should be trivia: tragically they are notions people still take seriously. About them we murder one another's children over and over!

I do admire the skill to reproduce the speech patterns and thought quirks of one personal pocket of time and birth-chance. But doesn't that skill lead toward a trap? Soon only a male Pole can write about the male Polish experience in St. Louis, only a Japanese can write about a tenth-century ronin, only an Irish woman could possibly write about an Irish woman, and only a Polynesian could know what it was to put up with Gauguin while he was on the island. No one can know anyone else. If that were really true, what use were the heart or our faculty for imagining? Literal realism, even while it mourns the walls that run with blood around us, helps keep the walls in repair. Who will say, let my Saxon blood sleep, let my Ugandan blood sleep, my Lebanese and my Korean blood sleep? Let my dreams wander roads and runways and let my waking name myself human, not Jew, Muslim, Christian, Albanian, not Canadian nor U.S.-ian, not brown, pink, saffron. Perhaps not even fiercely male or female. A bare, forked person.

These ideas, alive in the thirties of this century, were drowned out by the honorable cry for ethnic respect and also by a dire fundamentalist resurgence among religions. There is great, dear charm in the trinkets of family, type and faith. We cling to them as heirlooms in a big loneliness. But lovely as they are, they turn out to be cast of poisonous metal. We must learn *not* to put them much in our mouths or rub our wounds with them. They kill. Thora thinks that, even at her post as Mother Superior, shrewd old pagan that she is.

QRL
BACK ISSUES

— Scarce first editions of "perhaps one of the richest veins of original poetry, prose, and criticism in the literary landscape of the last half century."

THE 1940s

VOL. I, 4: *Poetry:* Stefan George, O. Williams, Garrigue, J.G. Fletcher. *Prose:* Brock, Heilman, Weiss $10
VOL. II, 4: *Poetry:* cummings, Taggard, Moore. *Prose:* J. T. Farrel, Kazin, Williams, Mizener, Snell $5
VOL. III, 3: Valéry Issue $5
2: *Poetry:* Austin, Graham, Hardy, Hoskins, Stallman, Stevens $15
4: *Prose:* Graham, Flores, Guerard,Weiss, Watts $10
VOL. IV, 2: Moore Issue $25
3, 4: *Poetry:* cummings, Sitwell, Koch, Patchen, Schwartz, Rexroth, 12 Japanese poets, Eluard, Apollinaire, Williams. *Prose:* Austin, Belitt, Bogan, Flaubert, Rexroth $10
VOL. V, 2: Pound Issue $5
1, 3, 4: *Poetry:* Watkins, Simon, Cavalcanti, Eberhart, Gongora, Merrill, Shapiro, Villa, Wilbur. *Prose:* Belitt, 3 Goodman plays, W. C. Williams, Zukofskynovella $15

THE 1950s

VOL. VI, 2: British Writers Issue. *Plays:* Lawrence Durrell and Ronald Duncan. *Poetry:* Campbell, Tomlinson, Ridler, Watkins, Nicholson $10
1, 3, 4: *Poetry:* Carruth, Duncan, Gregor, Herbert, Lattimore, Lorca poems and essay, Merwin, Martial, Schubert, Triem, Walton, Williams. *Prose:* Fiedler, Garrigue, Liben, Orlovitz $15
VOL. VII, 1, 2, 4: *Poetry:* Casanueva, Cummings, 8 Dutch poets, Ford, Golffing, Heath-Stubbs, Mayhall, Olson, Seferis, Williams' Theocritus. *Prose:* Elliott, Humphrey, Nakajima $15
Vol VIII,1 Leopardi Issue $5
2: *Poetry:* Ashbery, Lattimore's Bacchylides, Hughes, Kessler, Fitts's Martial, Levin, Wright, Zukofsky. *Prose:* Garrigue, Summers, J. Merrill play $5
VOL. IX, 2, Rexroth's "Home-stead Called Damascus" $5
4: *Poetry:* Char, Dickey, Koch, Finkel Hughes, Merrill, Nathan, Nemerov, Morse, Pack, Rosenthal. *Prose:* Rilke's letters to Supervielle $5

THE 1960s

VOL X,1-2: Hölderlin Issue $5
3,4: *Poetry:* Cummings, Nathan, Dickey, Merrill, Seferis,Rudnik, Snodgrass. *Prose:* Connors, Daniels, Ellison, Klabund $10
VOL. XI, 4: Montale Issue (on file only) $35
1, 2-3: Prize Award Issue: 2 plays by Holly Beye. *Poetry:* Andrade, Fargue, Gregory's "Ovid," Hugo, Levertov, Jarrell's "Faust," Vliet, Wright. *Prose:* Beye, Goodman play, Musil $20
VOL. XII, 1-2, 3: *Poetry:* Bly, Eberhart Dickey, Duncan, Gregory, Hughes, Ignatow, Lieberman, Simpson, Sward, Rosenthal, Sullivan, Urdang. *Prose:* Play by D. Finkel, 2 Chekhov stories, Jackson, Ludwig, Gardner. $20
4: Cocteau's "Essay of Indirect Criticism" $5
VOL.XIII 20th Anniversary Double Issues, 1-2: *Poetry:* Whitman, Hölderlin, Alberti, Ammons, Dickey, Gregor, Hecht, Jarrell, Jouve, Merrill, Levertov, Rosenthal, Shapiro, Stafford $10
3-4: *Fiction:* H.D., Ellison, Humphrey, Brooke-Rose, Eich, Gardien, Leviant, Oates, Lattimore's Homer $5
VOL. XIV, 3-4: *Prose:* Peter Weiss, Segal, Dostoevsky, Coover, Kleist $5
VOL. XV, 1-2: *Poetry:* Brock, Char, Garrigue, Guthrie, Hugo, Montale, Seferis, Weiss, Kinsella, Ponge $10
3-4: *Prose:* Borges, Coover, Friedman, Oates, Steele, Estrada, Kizer, Spacks $5

THE 1970s

VOL. XVI, 1-2: *Poetry:* Amichai, Ammons, Belitt, Carruth, Coover, Duncan, Enzensberger, Essenin, Ghalib, Gregory, Guthrie, Hecht, Howard, Hughes, Levertov, Perse, Plath, Sexton, Seferis, Simpson, Rich, Wilbur $35
3-4: *Prose:* Whitman, Coover, Ellison, Gonzalez, Merwin, Sartre $5
VOL. XVII, 1-2: *Poetry:* Ponge, Merwin, Wright, Char, Davie, Eberhart, Kinnell, Pastan, Rakosi, Solzhenitsyn, Finkel, Gogol, Hecht, Holland, Kunze, Plumly, Swann $5
3-4: *Prose:* Gardner, Busch, Eaton, Oates, Watkins $5
VOL. XVIII, 1-2: *Poetry:* Cavafy, Celan, Mandelstam, Carruth, Dubie, Lieberman, Merwin, Milosz, Novalis, Peck, Ostriker, Wright $5

3-4: *Prose:* Mandelstam, Coover, W. Morris, Kleist-Brentano, Moss, Willard, $5

RETROSPECTIVE ANTHOLOGIES:
A summary of works published over QRL's first 30 years

POETRY: A discussion of open and closed verse by W.C. Williams, Richard Wilbur, and Louise Bogan; and poetry over the past three decades through the work of 146 poets including Stevens, Cavafy, Nemerov, Ashbery, Rich, Solzhenitsyn, Whitman, Dickey, Bishop, Merwin $20p
PROSE: A Goodman play, a Zukofsky novella, diaries of Osip Mandelstam and Ben Belitt, stories, modern fables, translations by Ellison, H. D., Gardner, Humphrey, Coover, Morris, Borges, Garrigue, Merwin, Chekov $10p/15c
CRITICISM: Cocteau on painting, Flaubert on Aesthetics, Dostoevsky on religion, Lorca on Gongora, Seferis on Eliot, Sartre on Mallarmé, Weiss on editing $10p/15c
SPECIAL ISSUES: Combining 7 issues each dedicated to Pound, Moore, Kafka, Hölderlin, Montale, Valéry, and Leopardi, with articles on the writers andnew poetry, stories, or translations by Williams, Stevens, Bishop, Ransom, Bogan,Brooks, Rilke, Lowell; Eliot, Merrill, Heidegger $10p/15c

POETRY BOOK SERIES:
Publishing 4 to 6 prize-winning books in one volume: 1978 —

VOLUME XX: Burrows's "Properties: A Play for Voices," based on the diaries of Fanny Kemble, actress, abolitionist, feminist; important first poetry books by *Brian Swann* ("Living Time"); *Reginald Gibbons* ("Roofs, Voices, Roads"); *M. Slotznick* ("Industrial Stuff"); and *David Galler's* "Third Poems, 1965-1978) $10p/15c

VOLUME XXI: *Jane Flanders'* "Leaving and Coming Back"; *Jeanne Foster's* "A Blessing of Safe Travel"; and *John Morgan's* first book, "The Bone-Duster";

Canadian *Anne Hébert* tr. by *Poulin*; a play by *Sidney Sulkin* "Gate of the Lions." $10p/15c

VOLUME XXII: debuts by *Mairi MacInnes* : "Herring, Oatmeal, Milk and Salt"; *David Barton's* "Surviving the Cold" called "possibly this year's most distinguished" in *Hudson Review; Phyllis Thompson's* third book, "What the Land Gave"; Brazilian poet *Carlos Nejar* tr. by *Piccioto*; and Korean poet *So Chongju* tr. by *McCann* $10p/15c

VOLUME XXIII: *Jane Hirshfield's* lyrical first book, "Alaya"; *Marguerite Bouvard's* "Journeys over Water"; *Christopher Bursk's* evocations of the perilous adventures of childhood, "Little Harbor"; one of Poland's most splendid poets, and 1996 Nobel Prize winner *Wislawa Szymborska,* tr. by *S. Olds, Drebik,* and *Flint*; and Swedish poet *Lars Gustafsson* tr. by Gustafsson with Australian poet *Philip Martin* $20p/35c

VOLUME XXIV: *David Schubert: Works and Days.* Celebrates the poignant poetry of "one of America's best poets" (Ashbery). All of Schubert's mature poems are presented; in addition, a biography, composed of early poems and letters, with other's memoirs and letters, dramatically recreates this poet of the '40s. "A remarkable document: haunting, suspenseful, orig-inal, deeply moving" (Oates) Essays on Schubert by Ashbery, Ehrenpreis, Ignatow, Wright $10c

VOLUME XXV: *Reuel Denney's* poem on architecture, "The Portfolio of Benjamin Latrobe"; translations by *Swann* and *Scheer* of eminent Spanish poet *Rafael Alberti's* "Rome: Danger to Pedestrians"; *Nancy Esposito's* powerful first book, "Changing Hands"; *Larry Kramer's* unwavering exploration of family, "Strong Winds Below the Canyons"; and a poetic foray into a den of decon-structionists, "Canicula di Anna," by *Anne Carson* $15c

VOLUME XXVI: *James Bertolino's* third volume, "First Credo"; "The Diver"; by *Warren Carrier; Frederick Feirstein's* explorations of rowdy origins in "Family History"; vivid first books by *Julia Mishkin* ("Cruel Duet") and *Joseph Powell* ("Counting the Change") and

Bulgarian *Nicolai Kantchev* tr. by *Kessler* and *Shurbanov* $15c

VOLUME XXVII: "Sky in Narrow Streets" from dis-tinguished Welsh poet and doctor *Dannie Abse;* the premier Portuguese poet *Eugenio de Andrade's* "White on White" tr. by *Levitin; Joan Aleshire's* "This Far", a celebration of the possibilities and limits of language; *David Keller's* skillful first book, "A New Room"; and *Peter Stambler's* dramatic sequence on the Schumann family, "Unsettled Accounts" $30c

VOLUME XXVIII-XXIX: QRL's 45th anniversary includes *Reg Saner's* "Red Letters", lucid meditations on the rocky vastness of Colorado; *Jeanne McGahey's* remarkable "Homecoming with Reflections" (one of *Voice Literary Supplement's* "Best books of the year"); *Jarold Ramsey's* "Hand-Shadows", an unflinching journey through the wilderness of human relationships; and Australian *Craig Powell's* brave, trenchant work, "The Ocean Remembers It Is Visible $10p/15c

VOLUME XXX: *Jean Nordhaus's* graceful poetry of knowledge, "My Life in Hiding"; *Bruce Bond's* "The Anteroom of Paradise", explorations of composers and painters; *Geraldine C. Little's* absorbing "Women: In the Mask and Beyond"; *B. H. Fairchild's* powerful poems of the everyday, "Local Knowledge"; and *Judith Kroll's* "Our Elephant and that Child" pursuasive treatments of Indian realities and mysteries $15c

VOLUME XXXI: *Jeanne Murray Walker's* "Stranger than Fiction"; Israeli poet *Dan Pagis,* who "tempers outrage at absurdity with sad, knowing wit" (*Library Journal*) in "Last Poems", tr. by *Keller; Anita Barrows'* The Road Past the View"; Uruguayan *Cristina Peri Rossi's* "Babel bárbara" tr. by *Decker; Naomi Clark's* expansive "The Single Eye"; and distinguished French poet *Yves Bonnefoy's* "Beginning and End of Snow" tr. by *Sapinkopf* $10p/15c

VOLUME XXXII-XXXIII: 50TH ANNIVERSARY ANTHOLOGY: new poems by all the prize-winning poets in the Poetry Book Series plus poems from most of QRL's

important poets out of its first 30 years.

$20p/25c

VOLUME XXXIV: *Suzanne Paola's* confident first book "Glass"; *Frederick Feirstein's* poetic sequence "Ending the Twentieth Century"; Swedish poet *Werner Aspenstrom's* "Selcted Poems," translated by *Robin Fulton; James Bertolino's* "Snail River"; and *Paula Blue Spruce's* poetic play about Native Americans, "Katsina". 10p/15c

VOLUME XXXV: Lynne Knight's first full-length collection, "Dissolving Borders"; Jean Hollander's lightfooted "Moondog"; David Citino's blend of the lyric and dramatic, "The Weight of the Heart"; Barbara D. Holender's wily "Is this the Way to Athens"; and Romania's leading woman poet, Maria Banus, with her first book translated in the United States by Der-Hovanessian and Mattfield, "Across Bucharest After Rain". 10/20 $20p/$35c

VOLUME XXXVI: "Camel of Darkness," by the eminent Greek poet *Yannis Patilis,* translated by Gourgouris; *Warren Carrier's* elegant sixth volume, "An Ordinary Man; *Christopher Bursk's* "The One True Religion," a study of great myth making power; *Joseph Powell's* insightful and profound "Getting Here"; and translations of the fiercely strange voice of the Iraqi-born *Fadhil Al-Azzawi , translated by Mattawa*"In Every Well a Joseph is Weeping." 20c

LIVING

> "When you have a sudden thought, do you know where it comes from? Aren't you occasionally surprised by your own thinking? The poet is a person who simply listens to that thinking and takes it seriously and probes it and shapes it and begins to make something of it."
> —Theodore Weiss, from the film *Living Poetry*

POETRY

TWO UNIQUE FILMS follow the evolution of a poem across time and through the process of revision to its final version.

Living Poetry 1: A Year in the Life of a Poem

In 1987, the filmmaker, Harvey Edwards, followed Weiss throughout the year and filmed the creation and evolution of a poem, titled "Fractions," from the initial inspiration to the finished product—writing, revising, re-living the past and incorporating the present. It is a candid view of Theodore Weiss who, for half a century as poet, professor, and editor, has lived poetry.

> *Living Poetry: A Year in the Life of a Poem*, was the Blue Ribbon winner at the 1988 American Film and Video Festival.

Living Poetry 2: Yes, with Lemon

In 1995, Edwards learned that Weiss had re-written the "final" version. He returned to make a new movie with a different approach: a group of Princeton undergraduates, led by their professor, James Richardson, discuss the subtleties and complexities of this final version of "Fractions." The "new" poem is read by Weiss and his wife Renée on camera, intercut with the analysis and dramatized with re-enacted scenes from the poem. The new "Fractions" still contains the lyrical elements that distinguish the first film, but the canvas has been enlarged: from the depths of the past, Weiss plumbs the terrible moments of growing up in a small Pennsylvania town. Fires flash through the film—the childhood memory of his house burning sends the poet's imagination toward the larger fires of the world. At the same time a cup of tea and the kneading of bread in a warm kitchen become metaphors out of the daily for what, even in the face of catastrophe, remains.

> "Fractions" was published in Theodore Weiss' latest volume of poetry, *A Sum of Destructions* (1995).

Fiftieth Anniversary Anthology

Quarterly Review of Literature at 50

High notes from the greatest of QRL's acclaimed past
New poems from the present
QRL Poetry Book winners. This Fiftieth Anniversary Volume is a literary landmark.

"A national treasure . . . QRL's dazzling roster of writers is a tribute to their unerring eye for talent and their pursuit of excellence. . . . But though committed to bringing the rich catholicity of American voices to QRL's pages, the editors were never parochial in their leanings. They scouted the world of letters to showcase writers from Kafka and Celine to Celan and Mistral."
—*Parnassus*

"The Weisses were assiduous in publishing not only writers like Stevens, Williams, cummings, and M. Moore, but a great many of their younger, utterly unknown successors as well. The truth is, it was largely in magazines like QRL that much of the literature now studied as a matter of course in colleges and universities first appeared."—*The New York Times*

"The roster of young, little known writers presented in its early days reads like a page from a Who's Who of Modern American Literature."
—*Poets and Writers*

"The editors, whose eclectic international taste is to be commended, continue their search for the best in poetry." They now print 4-6 prize winning poetry books under one cover each year. —*Library Journal*

One of QRL's volumes was a "Favorite book of the year. QRL publishes books and pays authors real money." ($1000 and 100 books!)—*The Village Voice*

And QRL printed W. Szymborska 15 years before she was the 1996 Nobel Laureate.

QRL 26 Haslet Ave.
Princeton, NJ 08540
50th Anniversary — $20

NEW POEMS from:

Danny Abse
Rafael Alberti
Joan Aleshire
Eugenio de Andrade
Anita Barrows
David Barton
James Bertolino
Bruce Bond

Chris Bursk
Warren Carrier
Anne Carson
Naomi Clark
Reuel Denney
Nancy Esposito
B. H. Fairchild
Frederick Feirstein
Jane Flanders

Jeanne Foster
David Galler
Reginald Gibbons
Lars Gustaffson
Jane Hirshfield
Nikoli Kantchev
Larry Kramer
Geraldine C. Little
Mairi MacInness

Jeanne McGahey
Julia Mishkin
John Morgan
Jean Nordhaus
Joseph Powell
Reg Saner
Peter Stambler
Sidney Sulkin
Brian Swann
W. Szymborska